# Get Organized,
# Get Published!

# Get Organized,
# Get Published!

## 225 Ways to Make Time for Success

**Don Aslett and Carol Cartaino**

**WRITER'S DIGEST BOOKS**

CINCINNATI, OHIO

www.writersdigest.com

Visit our Web site at www.writersdigest.com for information on more resources for writers.

To receive a free weekly e-mail newsletter delivering tips and updates about writing and about Writer's Digest products, send an e-mail with "Subscribe Newsletter" in the body of a message to newsletter-request@writersdigest.com, or register directly at our Web site at www.writersdigest.com.

05  04  03  02  01          5  4  3  2  1

**Library of Congress Cataloging-in-Publication Data**

Aslett, Don
   Get organized, get published!: 225 ways to make time for success / Don Aslett and Carol Cartaino
      p. cm.
   Includes index.
   ISBN 1-58297-003-3
   1. Authorship 2. Authorship—Marketing. I. Cartaino, Carol. II. Title

PN147 .A724 2001
808'.02—dc21

00-51340

Editor: Brad Crawford
Designer: Rondi Tschopp
Cover designer: Stephanie Redman
Production coordinator: Mark Griffin

## DEDICATION

∼ *To all of those who* should *write, in hopes that they* will.


∼      *And to Ann W. Cartaino,*
          *who showed the determination,*
               *all her life,*
       *that every writer—and every person—needs.*

## ACKNOWLEDGMENTS

*Many people helped make this book possible, especially the following:*

• *The other publishing professionals listed in Contributor Biographies. In a world full of too much to do, they found the time to share their expertise.*

• *Karen Patterson, freelance writer, who assisted capably and cheerfully with many stages of this project, and "went the extra mile" to help us get to where we needed to be.*

• *Kirk Polking, who was as generous as ever with her lifetime of writerly knowledge.*

• *Jenny Beyhmer, Martha Jacob, Michael Hoover and Tobi Flynn, who lent encouragement throughout and helped improve the book in many small ways.*

• *The staffs of the Cincinnati and Hillsboro Public Libraries, and especially Laura Waln.*

• *Dr. Edward J. Holland and Pietro M. Cartaino, Jr., who helped Carol overcome a very large obstacle in midstream.*

• *Mert Ransdell and Jack Heffron of Writer's Digest Books, who made us feel the urgency of this topic.*

• *Brad Crawford of Writer's Digest Books, who calmly steered a complex project through a tight schedule, and was a real "comrade in arms" in the trenches.*

• *Oscar Collier, to whom Carol made a promise that this book fulfills.*

• *Howard I. Wells III, who helped Carol many years ago with the "stalling before starting" list and, in the here and now, with an "instant photo" when it was needed.*

• *Tortie Tanpaw and the makers of Diet Cherry Coke, who kept Carol going when the going got rough.*

• *And Clayton Collier-Cartaino, who managed to wait for Mother to finally be through!*

## ABOUT THE AUTHORS

### ∿ *A well-matched team for a needed book* ∿

A successful entrepreneur named **Don Aslett** loved writing (yes, even poetry!), finding it a source of satisfaction and popularity from the seventh grade on. His other love was cleaning and organizing, and he capitalized on this as a college student by starting in his freshman year what eventually became a large national cleaning business.

After his business was well under way, he began lecturing and teaching about cleaning, and to help serve the enthusiastic response that followed, he produced a little pamphlet: how using professional methods could save you 75 percent of the time you spend cleaning around the home and office. His audiences fought their way to his podiums to buy that pamphlet, so he self-published an entire book on the subject called *Is There Life After Housework?*

A copy of it found its way into the office of an enterprising publisher in Cincinnati, Writer's Digest Books. The editor in chief there, **Carol Cartaino** (formerly of Prentice-Hall), looked it over and said, "This has some rough edges, and this fellow is a little brash and overconfident, but there is a truly new approach to home cleaning here." So Writer's Digest published it. It's sold over a million copies now and been translated into many languages.

As good editors do, Carol saw a green light here, so she suggested that Don now do a question-and-answer book on cleaning. She even came up with the title, *Do I Dust or Vacuum First?*, and this little volume went on to sell an amazing 350,000 copies.

By now Idahoan Don Aslett and East Coast editor Carol Cartaino were a team and did one of the all-time books of the century, a book that has changed many lives and is one of the most frequently checked out of libraries in the United States—*Clutter's Last Stand*. Carol was so enthused about this book that she transplanted herself to California for a month to finish editing it, and to work with the illustrator, a Disney artist.

This unlikely team, Don and Carol, in the next seventeen years, put out twenty-eight more books together, and they are working on at least a half-dozen more that are actually in production and scores of others still in early stages. Some of their most popular books have been on decluttering your life and making better use of your time and energy to get more done, including

*Not for Packrats Only*
*The Office Clutter Cure*
*Clutter Free! Finally and Forever*
*Lose 200 Lbs. This Weekend: It's Time to Declutter Your Life*
*How to Handle 1,000 Things at Once*
*Keeping Work Simple*
*How to Have a 48-Hour Day*

# TABLE OF CONTENTS

# INTRODUCTION

Your byline on a printed page...every other person in the world dreams of it. But few achieve it.

Why? Because many would-be writers never actually move toward their goal—they get bogged in indecision, uncertainty, confusion, doubt, fear, procrastination and all kinds of half-formed ideas and intentions. Others get started only to soon find themselves adrift in a sea of scribbled notes, undone "to dos," piled papers and started (but never finished) manuscripts and submissions. Or everything else going on in their lives shoves writing aside.

Aspiring writers need something to get them across the gulf from thinking about it to doing it, from interest in being published to sustained action on it. They need something to show them how to stop milling around and start really moving toward the goal, to transform them from dabblers to doers.

The answer is here!

*Get Organized, Get Published!* will show you how to organize yourself and your writing efforts, to turn that rich treasure trove of ideas and experiences in your mind into stories, essays, articles and books that really see the light of day. It will help you organize not just file cabinets and computer files, paragraphs and sentences, but your energy and ambition, so you can move in clear, orderly, reassuring steps toward your goal.

## WHY ORGANIZE?

Being ready is the best guarantee of results there is, in this or any other profession. Planning and organizing your moves helps you through the entire writing process.

If you want to be a published writer, hopes and intentions alone won't do it—an orderly approach will. Consistency and organization are more important than genius and "breaks," even in this highly creative endeavor.

Too often when we hear the word organization, we think immediately of the physical side of files and folders and holders and gadgets. Maybe all we have to do is find the right clock, calendar or calculator. But organization is as much, or more, intangible as it is tangible. It isn't a purely physical thing—a lot of it is mental. An organized plan and approach, as we will explain in these pages, is as important as the right filing system or software package.

Why organize?

1. To be able to find things.
2. To be able to use them efficiently.
3. To simplify your life and work.
4. To make your time more productive.
5. To put *you* in control and shift things from a fight to fun!

## DON'T BE INTIMIDATED BY THE "O" WORD

Surprisingly, even free-spirited, unfettered individualists who take pride in doing their own thing are often intimidated by the "O" word—organization. Too many people interpret it as something that means restriction and bondage, but nothing could be further from the truth. Organization is the most freeing, turn-em-loose word in the world. Organization simply gives us order so we can get eight hours' work done in three hours, or so that if we only have minutes to write, we can get hours worth of writing done in them.

1. First: No one owns organization. There is no one way to do it. So don't assume you have to adopt any "master's" system. We can all have our own way to suit our own situation and temperament. You aren't like anyone else and will need your own system(s). We will show you how to mold, develop and grow into your own organization, adopting and adapting one principle at a time. You slowly grow into good organization, not hit it with a whole-hog, miracle, onetime revival shot.

2. Organization doesn't mean you have to have expensive files and containers and day planners. If you need equipment, you can make good use of things like inexpensive plastic trays from Kmart, and cardboard boxes (free). (See chapter fifteen.)

3. Organization is only a few things.
   a) Looking ahead, and at the whole picture.
   b) Going about things in the most effective and efficient way.
   c) Getting rid of any junk and clutter around you, or in your way.

So don't panic. Organization isn't tyranny; it is liberation!

This book combines all of the secrets and clever and workable things that Don Aslett, a successful writer, and Carol Cartaino, one of the best editors in the world, had hidden deep in their files and habits. First Don sat down and wrote wisely and generally, then Carol tapped into her own experience, and her hundreds of resources from more than thirty years of editing, and working with writers and publishers of all kinds. Since organizing is such an individual process—and no one has all the answers—she asked a wide variety of other publishing pros to share their secrets on these topics, too. The combination of Don Aslett's creativity and credibility and Carol's professionalism has given you a book like no other that serves up what writers really want and need to know. Go for it!

# CHAPTER 1

# *Want? Wish? or Will!*

Be honest—you've thought about writing. You can't read anything without thinking how good it would be to give your own message to the mixed-up world out there. We all believe we could straighten out some marriage, family, health, economic, government, school or traffic problem with our wisdom!

Just about all (at least 90 percent) of us have thought about writing.

Most of us (about 75 percent) would like to write.

Some of us (40 percent) *really* want to write.

A few of us (20 percent) start something, then let it go.

Fewer of us (10 percent) are "still working" on it.

Darn few of us (about 2 percent) actually finish a work.

Let's eliminate the "thinkers" here and look at the 75 percent (those who would like to write) that ends up as the 2 percent actually writing and see where the breakdown is.

First, writing has less to do with ability than you might think. All 75 percent can and do write effective and creative letters, school papers and business documents. Pro writing is just a simple extension of a good college paper or personal or business letter.

Certainly it's not lack of tools. We have computers, electronic thesauruses and dictionaries and other resources that make the logistics of writing easier than ever. Surely it's not a lack of subject matter—we are exposed to many more happenings and avenues of thought these days and much more information of all kinds (through mass communications) than the great writers of the past. And it's not a matter of money, either. Every one of us, whether we are at the bottom or top of the economic totem pole, has enough time and money to write.

## THE WORLD'S MOST HIGHLY DEVELOPED ART

Why the 75 percent to 2 percent fallout? Why do 73 percent of us go hungry for something we want? That is quite a weeding out, especially when you know as I do that if our reason or purpose for writing is strong enough, 90 percent of us can do it, and decently, too!

The answer: the world's most highly developed art—procrastination! We are all so highly developed in this skill that there is little room for improvement, unless you decide you'd like to become a writer. Then you can perfect procrastination! Writing is such a personal, hard-to-quantify thing that you can secretly put it off until later and still impress the public. In fact, you can put it off indefinitely and people still assume that book or article is coming...someday...or "soon" (one of the most popular words in the procrastinator's vocabulary). A single book, with the aid of some super efficient procrastination, can go on for twenty years without a word ever appearing on paper.

There are hundreds of "good reasons" out there as to why we procrastinate our writing plans, from pure laziness to "I can't afford it." We have all kinds of well-thought-out, documented, heartfelt excuses, astounding alibis and ripened rationalizations.

All would-be writers have their lists of things that are holding them back, and boy are they ever convincing. There's almost enough for a whole best-selling book on "why I'm too chicken to write like I've been wanting to all my life." You'll never get anywhere writing lists of why you can't, won't and haven't. Let's take a look at some of those reasons.

**EXCUSE: "I'm just too busy right now. My job and family life are too demanding, and my daily survival comes before speculative ventures like writing."**

This will always be so, so if you keep thinking this way, you'll never get started. Busy is the biggest blessing a writer can hope for. Writing fodder comes from exposure—struggle, sweat, experience, controversy, complication, conversation—up to your neck, even, buried in the problems and demands of daily living: young kids, sick parents, taxes due, health worries, house needs painting, hurricane coming, dog down with dandruff again. What more could you want to give you mood and material?

**You don't have to make time to write**—just add writing on to what you're already doing. Writing is just recording thought and action. You don't have to stop and find a formal writing space or span of time. The best manuscript you ever do may be pulled together from little thoughts or pieces you've jotted down right when something happened or when you thought of it. Tack your writing onto the tasks at hand, because the chores, and the cost of living will never go away and leave you to create in some quiet, isolated cabin.

When I reflect on my most productive periods of turning out published work, they were *always* during times when I was "overwhelmed"; my schedule was packed full and then some.

Since last year, for example, requests for my speeches and appearances have doubled, and I've spent half of my time in airplanes. I've also built two new buildings. My cleaning company acquired new contracts that almost doubled its size, and the number of salespeople with miracle products to show me have set records during this time. My wife and I used our home for a huge girls camp, and our garden yielded twice its normal vegetables to be picked and processed. And every other hour I'm on my ranch in the Idaho mountains in a pickup loaded with tools only young studs should be using—crowbars, shovels and post drivers—fencing through pine trees and boulders every spare minute. You get the picture.

But, in the seat of the pickup, in my toolbox, on the plane, by my bed, in my car or lunch sack—is my trusty yellow pad, steadily being filled with ideas, stories, lessons, insights, opinions and accounts. I write in between drinks of water, meals, riding up and back, on the tractor even! I don't have one conversation with a neighbor, government ranger, crew—anyone—that I don't get good writing material from! Being busy is like being in full-time writing school, for free! And what you write from this will be quality stuff, not idle speculations or something forced out at the keyboard.

Life is only going to get busier with every passing year, as your family, assets, opportunities and responsibilities increase. It will only be harder to write later, so you might as well launch into it right now, while things are hot and the alligators are nipping.

**EXCUSE: "I can't write right now because my life is in turmoil. My personal life is in such chaos that I can't concentrate on anything else. I must solve a number of personal problems before I can concentrate on writing."**

A liability to a writer? Just the opposite—this is the prime and perfect time to write. Your best work will be done while you are in the thick of life's battles—when all kinds of feelings, needs and ideas are welling up in you and on your mind constantly. What an opportunity. You are being exposed to so many things that your research is all done for you. All you need to do is capture them, and that can be done before, during or after your "turmoil," in minutes. If being busy and in turmoil—in other words, living—is your reason for not writing, then trade in your pens and unplug your computer, because you'll never write anything.

**EXCUSE: "I have too many distractions right now ... "**

See those two things below your ankles? They work well to transport you to a less distracting area of your life and place. You can also call in reinforcements to help with distractions—see chapters two and twelve.

**EXCUSE: "Writing will take me away from my duties at home, at work, in the community and at church. I don't want to neglect my family."**

All writing is a pure addition to life—not a subtraction—because it is so intensely personal. We all have our own inner thoughts, and they don't necessarily detract from our time with our spouse or family, or hurt the boss or the community. Anything you do that develops and improves you is an asset to those around you.

Many people today work to make enough money to support the lifestyle they want for themselves, their spouse and their children. They feel guilty if they want to do something for themselves instead of the family. But if they seriously explore their desire to write, they may be able to make that extra income working from home, in a way that is much more exciting and enjoyable. And find themselves happier, less stressed people.

**EXCUSE: "I'm going to do it ... later. I'll start when I get my life in order and everything is secure and caught up, when I retire," etc.**

Good luck, and be prepared for a big disappointment later! Things never get "righter" for writing. When all is clear and you are rich and relaxed, the kids are raised, etc., you are half worthless and in serious need of ambition. Most of us write better when there is some pressure on the pen!

**EXCUSE: "I'm waiting till I can afford a computer."**

Quit blaming lack of automation for lack of motion. Computers are nice to have, and they can make writing much easier. After your first few sales, you can always buy one. Meanwhile, surely you can afford the "rock-bottom writing kit"—a pad and pen.

At the library, you can take advantage of the computers they have for patrons to use—free!

**EXCUSE: "I can't type, and my handwriting is awful. And it's hard to find someone else to type things for me."**

This is no excuse at all—as we just noted, you can always write longhand, or hunt and peck on a typewriter. You can also find yourself a manuscript typist—and there are plenty of people everywhere with home computers and typewriters looking for a way to make a little money with them.

Or take a month out of your life and teach yourself to type. There are all kinds of textbooks and software programs for self-teaching. The keyboard of a computer has a softer touch than a typewriter and may be easier for an inexperienced typist to work on.

**EXCUSE: "I just don't know how or where to start."**

There is no official when and where and why and what when it comes to writing. You aren't losing anything by trying, or starting. All you have to do is you pick up a pen and touch the page. You just need to activate your first initial urges in this direction, and everything takes care of itself. It works out.

For more concrete guidance, see chapters three and four. There are also shelves full of other books out there (see Recommended Books on page 277), and a monthly magazine, *Writer's Digest*, devoted exclusively to helping you over this hurdle.

> *Everybody learns how to get started. That's what nonwriters haven't done. You sit down and hit the space bar and type T-H-E and find a word to follow it.*
> *—Carl Mills*

> *Writing is a craft like any other, like bricklaying. Or like music. Almost anyone can learn to play an instrument, even if not necessarily at Carnegie Hall level. The key is to sit down and* do it

*for some amount of time every day, even fifteen minutes. If you*
*work at it for two hours a day for ten years, you are bound to*
*become a pretty good writer.*

*—Robert Sloan*

**EXCUSE: "I don't have much formal schooling."**

This may actually be a plus. College can stultify your writing style.

**EXCUSE: "Do I have the authority to write? Surely I need to solve my own problems before writing to advise others about anything. Who am I to attempt to correct things, teach or advise other people on their problems, when I can't correct my own?"**

Your own problems are to a great extent what you will be weaving into your writing. This is often what makes us pursue a subject, and how and why we relate to it. If you didn't have some problems and questions of your own, you'd surely have too blank a mind to write.

Even if everything in your own life—house, marriage, health, morals or finance handling—isn't a perfect example to others, there is surely at least one or two areas where you have some authority (the "right") to write.

And even if nothing, not one thing in your life, is exactly as you would have it be, herein lies one great benefit of being a writer. Anything you write about, you learn well and have a tendency to live up to. Writing is the best self-improvement course you can take. You can tackle topics and research them when you don't know all the answers. In fact, knowing the questions is sometimes more important than knowing the answers. People have become great archaeologists, psychologists and physicists because they wanted to know how and why.

**EXCUSE :"I don't know what to write about. I want to write, but I don't really have anything to say."**

Then you must be a truly unique person. I've never met anyone without something to say about a lot of things. And when I meet you, I'll bet that in a one-hour conversation I will discover at least six subjects you are strongly opinionated, even passionate, about. There you have it. Find the one you really love (or hate) and get started. Once you start, your writing will feed itself.

You already own what you are as a human—where you've been and what you've done. What better to write about than that? If you want material, you have it not just in you but all around you. We are exposed to at least a hundred times the objects, people and events that any of our ancestors were. You probably have *five hundred times* the topics to choose from than they had. We now have access to even more on the Internet at the push of a button, and most of it is free.

The idea that you have nothing to write about is just plain old failure to pay attention to what's going on around you. We probably run into at least a dozen writing-worthy topics daily. So go ahead, do it—pick a point, a position, a pet, a picture in the mind, and start writing.

Remember the times in the course of an ordinary day when you or someone else suddenly broke into a grin or were amazed by something? Or during a dull, drawn-out meeting suddenly began chuckling to yourself? We've all had a flood of perception, anger, passion, power or greed sweep through us, or felt total disgust at having been left out or picked on. Writing can and will capture things like this before they pass away forever.

**EXCUSE: "But one of my manuscripts was rejected, and a couple of people criticized my work."**

Those are all just opinions. You still have that manuscript and all of the rest of your work, and other people and other publishers may have different opinions about them. Best-sellers such as *Gone With the Wind*, *Jonathan Livingston Seagull*, the Chicken Soup series and the Harry Potter series were rejected by scores of publishers before they hit the big time. Mistakes like this are made every year.

**EXCUSE: "I have no confidence. I read or hear about the awesome accomplishments of other authors and am overwhelmed. There is no way I could ever measure up to this, so I don't even want to try."**

The problem here is that we see these authors as super human, and it just isn't so. Writers don't always tell the absolute truth—we either leave out some of the gutsy stuff of getting there, or exaggerate our successes and the sizes of our advances. Outsiders, including those who want to write, lap up this stuff and tremble. But they might be just as good, or better!

An aspiring writer we know once tried to chase down President John Kennedy to hand him a bag of buckeyes for John, Jr., and Caroline as a remembrance of their visit to Ohio, the Buckeye State. He was wrestled to the ground by Secret Servicemen, arrested, interrogated for several hours and didn't even get to see the president. When President Kennedy heard what had happened, he personally called this fellow, apologized and asked if his children could still have the buckeyes!

This incident was this man's "claim to fame," but he had other stories to tell. He often talked about writing a book someday but lacked the self-confidence to do it. He died at age fifty-six, and all of his stories died with him. What a loss for the world.

Or consider what one of Carol's neighbors says:

"I'm just a housewife and mother, but somewhere inside me is an exciting novel. I am filled with ideas and stories I think could help people, encourage children and make the world laugh. But it all comes back to, 'Who am I? What makes me think anyone would want to read what I had to say?'"

Many people have wonderful stories to tell and often talk about writing a book some day. But one thing keeps them from doing it. They lack the self-confidence. They always say, "I'm not a writer. I've never done anything like that before, and no one would want to hear from me or care what happens in my life."

No one is going to believe in you if you don't believe in yourself. Every best-selling author had to start somewhere, often feeling just like you do now. You may not like what you write at first, but at least you'll have some confidence in your non-ability, and that is progress. It might make you mad or desperate enough to learn how to, and get better!

### EXCUSE: "But I'm not creative."

One of the feeblest and least valid excuses we hear from would-be writers is, "I'm just not creative or brilliant."

Really now, who do you know that *is* creative and brilliant? Some might appear that way (we always overestimate the abilities of others), and others may openly claim that status, but I'll tell you the combo that is really required to write: labor and love, a love of writing and immersion in life. Words don't come from just sitting at a keyboard or with a pad, and neither does creativity. Without some real-life experiences to draw upon, even brilliance is of little value.

### EXCUSE: "My topics have already been done."

That's for sure! As Solomon said so long ago, there is nothing new under the sun. Every year there are thousands of new articles and books on food, travel, sex, family relationships, faith, sports, animals and glamour, and there will be thousands more on those subjects next year and the next. Surely there is little in these subjects that has not been explored before. The fact that a topic has been done before doesn't mean that it can't be done again, and succeed in the marketplace. Generally, just the opposite. Selling a highly unusual or exotic idea is tougher than selling one that's been done to death, as long as you have something different to say about it. The fact that it's been done before means it's been on many other people's minds, and this is in fact why editors thought it would interest readers. When, for example, will "boy meets girl" ever go off the list of worthwhile topics? Now there is one to start on!

### EXCUSE: "I'm scared, so I won't do it."

Tell me one single bit of real harm that can be inflicted on you by writing. There is little financial risk here. All you might be out is some time, which you probably would have wasted in some idle meeting or in front of the TV. Name me one single thing to be scared of in writing. Rejection? This is a mere matter of someone's opinion, or a simple issue of supply and demand, not a lifetime judgment on your ability as a writer, or of you as a person. (See chapter eight.)

### EXCUSE: "It might take a long time. I wonder if I have enough time."

Well, folks, you have the rest of your life, and that should be enough time to do about anything. I wrote my first article when I was forty, and my first book when I was forty-five. I'm sixty-five now, and this year I started three new books. At seventy-five, I'm sure I'll have a dozen more new ones, and that many more done, and I'm just a janitor and a farmer. So think of what you can do!

The nice thing about writing is that you can do it anytime, twenty-four hours a day—while in church, in bed, during movies, vacations, while riding to work, in boring meetings or in the hospital. There isn't a single second in your life when you can't in some way be advancing your desire to write.

If something is fun, beneficial and emotionally profitable, what is too long? What would you rather be doing? I personally can't think of one thing more enjoyable than writing.

If we haven't covered your excuse for not writing, please add it to this list.

If you examine these objectively, not one of them is even close to a good reason to not start writing. They are all just what we first said—excuses to procrastinate, nothing more. "Can't, don't, haven't, won't ... because" are sad summaries of why we who want to and can write never get off the fence and do it.

If indeed you really want to write, there will be—there is—no obstacle to it. Baloney to all of those feeble excuses for putting off something that can thrill your body and brain like nothing else. Get on with it, man or woman, write! *Now*—in the tub, during your trial, during the game, driving home, while stuck in traffic. Do it!

## PLANTING, DIGGING UP AND HOLDING OUT YOUR OWN CARROT

One wistful glance at a shiny new book's cover and the thought that "it would be nice to be an author and have my own book" may not be quite enough to convince you to spend a good part of your life doing a book...but it is a start. If you count the plusses of what that book might do for you and forget the minuses (the hard work of doing it), you might just create your own carrot to finally begin writing.

What writing and publishing can add to your life:

1. A valuable habit of learning to look and listen, which will benefit every area of your life.
2. New avenues of thought and interest. One first book, article or story can lead to many others. Writing is a nonstop, never-ending education.
3. The satisfaction of expressing yourself (at last!).
4. Great experiences, travel opportunities and media exposure.
5. Flexibility to work on your own schedule from anywhere in the world.
6. Improved overall communication (writing and speaking) skills.
7. The ability to change lives and help people.
8. Confidence that you count for something (and have evidence on paper to prove it).
9. Prestige, and the opportunity to advance yourself. Even if your writing is not Pulitzer quality, people will be impressed once you are a published author.
10. Opportunities to meet interesting people from all walks of life.

11. New income ... maybe only pennies at first, but possibly some big dollars.
12. The power to make your mark on the world. Writing is the best way to leave a legacy. Long after you are gone, you can share your thoughts—who you are, what you care about and what you have learned—with others.

---

**Writing can overcome age and disability, loss of looks or lack of looks! No discrimination here.**

---

**Your ability, good or bad, won't be the starter or the stopper of a great career in writing. The key will be how much desire you have to actually do it. Mechanics can always be worked out with a little effort. It is the decision and the ambition to work at this career, almost at all costs, that will make for some great pages with your name on them.**

**You have the time and the resources, more than any humans have ever had before—just deciding to *do* it is when you become a writer.**

# CHAPTER 2

# *Finding the Time to Write*

The biggest demon most would-be writers face is, "I don't have" or "can't find" the time to write.

Today we are all battling two life-threatening forces—the "too much" coming at us from all sides and the fact that we are "too busy." We complain about this constantly, recalling the good old days before 250 TV channels, endless shopping malls and kids who have to be chauffeured nonstop to lessons and sessions, matches and meets.

Sure we are busy, and we are only going to get busier in the years ahead as family and job responsibilities, our skills and capabilities, friends and opportunities increase on all fronts. One big solution is just accepting the fact that you should write *all the time*.

## THERE IS ALWAYS TIME TO WRITE

> *There's no time that you can't write, if you've got the material.*
> —*Jim Joseph*

You don't have to have a special set-aside time to do your writing. You are a writer every minute: night, day, work, play, while shopping, traveling, showering, gardening and vacationing. Keep your work with you, even in the bathtub, on the hiking trail, in the hospital room, on the tractor and at dinner—something to write on, with and about.

Don't try to schedule writing into your life, just do it—every minute you are awake, you can be writing. No matter what or how many activities you are involved in—their value, their priority, their frequency—you can manage to write.

On my busiest days, when I'm weary from travel, I often end the day with more good stuff written than I do on any "off" time. How do I do this? Let's use one of my busiest days as an example.

1. In the hour I spent in the headquarters of my cleaning company before a recent trip, six employee abuses were brought to my attention. I took the time to record the pertinent facts and had fresh material for a book I'm doing on business management.

2. En route to my destination, I grabbed the wrong bag from the airport luggage carousel. Stopping to check and read the tags would have saved many hours of anxiety and frustration for both me and the other unfortunate party. A bad scene, but a great example for my book in the works on "doing it right the first time"!

3. Some jerk on the plane was using his cell phone loudly and irritating everyone. I wrote it all down and had some great new ammunition for my book on bad manners.

4. When I arrived at the hall where I'd be giving my seminar, some longtime readers and fans asked me to autograph their copies of my latest decluttering book. They related some incredible stories about junk and clutter to me in the process, and I jotted them all down.

5. During the seminar and afterward, members of the audience shared their observations about the challenges of modern cleaning with me, all super good. I quickly wrote all this down, too.

I came home with nine pages of great material without looking or asking for it, or taking any extra time to gather it. So take your writing with you everywhere; think "writing" all the time, until it becomes second nature.

For another example, my favorite book, *Clutter's Last Stand*, was written during one of the busiest times of my life. I was running three major businesses, had four kids in college, a ranch, was doing constant speaking appearances and promotion tours, and was building another home and a new commercial building. I literally didn't have a spare minute. Yet during that year, not only was that book done from scratch, but I made good progress on others as well. How?

Well, as one example, my wife's aging parents begged us to take a two-week trip to Alaska with them that summer to see their great-grandchildren, our grandkids. All the way there and back (four people packed into the front seat of a 1976 Ford pickup with no springs!), I had my writing folder in my hands. During the ride, I enjoyed the scenery, of course, but I also listened hard to the passengers' conversations, and thought and observed during all visits to stores and restaurants. I wrote as we drove, and for a few minutes each morning and evening, about the things we were seeing, hearing and living. Once we reached our destination, Skagway, Alaska, I sat on the street of that old gold-mining and now tourist-trap town with my writing pad and gathered pure gold information. Literally dozens of inspirations for my subject were there, alive and spontaneous, and I jotted them down. I also called and visited several times with my editor and coauthor. Thus a good part of one of my major books was written in about two weeks, in the course of a busy visit.

When it comes to time to write, you have all the time you are living, and that is about all you can ask for. If, sad to say, you convince yourself that you haven't the time or are going to wait until you get more time, don't count on being much of a writer—ever. The demands on your time will only get worse as you get older, so do it now, right now, every minute.

---

**The want-to writer's biggest excuse is "I can't find the time to write," but guess what? If you were relieved of everything right now—financial pressures, family responsibilities, work obligations, social commitments, your biggest excuse for not writing would still be—you guessed it—"I just can't find the time to write."**

---

## DON'T KEEP WAITING FOR A "LEDGE"

In the reality of everyday life, making a living, keeping up with the kids, keeping well, being at least a little bit spiritual, getting to our writing project seems almost impossible.

So we put it off or push it ahead, telling ourselves that someday there is going to come a "ledge" that will enable us to do it.

What is that elusive ledge? I'll describe mine, and I'm sure yours will be just like it: a niche, a space, a time-out where I can step off the merry-go-round and pant awhile and process everything. Where I can catch up and get ahead, and then move on at last to the things I really want to do.

All my life I've looked forward to that ledge, that nook I could duck into for a week or month or whatever and tear into all those overdue and long-awaited things. Like maybe when I break a leg and am laid up, or maybe a windfall of money will come, and I can stop working and really get down to writing. Maybe during a vacation or a trip, there will be a stretch of time to tackle all those additional article ideas I have. Believe it or not, but when I see a prison movie, I always sigh and think, "Man, if I ever were in there for a while, could I get a lot of writing done!"

I've been waiting for at least fifty years now, and that ledge has never appeared. I have a big family and many employees to help me, but that ledge to duck out of the line of fire for a few days has never come. In fact, just the opposite has happened. The longer I live, the more I have to do.

Even if you can manage to stop the clock, it probably won't aid your productivity. Most of the time when people do stop to catch up, they're so relieved to be stopped that they fall further behind.

The bottom line is, you are going to have to *stay* on the road and *write* on the road—en route, in the fast lane. You have to write on the run, and you can. The only answer is now. Today you have the time and ways and means to do it. All you have to do is start.

## MAKE WRITING AN "A"

> *If you really want to write, wild horses won't be able to pull you away from it.*
>
> —*Rohn Engh*

You have to make a real commitment to writing, or it will never make it to the "A" list.

Consider one professional we know, for example. He says, "I want very much to write, but I just don't have the time to do it. I work from 7:30 A.M. till 8:30 P.M., and when I get home, I just want to collapse in a chair." Yet this man belongs to civic groups and pursues a number of hobbies enthusiastically, from collecting antique veterinary gear to trapshooting to motorcycle riding and operating radio-controlled model airplanes.

> *I think one reason I've been so productive over the years is because I've made writing a priority in my life. I write (or*

*rewrite) every day, no matter what. Most everything else is of*
*secondary importance.*

*—George Sullivan*

Again and again the excuse pops up: "I've got so many interests and ambitions I can't do justice to any of them. How can I add my urge to be a writer to this long list?"

The answer is easy. **When we say we're "too busy" to do something, it usually only means there are other things we want to do more.** Once you truly commit and decide to write, you will have the time.

> *[After talking with many would-be writers], I have concluded*
> *that most do not want to* be *writers, working eight and ten*
> *hours a day . . . they want to* have been *writers, garnering the*
> *rewards of having completed a successful manuscript and seeing*
> *it become a best-seller. They aspire to the rewards of writing, but*
> *not to the travail.*
>
> *—James A. Michener*

## RECUT THE PIE!

Let me give you an example. In my time management and cleaning seminars, I often have an audience of typical modern homemakers, fathers and mothers, really struggling with the modern busy life syndrome.

I draw a circle and ask all the attendees to do the same. Then I tell them to slice the circle into wedges that show how and where they are using their twenty-four hours a day right now. Much moaning and groaning follows as the participants attempt to analyze the what and when of their activities. Most have more things to fit in than there is space in the circle, and suddenly the overall problem becomes clear. Things like jobs, commuting, cleaning, cooking, repairs, raising the kids, caring for the yard and pets, etc., use up every bit of the space. It is clearer than ever that the battle of modern life is "too much" and "too busy."

Then I have the audience draw another circle and put the leftover wedges in it. I call the first circle the "have tos" and the second the "want tos." Is this interesting! The second circle contains life's most valuable uses of time, like "spending time with my spouse and children," "expanding my hobby," "reading more," "learning to play an instrument," "working in the garden," "getting more exercise," "helping others," "getting in touch with myself and my Creator" and "finally getting around to writing my book." This second circle, which holds most of the activities that would truly bless and enhance our lives, is in fact the things we seldom get around to.

We can't throw out all the "have tos," or we would starve and our homes would fall to ruin. We can't throw out the second circle, either, or what's the use of living? Pulling wedges out of number two and simply substituting them for those in number one is often impossible. If circle number one is too tight, *you and I* are the ones who have to do something about it. We, after all, determine and control our own slices in the clock of life. No one else. That means we have to shrink the slices in that first circle to fit in the ones we want to wedge in. And we can. Remember—you choose and control the size of those wedges.

For example: Of the cleaning wedge, 40 percent of the time, effort and money here is usually spent on excess stuff—junk and clutter. Cut and control clutter, and your cleaning will drop 40 percent. That leaves lots of new room to transfer in some "want tos."

So take a hard look at all the things you're doing now, and all the time and energy they take, and "recut the pie" to make room for that slice we always wanted from our childhood birthday cakes—the slice with the writing on it!

## USE SOME OF YOUR SPARE OR WASTED TIME

We all think we don't have a minute to spare, but if we could push a button and have a count of our "off" (wasted or squandered) hours for the last year, we'd discover that most of us have at least fifteen hundred hours of "spare time." Write down exactly how you spend your time every day for a week—note all the big and little pieces spent doing what—and you'll see *tons* of useless activities. A lot of them are things you don't even enjoy.

According to "time science" experts, the average American in his or her lifetime spends:

Three years in meetings
Twelve years watching TV
Eight months opening junk mail
Two years on the telephone

Five years waiting in line
Nine months sitting in traffic
Four years cooking and eating
Three years grooming and dressing
Seven years in bathrooms
Three years shopping
One year looking for misplaced items
Twenty-four years sleeping

You could cut some of these things in half and only be better off for it.

Start today to replace dead-end activities and other less inspirational pastimes with writing. Steal time for writing anywhere, any way that you can.

Many people believe, for example, that in order to stay healthy, we need eight hours or more of sleep each night. Everyone has different physical needs, but because sleep can be an escape, we often overdo it. Many of us function very well on six or seven hours of sleep or even less. To make time for writing, reduce your sleep to just enough to get a good rest. If you find yourself drooping, a fifteen or twenty minute "power nap" sometime during the day is often enough to recharge your batteries and keep you going for hours. Once you start writing, you'll be so fired up you probably won't need a nap!

## CHOOSE TO WRITE

We may think our schedules are imposed on us, or largely out of our control, but every day, even in the most hectic conditions, we make many big and little choices about how to use our time.

For example, on one of the frequent trips I have to make "back East" from Idaho, it was cold and snowy, and the trip to Raleigh/Durham, North Carolina, took a total of nine hours, counting airport and air time. It was a full flight, and I got G25, the "embryo seat" next to a window. There wasn't enough room to take off my coat. Then came every traveler's nightmare: a 380-pound wrestler with two computers, chewing gum and an unceasing appetite, and he sat right next to me.

But by the time we landed, I'd written eleven of my best poems (even some romantic ones), some material for my autobiography and many sections of my latest book on dejunking, as well as capturing fifteen new ideas to write about.

I looked around on the plane and at the airport, where all of us had the same amount of time—nine hours—under the same conditions. I visually polled sixty or so of them on how they used the time:

Seven were reading hastily purchased paperbacks.
Twelve were sleeping (or trying to).
Eight were idly shuffling through magazines.
Fifteen watched a "B" movie.
Six ate continually.
Five stared into space.
Four were doing crossword puzzles.
Ten were engaged in an exchange of health status, or other chitchat.
Two fussed with their makeup and hair (for hours!).
Three were playing games on their laptops.
The rest were buried in newspapers.

Many potentially great writers never get past wishing, wanting, wondering or waiting for conditions or their mood to be just right. Everyone on that plane chose what to do with those nine hours. Writers choose to write.

## EDIT YOUR LIFE TO MAKE TIME AND ROOM FOR WRITING!

Good manuscripts result from cutting or editing out unneeded words, and a better chance to produce manuscripts in the first place can come from editing the "garbage" out of your daily living. If you really want to write, then you need to uncomplicate things and dump the diddly stuff that is taking up your time and emotion. Your writing projects can get double time from you if you give them the time instead of tending trifles and "to dos" that don't really need doing, at least not now.

So get out the pruning shears and uncomplicate your life. When you say "I will write," also say:

**I will find better health and greater energy** by quitting any harmful habits I have.
**I will focus less on food.** "Eat to live," rather than "live to eat." Have simpler, shorter, healthier meals.
**I will live in my house, not for it,** and clean by need, not schedule or habit.

**I will focus less on fashion** and other ego or "image" pursuits. Buy and wear clothes for coverage and comfort, for instance, not style and show.

**I will unplug the TV,** and spend less time on "the news," since sports, sitcoms, soaps, talk shows and the latest happenings in celebrities' lives have almost zero need of my time or energy to read about or watch. Remember that you want to write the news, not watch it.

**I will quit shopping as a pastime**—buy only what I need and then get back to my book!

**I will participate in the social events that are important to me, but stop wasting time** with ones that aren't.

**I will require everyone in my household** over five years old to take care of 95 percent of their own needs while I am writing.

In other words, narrow your life to the bare necessities: family, basic care of your self and home, your job and writing. Try your daily routine for a few days or a week without the timetakers you no longer enjoy. If you like the result, make it permanent!

---

How many of your "to dos" are unnecessary things you did, that now have to be undone? Such as things you bought or ordered that you didn't really need and that now have to be sent or brought back? Or the phone solicitation you sat and listened to, that left you with an insurance policy you didn't really want or need. Now you have to remember to cancel the policy after the thirty-day free trial period is up, pay a month's premium after you forget to cancel it and then call the credit card company to make sure the insurance is canceled from here on. Cutting back on these things can save you double time!

---

### Learn to say no

• Avoid organizations that require a long-term commitment unless you really want to spend all that time. There are those who feel that if you are a writer working at home, you don't have a real job, so you have time to sit on every committee or chair every meeting. Before you know it, your time is taken up with all kinds of outside activities and you haven't written a word.

Instead, say yes to one-shot commitments in the school and community like cleaning up after the fall carnival, gathering things for the fundraiser auction or chaperoning the after-prom party. This will keep you involved, but not overextended, so you still have time to write.

• As harsh as this may sound, eliminate (or at least control) the time spent with people who waste or hog your precious time. This includes folks who call to pass on the latest gossip, the repairman killing time until his next appointment, relatives who want to detail their every trial and tribulation, salespeople and telemarketers, and even friends who don't respect your desire to write. You can't be 100 percent social and get a lot done.

### Cut down on your caretaking

Writing does take time, but you can take that time away from mundane chores that are taking more time than they should rather than, say, out of your family time. For how to handle all of that "other" faster so you have more time for writing, see our books *How to Have a 48-Hour Day* and *How to Handle 1,000 Things at Once.*

### *Concentration should come before cleaning!*

Concentration on your writing should even come before cleaning. (Yes, this is America's No. 1 cleaning expert saying this!) The house doesn't always have to be ready for the white glove treatment. The shiniest floor won't be reflected in your writing, and if you devote too much time to polishing windows and silver, you won't be polishing many paragraphs. Household chores like cleaning, laundry, shopping and cooking can be cut back.

> *Write when your children are in school, and forget the housework! To be honest, when our children were in school and I was not working, I think I wrote to avoid picking up toys or cleaning house every day. To me writing was a more satisfying way to use the quiet time when the children were gone.*
> —Anna Lee Waldo

Much of what we call cleaning and maintenance is really junk tending—not just dusting and polishing things we don't really use and no longer enjoy, but keeping track of them, storing them, shuffling them around from place to place, insuring them, protecting them, organizing and reorganizing them.

Cluttered rooms take ten times as long to clean because we have to move so much out of the way to do anything, and then move it all back when we're done. And all those extra objects add up to hundreds of times the amount of surface to clean. You also need many more kinds of equipment and supplies to clean them.

Junk and clutter crowd us and stop us from getting to many of the things we really care about in life, including writing. They boggle our minds as well as our storage areas. See Recommended Books for guidebooks that will help you clean faster, get all of the "other" done quicker and clear out the clutter so you have the mental and physical space, and time, to create!

### Call in the cavalry!

Another way to free up time for writing is to recruit others to help you with time-consuming chores. If there is no mate or kids to help (and if you have them, they *should* be helping), find a professional. There are pro house cleaners, window cleaners, gutter cleaners, car cleaners, grass mowers, garden weeders, drivers, baby and pet sitters, horse waterers and trainers. There are even personal shoppers for gifts, grocery stores that will deliver your groceries, pharmacies that will deliver prescriptions and high school kids who will wrap presents. There are also professional helpers who sit with the elderly, assist the disabled, and walk and feed your dog or cat. Even if you only call in the cavalry when you are up against a deadline, it's worth it.

## THE "SECONDARY" SOLUTION

One big hurdle we face when getting ready to write is not a matter of spelling or grammar, or even our basic ability to write. It is bigger than all of these combined. It's the fact that for most of us who want to write, it will have to be a secondary thing. Sure we love it and want to do it more than anything, but we need to eat and pay the bills. Even those of us sworn to make a living at writing generally need a part- or full-time job to support us and our family, at least in the beginning. So for most of us, it falls into a second, third or even lower place in our schedules, which means it has a strike against it from the start.

If you work another job outside of the home, scheduling time to write is much more of a juggling act. Time management is vital, and setting aside time every day devoted to nothing but writing is important.

The bottom line here is that you have to make a commitment. You need to make this secondary activity as important as your primary ones—and want to write as much as you want to eat, play or exercise.

> *You have a choice of ivory tower or the power of concentration.*
> *Concentrate on your project, and you can write anywhere.*
> *Holding a full-time advertising job, I had to snatch time to*
> *write on my own. So I wrote most of my articles and first nine*
> *books on commuting trains. As a beginner, I'd write on a bus, in*
> *reception rooms, in the living room with our kids doing their*
> *homework and my wife sketching in an armchair so we could all*
> *be together. Care enough to concentrate wherever you are.*
>                                         —*Samm Sinclair Baker*

### Write before or after hours

Make some time somewhere for just you and your thoughts. Wake up a half-hour or an hour earlier, or retire a little later. Use this time to reflect on the day beginning or ending, and then write. Make writing a prologue or epilogue to your daily grind.

Unlike what most of us have to do all day at work, this is something you'll be doing, at last, just for yourself. Doing your own writing your own way, nights or mornings or weekends, isn't an extra chore but a relief and a pleasure.

### Write on weekends and holidays

A sacrilege to even suggest this? Not really. These precious breaks from our workday routine are meant to stimulate, refresh and uplift us. But much (if not most) of what we ordinarily do on weekends and holidays is play couch-potato, cruise, fight crowds and complicate our lives in noisy, expensive places. We end up aggravated and "hung over," in more ways than one. A good solid session of writing, on the other hand, is one of the best drug-free highs and cures for depression around.

I write best when snowed in or stormed in, or on holidays when I'm home writing and the highways are jammed with drinkers and gas burners. There is something satisfying and secure in being home with pen in hand. It also has the thrill of perversity—the feeling that you're getting away with something, and getting one up on everyone else by working weekends or holidays!

### Plan a writing vacation

When you get in the position to take a two-week or one-month vacation, stop. Take time off from work, but *don't* go. Stay home and write.

This stay-home writing vacation will end up being the finest of your life, perhaps the first real vacation you've ever had. You'll probably be at least several thousand dollars to the good, too, between what you'll save in gas, plane fares, hotels and not running around doing and buying things.

### Write whenever you're weather bound!

Writing is the perfect thing to turn to when other activities have been wiped from the calendar by rain, snow, mud or flood.

When we have a sudden change in our schedule or a big hunk of unexpected "downtime," we too often seem like people in jail—captured, confused and with no way to escape. Remember that the guys who escape—one out of one thousand—are the ones who use "the time" to start digging—in this case in your file of articles overdue to be written!

### Use time fragments

Seldom will you, I or anyone else have many full days or even half-days to just sit down and write. But as the old sage told the overwhelmed hunter, you can eat an elephant one bite at a time. Our days always have little stretches of fifteen minutes here and twenty-five minutes there when we have no choice but to wait around for something. You don't have to just twiddle your thumbs or cuss the cause of the delay—you can pull out your notebook (or laptop) and start writing. **You don't have to do nothing at all because you can't do a lot.** We're all looking for more time, and those time fragments add up, often to most of a day. Use them!

If most people had eight solid hours of clear time to write they wouldn't use them all, anyway—writing is too intense.

> *You don't think you'll ever have more than an hour at a time to devote to writing? Then break your writing objective into a series of small operations, each of which can be done in an hour or less. Sit down and list everything it's going to take to accomplish your writing goal—to write a book, for example. Such as: first think of what all the chapters might be, then outline*

*chapter one, then chapter two, etc. When you get to the actual writing, a one-hour goal might be to write one section of one chapter, or one or two pages of that section, etc.*

*If you only have one hour a day to write, make it a good hour—prime time. Not an hour after you get home from work and are tired and the kids are screaming and the dog wants to be fed. Find an hour within your schedule and biorhythms when you can really produce!*

                                        *—Jean Loftus*

---

Superb tools and subject matter cannot replace time—they can shorten it or make it more pleasant, but writing takes time. *When* you write is your call, but it is a call. You cannot bloom without a little bleeding—writing will simply have to replace or shoulder aside some of your other activities, personal or business. And this isn't bad, but often gives us no choice but to get better organized.

# CHAPTER 3

# *Making Your Master Plan*

Before you begin, you need not just a subject but a reason to write, an idea of where you intend to take the words you are going to put together. We aren't talking about some idea of someone else's—a spouse's or parent's expectations, or boss's demand. We are talking about *your* blueprint for bringing something to the table of your life, and just how you intend to do it.

The chapter will encourage you, even at the earliest stage, to have an overall writing agenda, a master plan or even a career plan, because it's hard to organize effectively if you don't know where you're headed.

## BLUEPRINT COMES BEFORE THE PRINT!

We can get away with "winging it" once in a while; lots of things just happen to us, some of them good, some of them much better than we deserve or hope for. And some not so good. Drifting through school or jobs or anything else always has some consequences. Some of us have made a lifetime habit of choosing things by default, which means we never really choose, we just ride along with what comes our way or happens to us.

You don't want to take this approach with your writing. If you are waiting for some random dream of turning out great pages to fall into place, it won't. The only thing that will fall is your dreams and wishes (by the wayside!).

We all get so tired of the "goal" talk we hear everywhere we turn that we hardly pay much attention to it anymore. We've almost worn that poor word out. We've become almost immune to the idea of good planning because we have so many tools, teachers and computer programs to direct and rescue us. We tend to think we can just bob along and the technological "current" will take us there. But "there" depends on "prepare" more than any other factor in writing.

I have great faith in your ability to write, but you also need a game plan—a clear-cut, self-made strategy. This is not just thinking ahead; it is actually reaching down into your wants and wishes and coming up with some kind of firm design for what you want to do with your message. You need a purpose, one that *you* pick, outline and commit yourself to follow.

One of the biggest obstacles to making a master plan is that we try to fill in too much detail when making one. There is just no way you can write every little aspect of your master plan before you start. Much of your plan will unfold by itself once you get started.

### Step 1 of any master plan: your reason for writing

It could be money, fame, revenge, ego, to prove to someone (or yourself) that you can, for a more fulfilling hobby than you have now, to present a spiritual message to the world, because you want to share your expertise or you simply have an emotional need to express something. You've got to have a strong, solid reason for writing, be it glory, altruism, rebellion, politics or love. There are lots of reasons to write (see chapter one if you need a few more). You must have one or several, or you wouldn't be reading this book.

A strong cause self-organizes you. Once you are dedicated to a do-it-or-die direction, you'll make it come to pass, come hell or high water, headaches or heartaches. The best organizer in life is "have to"— something so important to you that you find a way through any blockage. Perfect mechanics or procedure can never override mind-set. If your cause cools off in the middle of your writing enterprise, you'll never finish it.

Don't worry about form or format; just scribble it all down boldly: what you want out of your desire to write, what you are after, where you want to end up.

Once you do this, guess what? You just finished the biggest part of your master plan. Now you have the foundation and just have to decide what kind of house you want to build (decide what kind of writing will best accomplish your purpose). The design from there is fun, and you will know which materials to buy and where to get help.

Once you know why you are writing, you will feel less conflict, and it will be easier to persist and to make decisions.

### Step 2: Make writing a priority

Writing is so easy to let slide until later or put behind something else. We can procrastinate, forget or slow down, and no big finger in the sky points down at us. No immediate punishment is apparent.

But if you don't make writing not just a "to do," but a priority in your life, and keep it one, you might as well forget it. Putting it ahead of travel, socializing, sleep and playing is probably what it is going to take to produce something that will give you the byline you've been waiting for. And guess what? Writing will more than replace anything you may "give up" in the process of getting it down. Writing gives back what it gets, and once it is on paper, it lives forever, long after you are gone. People who missed it the first time can come back to it later, and it can lift their hearts and change their lives.

### Step 3: Choose a subject

Next start thinking of the writing projects you would like to tackle, the things you would like to share with others. There is nothing wrong with dreams, wishes and fantasies—in fact, this is some of the best raw material you can have for your goal, map or plan. Jot all of your ideas down—some of the unlikely ones may end up the winners. You can always weed out the weird or offbeat stuff later, but when you're planning, capture and record them all, just for the fun of it. Far better, when planning, to start with all of the possibilities before you weed down to the practicabilities.

Brainstorm the writing topics that you feel qualified to write about, or have a passion to write about, on paper or on computer. Which one stands out? Would be best for accomplishing your objective? Is easiest for you to start with?

If there is something you don't know much about but really want to learn about, don't rule it out. It's better to write about something you have a passion for, but don't know much about, than to write about something you know a lot about but have only a half-hearted interest in. Experience in a subject does give you some advantages, but a passionate interest is what will eventually bring out everything you have to offer. And if you like something and lose (it doesn't sell, or turns out to be a bad idea), at least you will have enjoyed doing it.

*I only write stories that interest me. I used to take any paying gig, but I was cured by a three-article stint for a women's magazine. It took me five times as long to do the pieces because I simply wasn't interested in the subject matter.*

—Kyle Minor

### Step 4: What *kind* of writing now?

Now you need to establish the *type* of writing you are most interested in and best suited for, such as fantasy fiction or historical nonfiction. This is an important part of your master plan: choosing the type of writing you will most enjoy and that will best meet your goals. The market guides and many good books on different kinds of writing will give you much insight here and tell you what you need to know. Here are some charts that may point you in the right direction, too.

## FICTION OR NONFICTION?

How can you decide, if you're not sure? This little quiz may help.

### List one:

- [ ] In school, you enjoyed writing short stories and imaginative essays.
- [ ] You usually see, and tell, things in the form of a story.
- [ ] You are not beyond changing details or exaggerating them to make a story more interesting.
- [ ] You have a lively imagination that often leads you into flights of fancy and "what ifs."
- [ ] You'd rather make up an imaginary person than interview a real one.
- [ ] You enjoy inventing characters, the things they would say and the situations they would get involved in.
- [ ] You would like to entertain people with your writing.
- [ ] You've thought of writing a novel or a script someday.
- [ ] You wouldn't mind having only a small chance, but a real one, of making big-time money as a writer.

### List two:

- ☐ In school, you enjoyed writing reports, theses and fact-based compositions.
- ☐ You are a practical-minded person.
- ☐ You enjoy searching out, gathering and verifying facts.
- ☐ You think and organize in an orderly one-two-three way.
- ☐ You have strong opinions that you are driven to express or causes you would like to advance or promote.
- ☐ You think of yourself as an expert in certain areas, and would like to capitalize on this.
- ☐ You read magazine articles and think, "I could have written something better than that."
- ☐ You would like to inform, teach and help people.
- ☐ You would prefer a more dependable income from writing.

Which list have you put more checkmarks by? If the answer is list one, you may be a budding fiction writer. More checks in list two suggests that nonfiction should be your game.

> *Listen to your inner voice. Write what you know and what works for you. If you know a lot about gardening, find a twist on that theme and write about it. Don't spend several years fighting against your natural writing focus such as I did for years, trying to write fiction instead. While writing different genres helped me as a writer, it wasn't putting my name in print, which is what I wanted. With two active children, my life is very family-oriented, and the parenting articles I write now are a continuation of my family life.*
> —Mary Jo Rulnick

## A TEMPERAMENT TEST FOR WRITING

Here's another little exercise that may help. Any good writer could probably succeed in any of these areas, but natural inclinations do have a bearing here.

*You have lots of patience and tenacity and don't mind working quietly out of the limelight. You like digging* deep *into things.*          =          BOOKS

*You are interested in a variety of subjects, but don't want to cover them too thoroughly. You like illustrations, feature stories and reading about current discoveries and trends.*          =          MAGAZINES

*You like to be in the middle of the action—on the scene and up to the moment on things—and would listen to a CB radio if you had one. You also enjoy political and social commentary.*          =          NEWSPAPERS

*You are familiar with the Web and its conventions and can write knowledgeably on a variety of issues, often on shorter deadlines than those for magazines. You prefer the informality of computer communications to the more rigid structures of print and can write copy that is punchy and colorful enough to keep readers from clicking through to the next site.*          =          ONLINE
PUBLICATIONS

## THE WORLD OF FREELANCE WRITING IN A NUTSHELL

Here is a quick overview of the publishing prospects for some of the most popular types of writing. It may help you decide where to steer your course. There are other books that can give you a wider range of possibilities.

**Nonfiction articles and essays:** An almost endless range of possibilities in subject matter, audience and income. Very open to beginners, and a good place to start. Article-size projects are easier to fit into a busy schedule, too.

**Newspaper stories:** Another good place to start, though the pay for freelance articles may not be high. A good place to get acquainted with the pleasure of being a published writer, hone the mechanics and gain valuable experience in observing, reporting and writing fast.

**Columns:** Not hard to start at the local level, and usually give you a lot of leeway for self-expression; you can write about almost anything you want, the way you want. Deadlines are short and frequent. You can work your way from a single column to more than one, and then to syndication or self-syndication. Self-syndication is easier than ever in the computer age. But, unless you are Dear Abby, you may not make a living on columns alone.

**Nonfiction books:** No real barrier to beginners, as long as: 1) You start with a truly fresh subject, one of broad appeal or one you have real expertise in. 2) You pick the right publishers for the type of book you are doing. (Read what the market guides have to say and look at who publishes what in the bookstores.) 3) You do a good proposal (see chapter eight and Recommended Books).

**Novels:** Could hit it big here, although you'll have a lot of competitors, and your work has to be good. It may be easier to start with "category," or genre, novels, since they often follow an established framework or formula.

**Poems and short stories:** Write for the pleasure of writing them, to self-publish or for prestige. Not easy to get them published, and if they are published, you may not be paid much.

**Writing for children and young adults:** An appealing field, but bear in mind that it's not easier to write short manuscripts like this well. You also have to be concerned with things like vocabulary level. Children's picture books, which are the first thing many people think of writing, are not the easiest place to start. The competition is strong here, including many well-established authors, and the illustrations in such books, which must be done by professional-quality illustrators, mean as much as the words. Children's nonfiction is probably the easiest place to start.

**Screenwriting:** A specialized form. But if you can learn how to do this type of writing (there are books and software available to help), and break in—there can be a big paycheck at the end of the tunnel. In the beginning, you need to network like crazy or find an agent well-connected in the field of dramatic rights. Once you have an agent, the need to live where the action is decreases.

**Playwriting:** If you love the theater and would like to write for a performance medium where the written word (not camera angles and fancy visuals) is still king, this may be a good field for you. Play publishers, organizations and theater companies all over the country are actively seeking new material. The financial payoff may be slow in coming, and unless your play passes the test of a long run in the Big Apple, that payoff may not be giant. But the satisfaction of seeing your work performed live is almost payment enough for many playwrights.

**Writing your life story:** Write for your family and family history, and the satisfaction of recording all the heartaches and triumphs of your time on the planet. Not easy to publish commercially unless 1) you are notable or famous in some way or 2) you have been in a position to see or experience things many people would like to learn more about.

**Writing copy of many kinds for business:** Including brochures, reports, ads and technical writing. It may not be writing the Great American Novel, but there are good pay prospects here, and steady work, once you get started. Businesses know the value of a way with words and are willing to pay what it is actually worth.

**Writing for the Web:** The Web is a fast-growing market for writers and encompasses every subject under the sun, but it also provides opportunities for self-promotion, self-publishing and interactive communication with your audience. While any type of writing can go online, commercial articles on the Internet are brief with short paragraphs like newspaper writing but as entertaining as magazine writing, and more relaxed than both. See the Recommended Books for more help here.

## YOUR WRITING PLAN, IN SHORT:

1. Why, really, do you want to write? What is the rock-bottom reason or reasons? What do you really want? Is it something writing can give you? (See chapter one.)
2. Where (really) is writing on your priority list?
3. What do you want to write about?
4. What form of writing would that subject work best in or would be the best vehicle for accomplishing your master plan?
5. What do you intend to do with it after it's written? Share it only with family and friends, or publish it more widely? If the latter, do you want to self-publish it, or persuade a publisher to publish it? This may depend on the subject and form of writing you have in mind.

### Write it down, now!

By now you should have some kind of outline of a master plan. Aim is always great, but your goals need to be spelled out and written down. Once you have them on a page or two, you will have a purpose that will start propelling you. This initial page of print will move you forward, almost on its own. Most of what you need for writing success is already in you, and a plan just organizes a way to get it out of *you*.

A master plan, written and maybe revised and then posted on the wall in front of you, will be your writer's pinup and prompter.

### It's never too late

Another dumb thing that we let erase our chances for accomplishment and fulfillment is thinking we are too old or it is too late. We should only get more serious about planning at fifty, sixty, seventy and eighty years of age. Too many of us think that when we get to be thirty, things are already set and we are on course and just have to follow the direction we are headed in. You never get through with your master plan—it just grows stronger and better as you go along.

## PUT YOUR SHOULDER TO THE WHEEL

After you've decided what you want to write, you need a way to make sure you actually do it. This means figuring out a way to assure the most essential ingredient of all writing: time in the chair, on the pad of paper or at the keyboard.

You must decide when you will do your writing, and how much time you want to put in on it each day or week. This partly depends, of course, on what you are planning to write and when you want to be finished with it. Try to choose a goal that is realistic and can be accomplished with the kind of writing schedule you have in mind.

> *Writing for a living is different from writing on the side. If you want to be a full-time writer, you will have to make a serious schedule for your writing and stick to it.*
> —Nicholas Bakalar

> *Most people already have a sleep routine, from ten, twenty or thirty years working at some job and driving up to an hour and a half to get there. They may not imagine that you can adopt a new sleep pattern that will give you time to write when you feel like it. If you didn't have that job, you could!*
> *So if you actually do produce several articles and get an "A" for them, you could start a whole new lifestyle.*
> —Rohn Engh

To be sure you meet your goal, you may want to set a schedule of production—exactly what you plan to accomplish daily, weekly and monthly—such as to write a certain number of words or pages per day, or an article per month.

You may want something much more flexible than this, such as my method of writing whenever you feel the mood and inclination. But for those of us with procrastination in our soul, a clear-cut action plan is better.

> *People try to schedule writing into their lives, but the best way to go about it is to structure it right into your life, make it part of your daily "routine" of eating, sleeping, getting dressed, feeding the cat, going to work, whatever.*
> *I always felt that I ought to exercise, for instance. I always said, "I've gotta do that." But what I needed to do was make it part of what I always do. Now the exercise machine is in front of the TV so that when I watch the news (which I never fail to do), I exercise.*

*You need to change your mind-set—make writing not
something you do from time to time, but part of your life.*
—*Jean Loftus*

### Remember: you own discipline now

You may have an idea by now of how important discipline is to a writer. When you were young, discipline was something that was always done for you. You had to toe the mark and follow the rules, and discipline was always preached at and sometimes forced on you. You were always told it was for your own good, and it probably was. But after all those years of being denied things because of "discipline," we developed a negative, even fearful, attitude toward that big, mean word. Because we associate discipline with being yelled at, being made to do things and struggling to do them, we still don't want much to do with it.

But now *you own it!* You are the one with the power to use it, for your own good. And it is your best friend, the most reassuring and helpful friend you will have in your whole writing career.

We often think we aren't very disciplined. But most of us are pretty well-disciplined once we decide to do something. Once you make the decision to write, discipline will be easier than you think. What you want to do is never difficult—even the toughest and most challenging parts of it. All of the efforts and sacrifices are worth it because your writing and its outcome are all yours ... forever.

Remember, the most disciplined armies and ball teams are the winners—discipline is their power and protector. Likewise, the trait a writer will use and need the most is perseverance, and discipline is its sole source.

Discipline doesn't restrict you, it inspires you, and it leads you out of the "hole" and into the light. Discipline isn't a confiner, it's just a boundary-setter, enabling you to organize and control your life. Discipline isn't a shackle to keep you tied to a keyboard, it is a chance to double and triple your talents. Discipline is the lines and guard rails on the highway to good writing, to keep you from running off the road, crashing or getting lost. Discipline isn't something you fight, but something that fosters you to freedom. Rules aren't there to ruin us, but to guide and nurture us, and to create order.

You own discipline now, and you can wield it like a sword to fulfill your dreams. Discipline doesn't *make* you write, it *lets* you write.

## OFF THE WALL, OR ON THE WALL?

One of the things that most helps me to reach my goals is to make them visual. I make flow charts for all my books just as I do for the operations in my cleaning business and as coaches do on blackboards to show the plays for their teams. Once the elements involved are sketched on a page or even hung on the wall, you can get a much clearer picture than you could ever get just thinking about them or listing them.

Which helps you more when you need to go somewhere?

1. Someone verbally describes the distances, turns and stoplights and number of miles.
2. Someone hands you a written description of same.
3. Someone hands you a map or drawing showing all of the roads, creeks, bridges and intersections all drawn out.

The answer is number three, hands down! So make yourself a big chart or poster of your writing goal or project and the steps leading up to it. It will give you a clearer sense of where you are going and where the words go, take things out of the abstract and into reality.

Best of all, now others can see and understand what you are doing and help you. Most of the time they just think you are crazy—now they will either know it or help you! **So make your action plan:**

1. Make a list of exactly what needs to be done to complete your first (or next) writing project. Taking something from a vague, general idea to a clear-cut, specific series of steps makes all the difference. Suddenly it is something you *can* do, not just *could do.*
2. Add a time frame—*when* you intend to accomplish each step.
3. Put your plan up on the wall or bulletin board, or hang it right in front of you.
4. Check off each step as it is completed.

## DO YOU HAVE TO BE "SOMEONE" TO BE PUBLISHED?

A neighbor of mine, who is a decent writer and wants very much to be a published one, sat in my office one day and wailed, **"Do I have to be someone to get published?"** (She'd just discussed several subjects that would make excellent articles before launching into a lament on how impossible it was for an unknown writer in a small town to attract the interest of the "mighty and powerful in the publishing industry.")

Since I'd urged her to get started writing seriously any number of times before, this made me mad enough to finally say: "No—I will almost *guarantee* you publication if you do the following" (let's start with articles, since they are easier, though the process is much the same for a book):

1. Write out a list of the subjects you feel strongly about and are expert in (we are all experts in many things from our life experiences).

2. Pick the one of these that other people would be the most interested in (testing your possible topics on others will help).

3. Find something in your life experience with this subject that would give you a new or interesting slant on it or provide readers with a new piece of information on it.

4. Look in *Writer's Market* and other market guides for magazines that are interested in these subjects and open to beginners (not all are). If a publication is listed in a market guide, the listing may say if it's open to beginners.

5. Send your article to them (if it's already written and they accept unsolicited submissions), with a brief cover letter. Or send them a good query letter. If your topic has a seasonal slant or connection, send it well ahead of that season.

*How to Write Irresistible Query Letters,* by Lisa Collier Cool, will tell you how to write a good query. See Marcia Yudkin's *Writing Articles About the World Around You* or Don McKinney's *Magazine Writing That Sells* for how to write a magazine article if you are not sure.

6. If you are rejected by one magazine, send to another, and keep sending till you get a "bite." There is nothing wrong with sending a query to several magazines at once as long as the publication accepts simultaneous submissions and you alert the editors to this.

7. After you are published, build on that success. Do articles on related subjects at first if possible, then branch out to other subjects (being a mini-authority on that subject will make it easier to get additional articles published). Then do a book in the subject area you've been most successful with, if you want to.

My neighbor would succeed, I am sure, if she followed this formula. She is not getting anywhere because she is not making a plan like this, and (equally important) then **steadily following it.**

## WRITING IS SO SIMPLE

You only have to conquer two disciplines to ultimately get published. Just *two*! If you can manage these, the other aspects that you probably are overly concerned with will either be sheer mechanics or will fall into place. The two?

### "Start" and "sustain"

Your success in someday tucking your own book or article under your arm will require both of these. As the old song about love and marriage goes—you can't have one without the other.

All want-to-be writers have failed on one or the other of these two. The never-starters, and at least half of all want-to-be writers—are talented enough but can't get off their wishbone and start wearing out their butt bone. The other half wilt when they discover writing requires a bit of will and work.

Chapters four and fourteen (in fact all of this book) will help you with these two simple basic requirements for publication—starting and sticking with it.

## MY GETTING PUBLISHED ACTION PLAN

1. The subjects I like best, feel strongly about, or am an expert in:

2. The one of the above that other people seem most interested in (I have tested this):

3. A new or interesting slant I could give this subject, or angle I could write about it from:

4. Some magazines that seem interested in this subject, and open to beginners (according to *Writer's Market* and other market guides), by degree of interest:

A.

B.

C.

5. I will have my query or article in the mail to magazine "A" by _____.
6. If "A" has rejected it, I am mailing to "B" by _____. I will first make any revisions in my query or article that make sense to me in light of the editor's comments.
7. If "B" has rejected it, I am mailing to "C" by _____. I will first make any revisions in my query or article that make sense to me in light of the editor's comments.
8. If rejected again, where I will be sending it next:

9. Where and when my article will be published:

10. My best idea for my next article:

Here is another action plan now, but for books.

## A SIMPLE ORDER FOR A SUCCESSFUL BOOK

☐ **1. Select.** Select and narrow your subject or subjects to your best shot, the one you have a passion for, have the most to offer on and the message you most want to get across.

☐ **2. Commit.** Make a total commitment to it. Change all those "I wants" and "I wishes" to a firm "I will." Absolutely no more trying, hoping, maybes, ifs and mights. (If you cannot check these first two, stop here and go back to dreaming.)

☐ **3. Plan it.**

☐ Choose the subject.
☐ Create an outline (organize it into chapters).
☐ Make a table of contents.
☐ A good title is important.
☐ What do you think the title should be?
☐ Make a rough cover for your book to help give it reality.

☐ **4. Survey the market.**
    ☐ Who will buy it?
    ☐ Why will they buy it?
    ☐ When and where will they buy it?
    ☐ Are there any foreign market possibilities?
    ☐ How will you use the book?
    ☐ Will you seek a publisher or self-publish?

If you will seek a publisher, research the best publishers for your topic in bookstores and market guides. Bookstores will show you who is publishing what most recently, and *Books in Print* (libraries will have it in hard copy and on disk) will show you all the books in print on subjects similar to yours. You can ignore any books, no matter how fine or formidable, that are now out of print. Get copies of the books closest to the one you have in mind and check them out. Not to copy, but just to be aware of their approaches, strengths and weaknesses. This will help you convince editors that you are familiar with the competition and can outdo it.

Write a good proposal (see *How to Write a Book Proposal* by Michael Larsen) and send it out.

☐ **5. Consult yourself.** Pull out every morsel of your own resources—everything you know and feel about the subject, and write it down.

Have you thought of perhaps a better title?

☐ **6. Consult the shelf.**
    ☐ Research near.
    ☐ Research far.
    ☐ Make others aware of your topic and plans so they can help you.
    ☐ Beg for help from anyone knowledgeable.
    ☐ Make an art or illustration file.
    ☐ (Remember, you want the best possible title.)

☐ **7. File everything related to your book or topic so that it's:**
- ☐ Neat and orderly.
- ☐ Well marked.
- ☐ Easy to use.
- ☐ Separated clearly into as many topics as it needs to be.
- ☐ Portable.

☐ **8. Rough it.**
- ☐ Consult your outline or table of contents.
- ☐ Then write.
- ☐ Put several copies of your draft in spiral binding.
- ☐ You've gotta have a good title!

☐ **9. Edit and add to it.**
- ☐ Read it yourself, with a "cold eye."
- ☐ Have knowledgeable outsiders read it.
- ☐ Get someone good to edit it, if necessary.
- ☐ Toss the trash.
- ☐ Add more where you need to.
- ☐ Rewrite parts that could be better.
- ☐ Recheck your files for things to add.
- ☐ Print and bind a clean copy of the revised manuscript.
- ☐ Keep looking for more good stuff.

☐ **10. Do artwork and layout.** What kind of look would you like the book to have? Find samples of what you like to show your editor someday. If you have a novel format idea, you might even have a designer do several sample pages or a couple of spreads to convince publishers of the merit of this approach. If your book will be illustrated, find prospective illustrators and get some sample sketches.

**If you are self-publishing:**
- ☐ Decide on page count.
- ☐ Design the chapter openings, the size and style of the text, and everything else in your book (a freelance book designer can do this).
- ☐ Come up with a better, and then final, cover or jacket design.

☐ **11. Publish (if self-publishing).**
- ☐ Make a list of places (bookstores and other outlets) to sell your book.

☐ Decide what kind of discounts you will offer booksellers.
☐ Decide how many copies you will print.
☐ Decide on a publication date.
☐ Make a media list and plan your media campaign.
☐ Design and produce any giveaways (bookmarks, postcards, etc.) you will use to help promote your book.
☐ Send out copies to the media.

☐ **12. Sell and enjoy.**
☐ Give to family and friends.
☐ Sell at seminars and speaking appearances.
☐ Give as gifts.
☐ Investigate premium sales.

## FORGET "SOMEDAY"—LET'S DO IT

Would-be writers are fond of the word someday. You can use this expression as one word, someday, or two words, some day, and the longer you wait, the more crowds in between the some and the day, the farther they get separated and the greater the chance that someday never comes!

I wonder, in our dialogues and conversations through life ("someday I'll visit," "someday I'll read," "someday I'll write"), what would happen if starting right now we were to substitute the word "today" for "someday"? Imagine the impact or outcome—wow! Do it now, make someday *today*.

---

If you aren't convinced yet, here is a little exercise that will help bring home the fact that "someday" doesn't stretch on forever. Sit down and calculate the number of years you have left on this planet (the average man lives seventy-four years, the average woman eighty). Multiply this by fifty-two, the number of weeks in a year, and it will make you think in a perspective you never have!

---

### When is a *better* time?

When is a better time to write than now? A mortician told me a while ago about a family that decided to search for something decent to bring to the funeral home to dress a middle-aged woman who'd died suddenly. (For years and years she'd always tended to look a little shabby.)

They discovered, much to their dismay, many boxes of beautiful apparel she had saved for a later time, which of course never came. What is "trunked" is too often defunct!

Do it today. *Get ready, set, write!*

---

**Where will you be one year from today? Still wishing to be a published writer, or well on your way to realizing your dream? Unless you have clear goals, discipline and a practical work plan, you may never see your work or name in print.**

**CHAPTER 4**

# *The Big Step: Getting Started*

## YOU'VE GOT TO START SOMEWHERE . . .

The world is full of people who want and wish to write, but never start. Starting seems to be the biggest obstacle in writing. Too many would-be writers scare themselves silly mulling it over and over, worrying and wondering, listening to horror stories and talking to others about all the negatives. Or believing exaggerated success stories that make writing sound impossible for them.

It's like building that dream house. People want it, and build it in their mind, talk about it, promise themselves and others that it will be done. But years slip by waiting for the perfect time and the perfect property, the perfect plan. In any area of our lives or aspirations, things don't just come together by themselves.

But once you put the money down on a piece of property and then walk around out on it on Sunday afternoon and pace it out and put a stake down where the house will go, magic happens. Everything begins to move and flow.

Great books or articles don't just come, either. Nothing just happens in writing—you have to make it happen. Waiting for everything you've been dreaming of to come showering down on you from an idea and handful of notes is futile thinking.

You can't wait to work everything out before getting to work. Never wait to start something important, something you really want to do. Starting has its own power—it welds you to the event, the desire. Starting is the official proof to yourself and others that you are really going to do it, which in turn makes all kinds of resources appear. Thinking it over, and even fantasy and daydreams (which you ought to take notes on), are good for a writer. But when the time comes to write, then write. You accomplish more through movement than meditation. Timidness in writing gets tiresome, not just to you, but to all those people you've been telling about your "someday" book for decades now.

At some point, you've got to quit sampling and circling and just bite off a chunk and chew. You learn to fight—and organize—in battle much faster and better than you do forever thinking it over.

Being afraid of writing is downright ridiculous. Who and what is going to hurt you? And writing is a low-capital investment. If you do it and lose it, or have to rip it up and start again, or it doesn't sell, or no one likes it, you aren't out much but ego (which may not be all bad). You did get some experience and a chance to set up some good habits and systems. Maybe this first fling was just the audition for the great book or article coming in the next ream of paper. No writing is wasted. A painter's best painting owes a debt to the thirty-eight terrible ones that came before.

You just cannot have the best, the most, or for that matter anything without *starting*. Right now, at two A.M. if necessary, during the worst part of your pregnancy, right after you've been fired, during your divorce, while struggling with your diet, when you are sixteen, when you are sixty-eight, or while it is raining.

## WAITING ONLY MAKES IT HARDER

Many people say to me, when I ask them about the little writing assignment I gave them for a brochure, newsletter, catalog or the like, "I haven't got to it yet, but it's sitting right here on my desk." Sitting isn't ready. Sitting isn't going anywhere. And worse, **the longer something sits, the older it gets, and the harder it is to do.** Staleness turns off a writer, or anyone else. It's true that finding the time, the tools, the place and the mood is all part of getting ready and organized to write, but *starting* will get you on your way and marshal these more effectively than anything!

Once you begin to write, it's amazing how much will just come. I'm a big believer in roughing things—just getting what you have to say down in any form at first. As you're doing this, new angles, new approaches, new aspects of the subject and entirely new ideas will flash into your mind. Don't let these distract or derail you, just jot them down on a separate pad and stick with your original focus. Once you have that down, go back and flesh out your new idea. Just watch—while you're developing the new idea, others will bless the old brain. All of this results from just starting.

## CAN'T SEE THE TREE FOR THE FOREST?

Many people who want to write never get started because they see the project as one giant task that appears overwhelming. If instead you envision a book, for example, as a bunch of individual pages someday bundled together, it seems much simpler. A page a day (which is nothing) would result in a nice 180-page book in a mere six months! Put a big bucket under a tiny drip of water and see how fast it fills. A book or article is the same.

## DO YOU NEED TO BE PERFECTLY ORGANIZED BEFORE YOU START?

You'll be the first if you pull it off! Organization is not an accomplishment, it is a constant process. Start when you're reasonably ready and the rest of your organization will happen as you write. Waiting for the ideal before you do it will never fill many pages. Once you accept that all need not be perfect for writing, you'll begin to get something done.

## THE BIG THREE

If I were asked to divide writing into three basic needs, they would be:

1. Materials: the equipment and resources
2. Mechanics: how to go about it
3. Mental willingness and ability

But I would not give these equal weight. The mechanics, which most people really get hung up on, I would not give more than 20 percent of the writing process. And the materials, as important as they are, amount at best to another 30 percent (with the mental resources far outweighing the physical ones). It's that last need, mental willingness and ability, that really tips the balance and determines how much we write.

So don't spend too much time lining up tools and technologies. All you really need is pen and paper, and a private place (and you can even get by without that if you have to).

Forget the idea of waiting for some new creative tool to help you break into print. "Boy, when I get a new computer (tape recorder, voice-activated software, etc.), I'm going to write my life story, a journal, that great book or articles for all the magazines." It's amazing how few tools and little time it takes to write when you are ready.

The success of writing is in the content, fresh from you, and how it gets into print physically (what particular means or machine you use) is not all that important.

## WHAT DO YOU REALLY NEED BEFORE YOU START?

We've tried to give you ideas for planning and organizing every area of your writing life in the different chapters of this book. But what preparation do you really need before you start?

1. Something to write with and on (paper and pen or machine). See chapter five.

2. A basic knowledge of English, including grammar and sentence structure, etc. If you think you might need some help, or a refresher, take a basic English course at a college or vocational school. Manuals on basic grammar and usage come in handy, too. You don't have to worry as much about spelling if you have a computer with a spell-check program.

3. Choosing a subject and organizing your notes and thoughts on that subject. (See chapters three, six, eight and nine.)

4. Deciding on the form (novel, short story, article, etc.—see chapter three) you want to write in.

This is all you need to start, so don't get lost in over-organizing. Some people spend so much time tallying and filing and re-filing and programming that they never get to the real program of writing.

## UNCOMPLICATE THINGS!

A life of constant complication will unfocus you and sap your energy. I can't tell you to just dump all your problems, but I can tell you that if you have a lot of unnecessary burdens in your marriage, job, finances, home, even your health—take some time before you write your "great novel" and shuck off as many of these as you can. Take a hard look at it all and get rid of the things you don't really want, that aren't really necessary, that don't give anything back for the effort you invest in them, that just end up problems again and again. We never get all the thorns out of our sides, but if you are carrying too much baggage into your writing career, you can't devote your full self to your work, and your work will suffer, in content, spirit and timeliness. Uncomplicate your life, and your writing itself will come easier. The peace and order of your personal life will carry over into your paragraphs.

## WRITING SEMINARS

Writing seminars can be helpful, particularly in deciding the kind of writing you want to do, or type of market you want to approach.

There is a great variety of classes and workshops in schools, and there are correspondence courses and annually conducted writing conferences. You must satisfy yourself that the time and money you spend somewhere is going to give you what you need. Here are some criteria to consider:

1. **Who is teaching?** This is a biggie. Are the instructors qualified to teach, from a long and strong background, or one lucky best-seller?
2. **What are they teaching,** specifically? Is it what you want and need to know, or is some of it eyewash only?
3. **Are you ready for the seminar?** You don't want to forget what you learned by the time you need to call it up.

You can spend your entire life attending seminars and conferences instead of actually writing, but these assemblies can work to your advantage if you use them wisely. Writing conferences give you the chance to meet editors and other writers, network with successful professionals, learn about new markets and writing opportunities, discuss problems you are having with your writing and maybe even get acquainted with an agent. Writing seminars, on the other hand, generally cover specific writing topics in depth and focus on the mechanics of writing.

Search the Internet for dates of upcoming writers conferences, or check with your local college, university, library or writers groups. A few helpful Web sites are the Associated Writing Programs (http://awpwriter.org) and Writer's Digest (http://www.writersdigest.com).

## A FEW PRACTICAL POINTERS ON STARTING

• If you do your drafts in longhand, use ink, not pencil. It has more commitment!

• Is dictation an easy way to start? Dictated copy (perhaps because we like to hear ourselves talk) has a high "blather" quotient—it's wordy, loose, sloppy, rambling. Though it comes out of our heads, it somehow doesn't seem to be run through our brains as writing is.

> *Since I couldn't type, I dictated an entire draft and then went through it and revised it ... and revised it ... and revised it. After so many rounds of revision, you begin to forget what you were actually trying to say. In this manner I discovered that the spoken word and the written word are two different languages, and good writing is easier done right on paper to begin with. I not only had to reorganize everything, but translate it from the one language to the other.*
>
> —*Jean Loftus*

• When you first start writing, don't worry about whether the spelling or English is perfect—just get down what and how you feel. You can edit and eliminate the awful, offensive or overly personal parts later, but get your first instincts down there, in writing. Once you have something on paper, it's easy to make it better. Do it now and perfect it later.

• It may help to remember that in anything you write, the spotlight is not on you, or on the magnificence of your writing style, but on the subject. Good writing is not just fine words put together; it is *about* something. Once you really get into your subject, the words will come easily and naturally. And you will feel more comfortable and less self-conscious.

• Specialized software for writers is available to help the writing process, especially for fiction writers and screenwriters.

• Don't hesitate to write and publish on any level in order to gain experience and accumulate clips—local newspapers and magazines, church bulletins, catalogs and newsletters. Many people have gotten started with letters to the editor!

> *To help yourself get started, break your project down into "blocks." Don't tell yourself you're writing a book, say you will be writing a page, or a chapter, or whatever does not seem too daunting to you. Breaking a project down into manageable parts is helpful.*
>
> —*Lynne Alpern*

Be bold with the editors at your local newspapers. Call them and ask what they are looking for. E-mail magazines and ask for guidelines, or consult their Web site. Tell them you are willing to provide them with sample articles for their consideration. Schedule a visit. Sometimes you can accomplish more in person.

---

Idealists like most of us writers have the tendency to hope, or even wait for the ideal time, mood or market before they proceed. If we live life waiting for the coast to clear, we will never land. We need to face the fact that things won't be perfect and *just start*. People who wait until the right time to sit down and write seldom do. If you wait too long, you'll never write anything but your own obituary for someone else to put on paper.

**CHAPTER 5**

# *Organizing Your Work Area*

Now is the time to set up your own miniature word city—the place that is going to house your talent. The actual room or space where you will write, call and interview, where you will set up your files and machines and store your inventory of tools and supplies.

A place to be used, not shown off, that can inspire you and speed you up, not tempt you into indolence. A place where you can be comfortable and tap all your resources efficiently, a place to conceive seeds that will grow into everything you've dreamed of harvesting.

This is another area of personal preference—the ideal office or writing place for one person might be a turnoff for someone else. I'm a spreader—I use acres of tabletop for my projects. If I can't see it, it doesn't exist. I have friends who are appalled at this and wouldn't think of having anything but one sheet at a time exposed. Whatever your style, you want an area that suits you and nudges you to go to work.

## THE FIRST QUESTION: WHERE

In the old days it was assumed that you found a cabin in the woods, put on a trenchcoat, stuck a pipe in your teeth, found a dog to lay at your feet and maybe a lover to sit by and cheer you on as you typed two-finger on an old typewriter. Today we imagine writers sitting in high-rise buildings surrounded by fantastic electronic gear that will even clear your throat for you. Neither image is really true. Writing spaces can be as unique as the people who use them.

### An office in your home

Most beginning writers have to use what they have available. We usually don't want to build a house addition or go out and rent a suite to produce our first pages of print.

But even working with what we have, we can and should alter, lay out and install things to produce a space that will really enhance our production. The following elements will help you get ready to write and encourage you to continue, whether you live in a forty-room mansion or a tent:

**1. Privacy:** Try to find a place where you can get out of the flow of family activities and everyday affairs. This may mean the back bedroom, attic, basement or a separate little building behind the house (see pages 60–62).

**2. Quiet:** This is an important consideration. Many people claim that noise doesn't bother them, but it takes its toll—even soft music. Part of your mind has to process it. When you're really writing you need silence, and the place that can best provide that is what you want. If you can, choose an office site that is away from the TV, doors, family room and kitchen. To improve the sound resistance of an existing room, you can install soft flooring (thick carpet!), sound-absorbing wall coverings, and sound-absorbing window coverings.

**3. Convenience:** Though we do want a quiet and private place, access and convenience can affect our accomplishments today more than ever. We rarely have days or weeks to write, but often only minutes, so choose your writing place accordingly.

**4. Space:** Writing is a physical act as well as a mental one, and we need room to set up our equipment to store the raw materials of our trade, and even to pace about and think, if that is part of our writing routine. Think through all the furnishings and machines you want and need (see pages 62–69). Don't forget space for storage—file cabinets, drawers or cabinets.

> *One thing the writer's office needs is plenty of storage space.*
> *More than you think you need now. File cabinets, shelves and*
> *bookshelves, and "slots" (cubbyhole devices).*
> *—Peter Seidel*

**5. Counter space:** This is a must, as important in an office as in a kitchen. A nice big desktop and plenty of table or counter space to spread things out and sort them on, to lay things out and put them together, will do more to improve your organization than any computer program around. Things you use or consult often should be visible and easy to reach.

**6. Shelves:** There are many good uses for shelves in a writer's office. Many writers like to store information in three-ring binders and keep them within reach. Shelves are, of course, also a good place for key reference books, project piles and the like. On a shelf sure beats in the way. (More about this on pages 68–69.)

**7. Light:** For both utility and atmosphere. Having plenty of light has a positive effect on you when you're writing. You never want to have to strain to see, and a brightly lighted office is more inviting and upbeat.

You will usually want general or overall lighting for the area, plus task lighting for your work station(s). If you want even more light than that, consider wall-mounted fixtures. Overall lighting can be provided by ceiling fixtures, recessed ceiling lights, or a ceiling-mounted light that drops down over your work area. Halogen lights make good task lighting, but they can get quite hot. When setting up your lighting, remember that you want to avoid reflections on your monitor.

Fluorescent provides the most light per fixture, but the pulsating strobe effect bothers some people, and can cause problems with some computer monitors. If you opt for fluorescent, you will like the effect of daylight, warm white or color-corrected bulbs much better than the old standard bluish-white. Fluorescent fixtures with electronic ballasts are less likely to bother your monitor.

Whenever possible, skylights are a great way to get natural light.

**8. Climate control:** Fresh air and good climate control are a must—the temperature of the room will eventually be your brain temperature! Adjust the room to have ventilation and the right temperature. You don't want to freeze or have sweat dripping on your pages. You need no distractions when writing.

A window in the room or area can provide fresh air and a view of some kind (hopefully a nice one!) to switch your eyes to from time to time. This will help prevent eyestrain from too many hours staring at monitors and papers.

**9. Security:** Not that anyone is necessarily going to steal your stuff (machines or ideas), but a door on the room keeps wandering eyes off your rough drafts and idle hands off the phones. No one will toss something by mistake, and the cat won't have a chance to try typing or make a plaything of a neatly finished proposal. You'll feel better knowing you're going to find your work area just like you left it.

**10. Phone:** Make sure you have enough lines and jacks for all the phones and phone-line-using machines you have in mind. You may want to position the phone so that you don't have to move to answer it. A headset phone will enable you to type as you talk, and a soft ringer will be less intrusive. Wall-hung phones won't take up any of your precious desk space.

See chapters twelve and fifteen for more on phones.

**11. Power:** Make sure your intended office has adequate and well-placed power supplies and outlets. This may take some thinking and some additional outlets or circuits. It's best to have a separate circuit for your computer.

Surge protectors and battery backups for valuable computer equipment are wise investments if power is at all erratic.

**12. Make it fit:** Make your work station fit not just the space available, but your personality. I'm a surface writer—I want things out, in sight. I know writers who produce an unbelievable volume of work and whose desks and counters don't even have a germ on them, even when they're working on thirty projects at once.

The position of everything in your office, from your files to the wastebasket, should fit your physical and mental flow. Be bold enough to design or adjust your office so that it truly fits you. You will feel more comfortable and productive, and it will help keep things clean and uncluttered, too.

Keep your eye out for systems that suit you and adapt them to your own needs. Tailor your tools and furnishings to your height, weight, temperament, schedule, situation and ways of doing things. Borrow all kinds of ideas, try them on, and take and use the ones that fit you. No one owns organization, though some efficiency experts might create that impression.

**13. Self-contained:** Make your work area as self-contained as possible. The less you have to go out into the outside world when you're working, the fewer distractions you will face. This might mean a bathroom in or near your office, an outlet for the coffeepot you can't write without or a fax machine to eliminate the need for trips to somewhere that does have one.

---

**Some of the possible places to put an office in your home:**
1. The basement
2. An extra bedroom
3. A walk-in closet or former pantry
4. A utility room
5. A sun room
6. A foyer

**7. The attic**

**8. In a corner of a heated garage**

---

Where your writing headquarters is located is not as important as privacy and, for most of us, quiet.

**The bottom line is:** taking your writing from the bedroom or the kitchen to the "official cave" makes a statement to family and yourself that this writing is really a "go" in your life and not some passing fancy.

> *It's important to have a room of your own, for the sake of organization, and for a psychological reason, too: so that when you walk into that room you know why you're there. Everything I do in this room has something to do with writing.*
>
> —*Nicholas Bakalar*

> *Experiment, before you set up your office, with working in different kinds of places—places with a good, expansive view and cubbyhole-like, closed in places. How do these different settings affect you, where do you do best? A beautiful view would delight some of us, and distract others.*
>
> —*Peter Seidel*

> *Real writers, regardless of their publication status, work on their craft every day, and will be more productive in a work space they've made their own. I'm fortunate enough to have a whole room to myself, but with a little creativity anyone can find "their" space. Stephen King claims he wrote* Carrie *at night, using a tiny furnace room no larger than a closet as an "office." Mary Higgins Clark has said she wrote her early novels on a kitchen table, working for hours after her preschool children were asleep. For that bit of time the table was* her *space.*
>
> *A writer who believes in the importance of his work (why write if that's not the case?) will make space for it. The space will be personal, a place containing whatever the writer needs to focus on the lonely, isolated business of writing.*
>
> —*Robert Sloan*

*If you can't assign an entire room to your writing, an area of an existing office can work, or shared offices. You can also set up an office in the master bedroom or the family room. The furniture can be arranged to make it seem like a room within a room that will give you the privacy you need. The big plus of family room sharing is that young children can play alongside Mother while she writes and not feel so separated from her.*

*If you must share your writing area with an at-home business or family office, then the challenge is to deal with things and put them away regularly in their assigned area so that they don't become a distraction for your goal of writing.*

*—Pauline Hatch*

## A TRULY SEPARATE OFFICE OF YOUR OWN

Working at home is great, but even better is working in a separate building at home. A building that puts you many feet, and one or more closed doors, away from the constant distractions of the house itself and the rest of the family. My coauthor Carol works in a metal "pole building" across the driveway from her house, and her partner, the literary agent Oscar Collier, did much of his writing in an artist's studio that he built himself on the sandy soil of a Long Island estate. Up on a hill at my ranch in Idaho, I built a fine three-thousand-square-foot concrete facility to house all of the tools and machines I need to run and maintain my ranch. A smaller version of this would make a super writing studio.

If you can afford, or have the space for, a separate building, this would be ideal for many of us. When planning your writer's retreat, consider:

- Thick (or at least sound-resistant) walls
- Sound-absorbing wall, ceiling and floor coverings
- A good-sized window or windows, placed according to where and when you want the sun
- Skylights
- A generous number of well-positioned power outlets
- An efficient heating and cooling system
- Sink or half bath
- Whether you want a separate electric bill for your retreat, or you want to run it off the house current

- Plenty of built-in bookshelves, and even built-in desks and work tables
- A small deck to sit on and ponder the project at hand
- Access/walkways from other areas
- Parking for yourself, and John Grisham, when he comes to visit
- Solid-core door with good lock!

Until you can afford a cedar-shingled A-frame or full-scale office addition to your home, here are some low-cost places to have an "away from the house" office at home:

1. A freestanding garage, or part of an attached garage.

2. A separate office building of inexpensive construction, such as the pole building mentioned earlier.

3. A workshop detached from the house.

4. A greenhouse or boat house.

5. A finished corner of the barn, or even a finished horse stall.

6. A storage building or shed somewhere on your property (Carol has some sturdy old concrete-floored chicken houses that could be converted to offices without too much effort). There are companies that make movable buildings complete with windows and wood floors. These are meant for storage, but they could easily be low-rent writer's retreats. You don't even need a foundation or slab for them—they can just be toted to your place, leveled and set up on concrete blocks, which the company will supply. Nearly every lumberyard offers small utility buildings perfect for this purpose.

7. Trailers, or mobile-home units (available used as well as new), already have a kitchen and bath. And the portable offices, called construction shacks, used on construction sites are by no means shacks, but very efficient offices. Or write in the camper or motorhome that you only use a few times a year!

8. A spare room in a business office of any kind, on or off the premises.

Do you want an office outdoors? Maybe not. The idea of working out on the lawn or the deck is always appealing, but trying to do paperwork outdoors has its problems, from wind scattering or blowing your pages around to excessive glare from bright sunlight.

---

**The wonderful thing about writing, for fun or for a living, is that you can do it anytime, anywhere! You can do it in your living room or**

kitchen, in a bedroom or dorm, a barracks, in prison, in a tank, on a tractor, at the lake, or in a chicken coop, in Idaho or Ohio. It doesn't matter for the basics, or when you're just getting started. But like the man who makes fine paintings or furniture, when you can arrange something a little better, a little bigger or better designed for the purpose, it will enhance your productivity.

---

## YOUR WRITING EQUIPMENT—MODERN OR OLD-FASHIONED?

*Dear Don,*

*I hope you are taking note of my up-to-the-minute, twenty-first century letter writing device. It's called a word processor. Is there anything I could point out about its precision, the beauty and diversity of its type, its impeccable spelling ability, its error-free finished copy, its speed, its memory, not to mention its style . . . that would influence you to consider adding your pathetic old manual typewriter to your Junk Museum? Give it up, Don. That poor old thing deserves a spot right next to the canvas goat nursing bra! Or the two-faced gargoyle magazine stand . . . or the hydraulic napkin lifter. Or maybe it could be nestled next to the battery-operated "Flake Off" dandruff removal brush . . .*

*—an excerpt from a letter from a writer friend*

I love what computers do; I own hundreds of them in my various businesses, and profit greatly from them. I keep my people in the best upgrade going, but I don't have one myself, I haven't touched the keyboard of one yet, and I'm putting out many books every year.

Whether I'm an old fogy, stubborn or unteachable is irrelevant. My point is that you can write a lot of good stuff, anytime, anywhere, in any style with a free pen and a two-dollar pad. So don't get caught up in the "I can't start without a computer" syndrome. It's amazing how few tools it really takes to write when you are ready.

Even in the computer age, automation can't replace preparation or inspiration. Brilliant things were written five thousand years ago in primitive conditions with primitive tools. Some of the greatest writing ever was done by candlelight with a leaky quill pen. Nothing is old-fashioned that captures feelings, facts and figures for the public to read.

I get guffaws from everyone who sees the old manual typewriters in my three plush offices. But I usually bang out three times as much copy a day as the folks who spend their time sorting through the jokes and trivia of thirty e-mail messages daily. Old-fashioned? Maybe, maybe not. The results make the final judgment.

All of my initial drafts are done on a yellow legal pad with a motel pen (Marriot's are the best) or an old 1969 manual Olympic typewriter. I'm fast as lightning, spelling words just enough so they can be recognized and capturing my thoughts any way I can.

Before you submit a final draft to a publisher, it must be typed—editors won't read handwritten manuscripts—but if you don't have a typewriter or computer and don't want to learn to type, you can hire someone to type your finals (see chapter one). The success of writing is in the content, fresh from you, and how it gets into print physically (what particular machine you use) is just simple mechanics.

**Computer considerations:**

- If you're only using a computer for writing, just about any reliable computer will do. If you plan to have Internet access (and you should), a 56K or faster modem is best. If you require a really fast Internet connection, look for an Internet Service Provider (ISP) offering digital cable access.
- A larger monitor, say 15″ or larger, will display more copy and make viewing, and editing, easier.
- On the Internet, make sure your ISP has a local dial-up number, if possible, to avoid long-distance charges.
- Your local community college or an experienced friend can teach you the basics of using computers and word processing software.

*The first computer for a beginning writer? Any relatively new computer will do. If you're buying one, get a good cheap one, but not too cheap. If you have no experience and no support, I suggest [Macintosh's] iMac; if you write and go places, a laptop.*

*Go to the library, or a college computer lab, a large computer store, or even a friend's, play around with computers for a week or two, decide the features you like, want and need, then shop around to find what you feel comfortable with. Talk to someone who buys computers for others, and say, "Hey, I want a good* cheap computer to get started." Someone who buys thirty or forty computers a month really knows.

The smartest thing I ever did was buy my daughter's old computer for a hundred dollars. I wasn't afraid of damaging it in any way. It wasn't the latest thing, but it did everything I needed. I did some of my best writing on it because I wasn't intimidated by it at all.

To get a used computer, you can go on the Internet and go to sites such as http://www.dellrefurbished.com. Dell is the largest producer of PCs and sells machines here that have come back to them and been refurbished.

—Carl Mills

A primary consideration in choosing a computer is the initial learning curve. Macintosh is easiest to use, because it has intuitive interfaces. Apple wrote the book used as a guide by all programmers to human interface design.

—Ed Rach

What word processing program is best? Whatever you like to use. If you've never used one, then buy the one most people use. There are times when going along with the crowd is not a bad idea. So buy Microsoft Word. Many people like to use Word Perfect, however, because it allows you to tinker more with the text.

If you're going to be working regularly with someone, getting the same program they have will make things more efficient.

—Carl Mills

I am a poor typist, as well as dyslexic, and on the old typewriters, I made so many mistakes and then had to make so many corrections or do the whole thing over that it was too frustrating. A computer set me free. It was invented just for me. Word processing corrects my errors, and it can be revised easily and endlessly. A spell-checker also quickly locates my ytpos (typos).

—Jenny Behymer

The computer has opened many avenues for me. I teach a nonfiction writing course online. I can correspond with editors and

*e-mail last-minute assignments faster than I could without it. With e-mail, I can pitch ideas and articles without spending a dime on postage. All this for a person who is computer illiterate.*
—*Mary Jo Rulnick*

*The computer has been a boon to me because it facilitates rewriting. And when you write for kids, you spend most of your time rewriting and rewriting and rewriting.*
—*George Sullivan*

*On a computer, I can rework a document twenty times or more without a significant amount of effort. Typing on a computer is so easy that I can explore various methods of presenting information and then offer the editor my best.*
—*Kelly Boyer Sagert*

## Other key office equipment

1. An answering machine and caller ID will help you screen calls and allow you to return calls at your convenience. (More on this in chapter twelve.)

2. E-mail services and a fax machine enable you to send messages anytime, day or night, without a time-consuming conversation. It's better to have a separate fax than direct fax right into your computer. The latter puts you at the mercy of any idiot who might decide to send you something harmful.

3. Internet services for research purposes will save you many hours in a library.

4. A multi-line phone gives you a dedicated line for the computer or fax, or both, while keeping one line free for phone calls.

5. A small office copier lets you make copies at home rather than having to go elsewhere.

6. A postage scale and supply of postage eliminates trips to the post office.

7. A generous pile of office supplies, especially paper, and printer, copier and fax toner cartridges.

8. Filing boxes for disks so they are stored away from damaging effects.

9. A camera can be very handy to keep on hand should a photo opportunity present itself. Consider buying a good-quality camera that does not cost a fortune to take pictures to supplement your copy. And learn how to

use it. Take a photography course at a university branch campus, community center or photo shop. Pictures help sell stories and books.

### Furnishings

You don't need a matching computer-gray, ergonomically designed office suite or a two thousand-dollar mahogany desk to get started. You can make do with what you have and gradually add and replace things. Office furnishings can be found not just at office supply stores and showrooms, but—more inexpensively—at used office furniture outlets, auction houses, yard sales and moving sales.

#### Desk

Go for the biggest desktop you can lay your hands on. Big desks of all types and sizes can be bought inexpensively at used office furniture outlets.

If you don't have a desk, buy an inexpensive wooden door at a home-supply store, put three coats of polyurethane on it, and some sturdy boxes or short file cabinets under it and bingo—an instant executive-size desk. Two of these and a clean floor will give you acres of room to lay out and view your ideas.

## THE WRITER'S OFFICE

### Bare bones
desk
good chair
large table(s)
a writing machine: either a word processing computer or a typewriter (preferably with memory). If you opt for the former, you will also need a printer, Internet access and a place to store disks and CD-ROMs.
good lighting
phone
calendar
places to file things, such as file cabinets or stackable containers
bookshelf
key reference books
scissors
stapler and staple remover
tape dispenser

letter opener
pencil sharpener
ruler
wastebasket (more than one, in handy places)
paper
notebooks
pens, pencils, erasers
highlighters
envelopes, mailing supplies
paper clips and holder
rubber bands
rubber cement
paper towels/tissues for cleaning glasses, monitors, etc.

### Desirable but optional
answering machine
headset for phone, or speakerphone
fax
copier
calculator
scanner
tape recorder
copy holder
visitor chair
couch or upholstered chair
postal scale
place to store toner, copy paper, etc.

### Advanced
lucite frames to display copies of your books
framed artwork from your books
shredder for unfavorable reviews
uncomfortable chair for unwanted visitors, or critics

### *Tables*
Now hit a used office furniture store or the local "mart" and get a couple of tables. Folding banquet tables are fine for the purpose. Laying out your work has lots of benefits—physical, mental and psychological.

And picking up something can be easier at times than opening a computer file and printing it out.

### Chair

Spend some time picking out your chair, because you're going to be spending a lot of time in it. A used office furniture outlet will have scores to choose from. You want one that is comfortable and that swivels and has casters so you can roll around from one work area to another, or the desk to the file, without getting up.

Never choose a chair just by looks. The only way to choose one is to pull it up to a desk or whatever, close your eyes and sit in it for several minutes. How does it fit your leg length and feel to your back and rear? It should have an easy to use (preferably gas cylinder) height adjustment.

### File space

Buy some filing cabinets or whatever you intend to use to do your filing (see chapters six and fifteen). You can get used one-drawer cabinets (that cost $250 new) for as little as twenty-five dollars at a used office furniture store. It's amazing how many books and articles you can store in one filing cabinet.

Overkill on drawers, cabinets and other places to file things—it's better to have too much room than too little.

### Shelves

You need to have your key resources right around you, or just steps away. Having to leave your writing space to chase after something really breaks your flow and invites distraction.

While more and more reference material is on computer, or online, and can be reached without turning from the monitor, there are still times when you want to consult hard copy—dictionaries, phone directories, market guides and other reference books. These should be on a nearby bookshelf and as up to date as possible. Bookshelves and cubbyholes are also great for storage and a good way to keep projects separate.

• Bookcases make great project pile organizers, and you can find a great selection, wooden and metal, at used office furniture outlets. Taller is usually better to take advantage of the space the case takes up.

• You can get a lot of storage space from a wall full of shelves on standards. But if you take this approach, don't try to hang the standards on bare sheetrock. Have a carpenter (or the home handyperson) install strong enough supports on the wall to hold what you intend to put on here—books and papers are *heavy*. You don't want to be wiped from the scene by a shelf avalanche before your best-seller is done.

• Even better than shelves for making the most of wall space is the following design from a literary agent's office: Build yourself a couple of tall plywood "bookcases" with not just shelves (about twelve inches apart), but also dividers in the shelves, and slots in the shelves that enable you to change the position of the dividers. This will give you a cornucopia of big cubbyholes that can house books, magazines, manuscripts, mailing materials and project piles equally well.

### Mailing center

To aid with the all-important business of getting things not just written or made out, but actually mailed, it helps to make a little "mailing center." This can include things like stamps, envelopes of different sizes, mailers, Jiffy bags, manuscript boxes, labels, rubber stamps and packing tape, all assembled in a convenient spot with some counter space to pack and unwrap things. Don't forget a highly visible outbox for things ready to go!

### Bulletin board

If you have one, you need a *big* one, so use the wall itself if you want to. Bulletin boards are great for those temporary reminders, as well as for flow charts, to do lists and important notices. You might even like a bulletin board with built-in dry erase board.

You can also use them for things you want to display, admire or show off to those who might drop by the office.

## MAKING THE MOST OF YOUR SPACE

*The first thing you need to do is decide exactly what the functions of your office room or area will be. Then you need to get everything out of here that will not contribute to those activities. After you move out the things that don't belong, then you need to decide exactly where to put everything else.*
*—Pauline Hatch*

1. Have a floor plan so that your desk, computer and printer, file cabinets, worktable, phone, fax and copier can be conveniently close, but not on top of each other. Make as step-saving an arrangement as you can. Consider whether you are right- or left-handed.

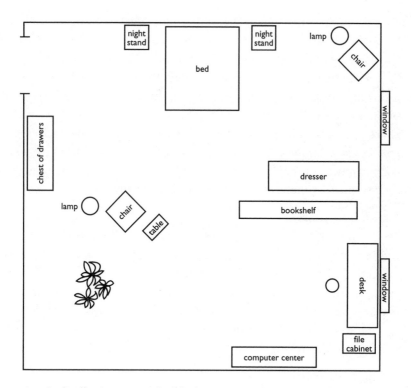

*A writer's office in a master bedroom*

2. Consider asking a student of architecture or office design for advice.

3. After working out a floor plan, set up your office and try working in it. You'll soon see where improvements or changes might be made for efficiency or convenience.

4. Office supplies: If you keep things together and always in the same place, you won't waste time digging and searching for things. And it'll be clear at a glance what you do and don't have. If you don't want to spring for an office-supply cabinet, you can use a closet or old wardrobe with shelves.

> *It's important to have everything in one place so that when you're ready to work, you can work. If you have things scattered about, every time you do a job, you have to get ready to do it all over again.*
>
> —*Deniece Schofield*

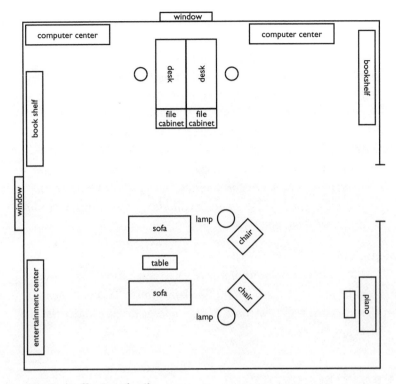

*A writer's office in a family room*

If you work at a computer, you want shelves at arms length for the reference books you use most often, with the ones you use most often closest. The shelves should be spaced such that you can reach things without leaning or stretching. Paper references are sometimes easier to use than the multilayers of a computer reference system.

If your work center is a computer, consider a U-shaped setup, so while sitting in your chair, you can swing around and reach anything you need—book, paper, tool or project pile. Or you can stop typing and swing around and edit or read, or work on paper for a while.

To get a U-shaped arrangement, you don't have to go buy an expensive "computer workstation." You can set your computer on a desk, and then put long tables on the left and right of you. This way you just have to make a forty-five degree turn from the computer to reach or do something else.

*In the U, have the equipment you use most often closest to you. I have my scanner and printer right next to my computer, so I can just reach over and pull off the freshly printed proof or scan something in, without getting up from my chair. I have the phone (with built-in copier) a little farther away.*

*Copy stands (that attach to your monitor, desk or the tables on the sides of you) are a big help when you are typing from something, and more than one is even better. You can use one for the report you need to excerpt from, one from a book you are referring to often, one for another source, etc. It's much easier to just move your eyes from one to another, than to pick them up and hold them open, etc.*

—Ed Rach

*I don't have to get out of this chair to reach anything from a ruler to a postal scale to a three-ring punch. There are pencils, pens, even refills for those pens in a large drawer under the keyboard.*

—Robert Sloan

## A PORTABLE OFFICE

If you don't have an office, can't make one or can't get much done in the office you already have, because of constant interruptions, there are other options. Guess where 90 percent of my writing is done? On the go! These are some of my most productive alternate offices:

In my car
In church
On the plane/in the airport
In motel and hotel rooms
In the garden
On my tractor
In the jungle and banana grove of my Hawaii home
In my shop
In meetings anywhere
In TV/radio studios
In classes and seminars

All I need to take advantage of any of these places is a couple of pens and legal pads and some atomic earplugs.

*I keep everything relating to a book in progress in a portable file box with a lid and handle. I keep the box next to my computer when I'm typing, and carry it with me everywhere so that I can work while waiting in the doctor's office, or wherever.*

—*Deniece Schofield*

When setting up your office, ask around, and see what other successful freelancers are doing and using. You don't have to copy them, but it might help you to see things more clearly. There are plenty of options around, so just line them up and pick one.

You do want a comfortable and well-equipped office, but if you visit the stationery, office supply and furniture stores too much, you'll end up a shopper and shuffler instead of a writer.

## CHAPTER 6

# *Organizing Those Irreplaceable Raw Materials*

There is nothing more important to organize than those irreplaceable raw materials of our trade: notes and ideas. How we record them, and even more important, **what we do with them,** can make all the difference between success and failure as a published writer.

Good writing draws upon a lifetime of experiences, impressions, observations, information, facts, stories, quotations, examples and human interactions. The key is to bring all of this together in an orderly way so that it can be weighed, sifted, culled, kept and assembled to create the finished product and spark ever more resources. This means not only never failing to write it down "on the spot," but getting your notes, thoughts and ideas from scribbles on napkins, 2 x 4s, envelope backs and notebook pages into a well-thought-out and easy-to-use filing system.

In this chapter you will learn how to set up a sound foundation for your filing, how to "capture" and file all kinds of things, and then how to keep track of everything everywhere.

## THE QUILT PARALLEL

At county fairs, community craft shows or church bazaars, I spend most of my time inspecting and admiring the quilts. The finished product, like a finished book, is a the result of putting hundreds of pieces into a carefully preconceived pattern. Quilt making, like writing, is a process that takes skill and accuracy, and the design and layout of the pieces can parallel perfectly with your initial outline or plan for your book. And quilts, like books, need enough of certain subjects to carry out a thought or pattern.

But the real brilliance, the foundation of the quilt, begins with the spotting, keeping and cutting of the raw material—the vision of what that old garment will look like when presented to people in some order. The usable is artfully stripped out of the original source and stored, sometimes for many years, before it is used. Buying material for a quick quilt never conveys the feeling or depth of one made from pieces clipped from all the fabric of your life. You've got to tap yourself and everything around you. Books are much the same. You don't get ready to write just sitting in a library or tapping into the Internet. You've got to tap yourself, early and often and thoroughly.

## CAPTURE IT FOR YOUR COPY!

We writers spend a lot of time worrying about "good stuff" getting edited out or forgotten, or otherwise slipping through the cracks during our writing. This seldom is a serious problem. The real disaster, and a much more common one, is letting good material slip by before you ever put pen to paper.

A feeling, an idea, a revelation, a suggestion is prime, you are excited by it, and everyone you share it with is, too. So you say to yourself, "Man, that's dynamite! I'll get it down on paper later." And then it is gone—you either can't find it or don't remember it. Things like this have to be captured and cataloged in your collection if they ever are going to enrich the copy you intend to write.

---

**Every day thoughts, ideas and writing opportunities come out of nowhere, strike you and then bounce off into infinity. No matter how good they are, you won't have them when you want them unless you capture them.**

---

### The art of taking notes

"Taking" is an apt word for notes, because that is exactly what you have to do—it almost has an overtone of stealing. But every writer either has to be a good note-taker, or have a never-ending memory and recall. For most of us, note-taking is easier.

There is no day or hour set aside for note-taking; you do it twenty-four hours a day, everywhere and for any reason that might interest you. Take notes whenever your instincts tell you to, if there is any chance at all that something may feed your writing interests. And **take**

**them now,** don't sit, lie or stand there thinking it over. Record the action right during it! If you wait to do it later, even if you remember all the details, you will lose intensity. What you jot down in the midst of an experience (such the time you spent searching every house, hill and valley in a seventeen-mile stretch for a lost cat, in the heat of July, while five months pregnant) will be different from what you might write about it, recalling it some calm, cool and unburdened moment a year later.

---

Everything and anything that registers *wow* in your life (it might be butterfly collecting or bungee jumping for you, but for me it's an easier-to-clean kitchen counter design), *grab it right then.* Write it down, clip it out, take a picture of it, photocopy it, make a sketch of it, get the address, send for it, tear it out. These gems are everywhere—on a label, in a magazine, in a movie or during a conversation. Some of my best information comes "on the run."

All note-taking requires is a pad and pen or pencil. Most of my notes are handwritten. Not because that's faster, but because much quality material comes to me, or I come across it, when I'm far from my typewriter. I'm much better off scribbling it down right then than trying to type it beautifully later.

Sometimes you can grab a handout or brochure and reduce it to the bit you want to keep, and this is note enough, probably better than your own handwriting. If I hear a speech or presentation that is even close to one of my target subjects, I get a copy of it if I can.

You should always have paper and a pen with you once you are a writer. Never go anywhere without them. The best notes come when they please, or in the middle of something else, not when you are ready and waiting.

I won't even run the bases in baseball without a small pad and short pencil in my pocket. When I'm doing something active, I have a piece of paper folded into something not much bigger than a business card. When I'm driving, there is always a yellow pad next to me on the seat. The result looks a little first-gradish, but I have it, and I can class it up afterward. Some people keep note cards, notebooks and Post-its all over their houses so they can immediately write down thoughts before they lose them.

Be careful with brevity when jotting notes. Abbreviations are easy to remember for about two weeks; after that, even the best wrinkled brow cannot decipher some of the scribbles and partial words we've jotted. I've spent my share of time trying to decipher notes I jotted while driving rural Idaho mountain roads. I know there is a brilliant idea in there somewhere, but I may never recover it. I hate this.

If you take notes in some awkward situation, read them over quickly as soon as you can. Often you can add a few letters or words right then that will make decoding much easier.

---

### Capturing conversation

No one, not just would-be writers, should get locked into looking for material on the written page or Internet only. The best raw material for writers, the most alive, the most personal, the most original, the most spontaneous material comes *free*, simply from conversation. Absolutely brilliant, humorous and wise material is pouring out all around you, every day, from when you get up in the morning to when you go to bed. Capturing the spoken word is my key power in writing. It is absolutely authentic and up-to-date, and there is plenty around to gather to edit down to the gems. The flavor I've so often been praised for in my thirty-plus books is predominately from conversation, or the spoken word. If you know how to capture it, you can be "writing" all the time, even while you're working, playing, resting, visiting or waiting. All of that great stuff is out there, and it's yours for the taking.

Just be sure to capture it verbatim.

For example, no one says more clever or funny things than young children. When a kid says something spontaneously, it gets many laughs and all kinds of admiration. That often doesn't happen when we repeat the same thing to others—we may get ho-hums, or blank stares that say, "What's so funny about that?" The problem is, we didn't say it exactly like junior did. We got the general point across but lost all the charm. When the child said it, he reversed nouns and verbs, subject and predicate, made up his own words, and so on.

Likewise, the other day I heard someone remark that her father-in-law drove crooked because "he farmed everyone's ground from the road." Everyone laughed. When I used that a day later, no one smiled. Finally I realized I'd said: "He farms from the road" (leaving out "everyone else's ground," which is what made the expression memorable).

Whenever you hear good dialogue, make sure you capture it—write it down. I've picked up some great stuff from coffee breaks, town meetings, living room and dinner table conversations, in doctors' offices, at lectures, listening to the people around me at malls and even from talk radio and TV. Everyone out there is a walking, talking book, so don't miss out. Don't just try to remember it for later. You never will. And what you do salvage when you try to call it up from memory alone will be neutered.

### Keeping notes overnight is long enough!

You took a note or clipped something because it related to a thought or need. So don't waste it. Notes tossed into a pile to "process later" can easily become valueless, just be a puzzle and exasperation to you. You will forget what they were about, or no longer be able to decipher them.

Don't leave your notes unsorted for more than a week. Type or file or organize them somehow, so they can move on to the action column, out of your dreams and into your plans. Process notes promptly—it only takes minutes, and will reward you monumentally.

The biggest reason to review notes quickly is that even the best of us have a hard time keeping up with someone speaking rapidly in an interview, for example. If we transcribe those notes within twenty-four or forty-eight hours, we have a much better chance of filling in the gaps and deciphering scribbled abbreviations. Don't tuck things away until they are meaningfully translated, or you may never manage to translate them.

### Identify it now

I cannot stress enough the importance of labeling resources now, before they go anywhere. **There is a reason why you wrote it down, clipped it or grabbed it.** Label it the second you save it. Then no matter what happens to it after that (in case you're a poor organizer), you can find and place it faster.

Having the finest notes, articles, clippings, drafts, or whatever without a big, clear identifier on them is just like having a box or book of recipes without titles. All that good info is still there, but you have to read half or three-fourths of the copy to figure out and identify each dish (if you even can). You wrote, cut out or kept that bit of information for an idea or reason. Write it on the piece—now. Trying to figure out the what and why of a morsel or scribbled message to yourself months later is pure misery.

### Symbols can simplify

Ever notice that when ideas, information and inspiration begin to flow, they often come in floods? Then you have to frantically collect all this and can easily end up with a "pile to file" (often requiring you to reread and study things to figure out where they go or what you saved them for).

When collecting resources of any kind, the minute I grab them, rip them out or jot them down, I "brand" them in the upper left-hand corner of the page with a little shorthand symbol.

For example, anything destined for my autobiography (which I've been working on almost every day now for twenty-five years), which has the working title of *How I Made a Million Scrubbing Toilets,* I use the symbol $. So my notes look like this:

$ The story of the dead rat under the employee cafeteria

$ When dad had me arrested for shooting the sage hen out of season

I have a symbol for every one of my writing projects, and it helps keep things instantly recognizable and organized.

When I type my rough notes off of my notebooks or whatever onto a nice clean sheet called "Write and record," I put one of these little symbols in front of each word, sentence or paragraph. Later, when I snip these sheets up and distribute them to the appropriate files, there is no delay, error or uncertainty as to what things are or where they go. In fact, I generally don't even read these things as I am sorting them— I just see the symbol and send it on its way.

Here are some others of mine; I'm sure you can think of even better ones for yours.

| | |
|---|---|
| **200#** | *Lose 200 Pounds This Weekend,* a book on dejunking |
| ∧ | (a steeple) A church book I'm working on |
| **BB** | "Boss Book": A book on how to be number one with your employees |
| **2000** | My "new century" cleaning book |
| **Sweep!** | A book on littering and the environment: *Am I My Brother's Sweeper?* |
| **GOGP** | This book, coauthored with Carol Cartaino |

Things I feel are especially important or worthy of further expansion I write "key" in all capitals by.

This makes it easy to recognize and place material instantly, no matter how many projects I have in the works at any given time. These marks are for your own personal identification of things, so (unless you have an office helper), it doesn't matter if anyone else understands them.

---

**Sorting up front is smart, smart, smart. A good idea isn't a good idea unless it carries a finish line label of "good idea for what?"**

---

## Sort and separate as you go

Having a lot of material to draw from is wonderful, unless it is all in one big pile. Sorting is something we all dread and can be avoided so simply.

A subject is like a bolt. When all the subjects, or all the bolts, are tossed in one place, file or pile, you spend most of your writing time digging and hunting. In my farm shop, I have tens of thousands of bolts and nuts, which I use often to build or repair machinery. The bolts are separated in bins by size—¼, ⅜, ½, ⁵⁄₁₆, ¾, ⅞ and so on—and in some cases by length, so when I need a bolt I can find the right size instantly. This saves hundreds of hours of searching, and it is just as easy to put a bolt under a size as it is to toss it in a pile. Something can be placed in a specific place as easily as in a general place. And then **you have it when you need it.** So once you have something, put it in the right computer document, on the right list or in the file. Don't make it a two-stage process.

As a writer you know your different subjects, so right from the beginning, start organizing material under its respective subject or project. Don't have one big file that says, "Writing." The same goes for files on disk. Use clear names for folders and subfolders to make access painless and efficient.

When the box or file on an individual subject gets too big, I subdivide it into rough chapters, and then instead of tossing things in the general subject file, I place it in its chapter. If you proceed this way, it's amazing how far along a book will be before you officially begin to write it.

You can also have a catchall, or one single location: a box, an envelope or file folder, whatever, that you can quickly toss all such items in. Just put it all in this one central location. Every week or so, take a few minutes to remove all the saved scraps and pages from your catchall, and put them in their respective files or make new ones as necessary.

Once you have a system in place, the amount you save under any topic is irrelevant. Your brain and room can handle any number of writing projects at once if you keep subjects separated (and things labeled) as you go along.

## SETTING UP YOUR FILING SYSTEM

We want to not just save, but be able to find and use, the treasures (sto-ries, ideas, anecdotes, articles, pictures, jokes, quotations, contacts, etc.) and important papers such as bills, contracts and releases that too often get lost in clutter. This means some kind of filing system. The basic pur-pose of filing is to keep things and be able to find them fast.

All of my books get their start as a simple file folder.

Building quality files costs little time or money and is the best resource you can have. You can have forty or four hundred categories as easily as four—it just depends on your reach and interest.

Don't be a sheep in your organizational system, or in anything. Unless a filing or organizing system complements the way your mind works, it will be of little use. Before you start your filing system, think about its purpose and intent. There is no one way to file—you can and should do it to fit your personality, goals, interests and projects.

### Filing tips

• Find one place for all your files. You might only need a small box, or if you're like me, you will want a number of large file cabinets.

• Look in an office-supply catalog, and you will see not just the usual vertical and lateral file cabinets, but all kinds of filing units, including files on rollers, those that fit under workstations and open file shelving units for highly active files. Pick the best kind for you. You can also use some of the ideas on pages 87–89, or my own system of drawers and boxes (see chapter fifteen) to fit more and bulkier things.

• Be sure to allow enough room in your storage containers for what you will be gathering. Once you start serious work on a subject, single files will triple, and new categories will bloom. Overstuffed files will become clutter, and mean damaged documents.

• Have the bed ready so you can jump right into it—have the files, the drawers, the space ready and waiting before you need it, not after you come staggering home from a great event with all kinds of great new ideas and notes and clippings and literature.

• File headings on a file, box or drawer, are free (or don't cost much to make), so don't be sparing with them. Make all you need. I make a file for every single separate subject or talk I will be giving so I never spend a minute shuffling through papers.

• When you're naming files, follow the way you think. Your files are personal and should follow your thinking patterns, not someone else's. What's easier to remember and retrieve than "Funny quotes," when you need to give a speech or presentation? You can be as creative as you want in naming your files, but avoid cryptic or confusing labels, or what goes in may never come out.

• See chapter fifteen for ways to use color to distinguish your files.

• File it, don't pile it. Even the best material becomes a burden the minute it has something on top of it and you have to look for it (the old "I know it's in here somewhere" bit). Your goal is to be a professional writer, not a paper detective.

• File it in the rough. Don't try to groom and perfect things until you need to use them, because some of them might end up to not be worth it, and most of them will be shaped by what you decide to use them for or with.

• Whenever possible, reduce the size and bulk of what you file. Don't file the whole magazine, just the article you wanted.

• Small pieces of paper and little snippets of copy can fall through the cracks of our minds and files and desks, and the wind will blow them away if you happen to be working outside. Tape, glue or staple small things like this to a full page (the back of old drafts, etc.) before you file them. This also gives you space for any notes you want to make on the item. Anything too big to fit in my files, I reduce the size of by photocopying or neatly folding.

• The key to a functional file system: Refile things daily, or twice a week. The sooner you refile, the fewer mistakes and lost things there will be. Filing only takes a minute and can be done in idle time, such as while watching TV, when you're not feeling creative or you can't sleep.

• If have a lot to file, sort everything before you file to save time (so you only have to find and open the "Aardvark" file once).

• Keep your files fresh. Of course new stuff is coming in all the time, and hopefully, as you begin to write, some stuff is coming out of those files, too. Once something has been used in your writing, checkmark it, put a line through it or move it to a different kind of file. Periodically, clean out obsolete or dated information you've either replaced with new, or know you won't need.

Your "writer's reservoir" will not become polluted unless you toss trash into it—unmarked and unidentified things—or fail to return things you've already used to it. When you read through a file, box or drawer and see that something is outdated or off the point after all, toss it. You continually clean house in files, just filtering the water in your reservoir.

• Never lend your files! Not to anyone, not even to close family, sweethearts, members of your church or even your children. Show files or copy them, but never let go of them. They may get pirated, or lost or damaged. People are pretty careless, by and large, and rarely return things promptly. If you want to share what's in one of your files, copy it, keep the original and give the copy away. Recovering or regaining lost information or material will cost ten times what it did originally in time and money, and a hundred times the emotional energy.

If you follow these rules, when you need to use a file or drawer you will have what you need in it. It is fun, even before you begin to write about something, to sit down with it on your lap and just leaf through it once in a while to remind yourself of what is there. This is a pleasure and always a surprise, and it refreshes your inventory in your mind.

I find that the best way to use one of my files or drawers is to find a large, clear table or floor and dump everything out on it and roughly organize it by subject or order. This only takes minutes, and then you can quickly see where things go and what you might use.

If you end up with forty or fifty snippets you don't need or can't find a place for, great! Look at all the great options you just had. When you're finished writing, move any of these raw materials you might need to refer back to, to a file folder within that book or project. Then put the rest of the "reservoir" file back. I bet that before your book or article is finished, you'll go back to that file a couple more times and take some more things out to use.

## WHEN FILING ON COMPUTER

• Create as logical and orderly a system as you would with paper files, putting all related documents into clearly named file folders and setting up folders within folders, or more than one file folder for a given subject if necessary. Name the documents, too, as clearly as you can, so you can find things quickly.

• Try not to daydream while your computer is asking you where you want to file something because you can misfile things quicker on computer than in a file cabinet. And if you don't remember what you called the file, you may never find it (or spend an hour opening and closing documents looking for it).

• There are computer programs specifically designed for filing notes and ideas, including InfoSelect and PaperPort. They make it easy to enter notes, to find all your notes on a given subject quickly, and to group and combine notes in different ways. There is even a program— The Paper Tiger—designed to help you set up and manage paper files more efficiently.

*I tried for years to get better control of all the information I wanted to keep track of, but all I did was end up with mountains of pieces of paper and notes. Finally I found a better way: one that makes the whole process much easier and faster. I computerized all my notes and records. I now use this approach for almost all my filing, and it's cut my paper files by over 60 percent.*

*There are several software programs that work well for the kind of "idea management" I'm talking about, and most of them cost well under a hundred dollars. The prerequisite for any software program I use is simplicity and a very short learning curve, so I chose the PaperPort Deluxe software from Visioneer. I also bought their edgefeed scanner, which is a nifty device about the size and shape of the cardboard center of a roll of paper towels. This sits between my keyboard and monitor and is activated by simply sticking a piece of paper into its slot. This launches the PaperPort software and scans a document even if you are in the middle of doing something in another program. After it scans your document, it delivers you back to the program you were working in. It does a nice job on color or B&W (very good file quality, but not publishing quality).*

*Most of the software packages such as this, designed to keep track of miscellaneous things like thoughts and notes, also include OCR (optical character recognition) software, which makes conversion of typewritten or typeset material into Microsoft Word, and many other programs, easy. Converting the text in this way allows the software to search for individual words or groups of words, making it unnecessary to cross-reference your file folders.*

*Using PaperPort is very intuitive and is similar to Windows Explorer itself. The software also has a great set of tools, including such things as a highlighter, a Post-it note type tool that allows you to add notes which can be printed or suppressed, and one that enables insertion of a picture or other graphic. Other tools permit you to crop or enhance a picture. A tool I find indispensable is the "stacker," which works like a paper clip allowing you to group several items together, or to pull them apart. There is also a "Link Bar" to which you simply "drag" an item to send it to a fax machine, OCR, word processor, image processor (like Photoshop), printer, the Internet, etc.*

*Software such as this is a powerful aid to getting organized. Of course, you still have to do the work—the thinking—but these programs may just leave you with enough time to do it!*

—*Michael Patton Hoover*

---

**The rewards of faithful filing are many, including a feeling of control (when you need something, you can find it), and a neater, cleaner, more efficient office.**

---

### Make an anecdote bank

Writers develop a keen sense for anecdotes over time—we immediately recognize a happening or incident that will make good copy. Whenever life serves up one of these, quickly write it up and put it immediately in the file it belongs in. Or write a concise, few-sentence description of it and put it on an anecdote list so you can write it up later, when the perfect topic appears.

Example: Carol ordered a custom-made, solid-oak bookcase once to fit a certain spot in her office. She went to great trouble to figure out how many shelves were needed, what size they should be and exactly how high and wide the bookcase should be. She gave all these measurements to the cabinetmakers over the phone. When they called to say this handsome piece was ready, she drove in excitedly to pick it up. There it was standing proudly against the wall—and she was stunned. All the measurements were correct, but the height and width dimensions were reversed so that the bookcase was wider than it was tall.

A great story to demonstrate the importance of leaving nothing to chance when giving instructions. Carol could either write it up now, and drop it right in the file for the article she is planning on that subject or put a line in her anecdote bank that says, "the bookcase I had built that ended up with wrong-way shelves" and wait for an opportunity to use it.

If you write only a brief description, make sure it's clear enough that you will be able to "decode" it later. The meaning of things like this may be crystal clear now, while the experience is fresh in mind, but time can fade details and memory. So don't jot down "the driveway story." Better to say, "The time the highway department offered to widen the end of the driveway so the snowplows wouldn't run onto the lawn when turning around. A big crew spent a full day doing it, and when the first snowplow proudly used the now much wider driveway, it ran over onto the lawn."

However you file or identify your stories, be sure to do so, especially the ones that come from others, where it will be even harder to remember all the details later. Nothing is worse when you are ready to write than knowing you have the perfect story for the purpose . . . somewhere. If someone sends you a letter with a great little story for some purpose in it, copy that page (making sure you note what it's from, if it isn't already identified), and drop it in the file.

Be sure to save those stories! Jot them all down—if you have ten to choose from, you can pick the best two. Just be sure to keep the other eight where you can find them and consider using them for something else. Real-life stories bring any subject to life.

Use your own stories and examples first—they have more authority, are fresher and of course more fun to write!

### The delights of duplication

Today copies can be made in seconds, for pennies, eliminating a million excuses and stress-outs for lost copy. Be generous with copies! I usually duplicate anything I have instantly, so this means I have two copies of what I write and what I collect, in two separate places (in case of fire or flood, etc.).

1. In my books, nothing exists until it's in hard copy. Always have hard copies of anything important, just in case.

2. If any doubt exists as to what chapter, or even what book or article, something belongs in, make several copies of the item in question and place a copy in each.

3. Once I have a lot of time and energy into a project, I make copies of the whole file or pile and keep them in different locations, preferably two different buildings.

4. If you intend to work on something while traveling, never take the originals if you can help it. Bring copies, instead, because carried-around

pages always get beat up, wrinkled, wet, greasy, etc.

5. We can be haunted, driven to distraction by the thought of lost copy (it may not have actually been that good!). To prevent this, when working on computer, be sure to "save" every fifteen minutes or so—your computer probably has an autosave feature that makes this easy to do. At the end of the day, and the end of the project, make a backup copy of all of your files on that project. Using a Zip drive, made by Iomega, is the most efficient way to do this, because it copies quickly, and Zip disks hold far more information than floppy disks.

---

**The big three of handling resources:**
- **Collecting**
- **Culling**
- **Calling up!**

---

Anything you cannot find immediately is *piled*, not *filed*.

## FILING IDEAS: POINTERS FROM THE PROS

*I believe in the folder system—one folder for each chapter. By the time you make up your folders, you've already done an outline for the whole book. Not that you may not end up changing this as you work.*

*I make copies of my outline and staple one to the front of each folder, with the chapter that folder represents circled or highlighted. I also draw a big number "6" or whatever right at the top, where I can see it easily.*

*Once you have your folders set up, you just toss things you've written into the appropriate folder. I don't put these folders in a file cabinet. At office-supply stores you can get "sorting" or "posting" tubs—steel boxes with slanted sides that are wider at the top than the bottom, have handles on the sides for easy carrying and nonslip coatings on the bottom. When you put your book files in one of these, you can find the folder you want more easily and review what's in it without taking it out. If you can't find a box like this, use any kind of portable filing box.*

*Amongst my folders for every book I have one for the "most precious" things I've thought of or come across, the things I can't afford to lose or forget to include. With a file like this, whatever you want to call it, you can easily check to make sure you used them all.*

    *I also have an idea folder for each book, in which I put any-thing by way of notes to myself on that project, such as "think the outline needs to be rethought," "need a character who is/can _____," or "Chapter eight is lousy because nothing much happens in it. Need to add some danger or problem to it."*

—Frances Spatz Leighton

*I keep a loose-leaf notebook in my sewing room divided into sec-tions: quilting ideas, children's clothing, adult clothing and craft projects. As I get an idea or clip a picture or article I simply tape it on a page of notebook paper in that section of the notebook. As I try an idea, I mark it "keeper" or discard it.*

    *I keep a similar notebook on home decorating and gardening. I clip pictures or good ideas I come across and add thoughts for changing or applying the idea in the margins of the page.*

—Beverly Nye

*As I am thinking about a novel, I fill a file folder with clippings, articles, quotes or whatever on it. I visit the city or country the story will be set in, at the time of year the story will take place, and note what things look like, what flowers are blooming, etc. I also talk to a lot of people there. A while ago, for example, I vis-ited the Center for Disease Control in Atlanta and talked to top experts there about an insidious "pig virus" one of my novels would be focusing on. I take pictures of places I am thinking of having action take place in and put the pictures in an album in some kind of order, with identifications. A movie camera would be better because you could pan scenes and see relationships.*

—Don Donaldson

*You can use a handheld recorder to take notes on things while driving, or a laptop with a voice-activated program. I often dic-tate things as I drive back and forth to school—this is some of my best thinking time, when I'm alone in the truck, an hour and a half each day.*

—Hollis Stevenson

*At the beginning of each new book project, I purchase large
envelopes that I label with my proposed headings, and I gather
all transcribed notes, newspaper and magazine clippings, journal articles and file them—as I come upon them—into the
appropriate chapter envelopes. This way I start work on a chapter and everything is in one place in front of me. Later, when I
need to check a reference, I just go to the envelope, and it's
always there.*

*—Janice Papolos*

## ORGANIZING VISUALS FOR PUBLICATION

"Word people" like us writers may be slow in recognizing the importance of visuals—art and illustrations of all kinds. In this day of TV,
video and digital everything, graphics are a great help in competing
effectively with all this and selling your work. Pages and pages of
straight text with a bit of different type or margin adjustment here and
there just doesn't do it anymore. Don't overlook the possibility of
including things in your book or article that people can look at instead
of read. Used well in a book, illustrations and photos do wonders to
help get a message across.

I always collect art and visual ideas for my writings, and they all go
in a file called (you guessed it) "Art and visuals," which I feed constantly as I go along. Picking up art ideas for your writings is exactly the
same as picking up notes or any other research: When you see or think
of something you like, clip it or make a little rough sketch of it yourself.
We always hear people (maybe even ourselves) saying, "I can't draw,"
but who really can, except the few people who are truly artists? We can
all make rough sketches and stick people, so do it. Get your illustration
idea down somehow and drop it in the file with a note that identifies it
(in case your stick men didn't do the job)— how it might be used, or
where it goes.

### Photos

A lot can be recorded or captured in a photograph, often better than
you can describe it in words. Cameras are inexpensive and easy to use,
and film is cheap today. If you can't find an illustration of something,
photograph it yourself, or get a friend who is a serious amateur photographer to do it for you. Even if a more professional photograph is

eventually needed, you'll have something that gives a clear idea of what you're after.

Remember, negatives are easily lost and damaged and hard to look through. Order doubles or triples of prints when you have them processed. This doesn't cost much these days.

Better yet, shoot slide film. You'll get clearer images and better color, and turning slides into prints is easy. Shooting slides will call for a light box, a screen, and a slide projector, all of which you should be able to pick up inexpensively.

There are also digital cameras now that don't require film—images are input directly into a computer that then prints (or transmits) the photo. This is not a thrifty way to go, but it is convenient.

*The most important thing about organizing your photos or illustrations is just that—having some kind of organization. You need a system. It doesn't have to be complicated, just a plan that will help you find what you need when you need it.*

*My husband and I are photographers/graphic illustrators, with most of our work filed as color slides. When we started out twenty years ago, we had no idea what kind of filing system we'd need. So we began with something simple—a category for each of the places where we did a lot of photography. We had one for Yosemite National Park, one for the Pacific coast, one for the town we live in, one for studio still lifes, etc. Each category was then broken down. Yosemite had shots of Half Dome, El Capitan, shots with people in them and so on. At first they were labeled at random—"A" for El Capitan, "B" for Half Dome, "C" for people shots, etc. Then as photos multiplied, an alphabetical approach seemed better. El Capitan got filed under "E" and Half Dome under "H," but still maintaining the basic categories.*

*We used a loose-leaf binder for each category, such as Yosemite. Within the notebook each subject—Half Dome, for instance—had its own plastic page or pages of twenty slides each. We built shelves into a closet to hold the books. It's not a perfect solution; there are some things we may never see again. But it's a very simple system, which hasn't changed much over the years, and we can still find almost any photo in the thousands now on file.*

*Your filing system can be simple or complicated, depending on how much material you need to keep track of. If you have primarily illustrations, consider manila folders and a filing cabinet. I have two filing cabinets, each of the two-drawer variety, that I use to support a hollow-core door. It makes a perfect desk with room to file all of that material that freelancers seem to collect in huge amounts. A simple alphabetical system should allow you to find whatever you need. Illustrations too large for a filing cabinet would require some special container probably available at an office-supply or art store.*

*If you have lots of illustrations or photographs, and you have the background for it, some sort of computerized system, such as a database, might be the answer. From our point of view, to start now to put everything into a computer file would take far more time than we're willing to spend. But if you're just starting out, you should consider this possibility.*

*With a database you list (and file) all your artwork, whether photo or illustration, numerically. You also enter categories to help you find what you want. For example, a photo of the Grand Canyon might be listed under Arizona, Grand Canyon and possibly national parks. If you categorize well, your database can give you a list of all the Grand Canyon photos or those on any other subject, and unlike our system, things probably will not fall through the cracks. For us, there are two possible downsides. One, if I'm seeking photos of the Grand Canyon, I now have to go through a lot of binders to find them, instead of only one. Secondly, computers do crash. So if you choose this route, backup, backup, backup.*

*Lastly and perhaps most important, once you have a system, use it and maintain it. File new material that comes in and put things you've used recently back in their proper places. If you do it right away, it only takes a minute. It's far too easy to stack things on your desk to refile "when you have the time." When the stack gets about a foot high, it's almost impossible to find the time. Then, when you need something, it's nowhere to be found.*

*Organization is a great timesaver, and it's easy. Find a system that works for you, and use it.*

*—Carol and Mike Werner*

*In our book* Sell and Re-Sell Your Photos, *we tell readers to put their photo cataloging info on 3" x 5" cards, whereas now many computerize it.*

*On the Web there are free cataloging programs, photo albums you can put your pictures into. They are free because there are ads in them. You put your prints in them, assign numbers to them and can share them with anyone you want. Just tell people they're at URL _____.*

                                        —*Rohn Engh*

---

All of the material you have gathered but not used in writing yet is your reservoir. It collects and builds up just as a water reservoir collects the tiny trickles of water running down hills and valleys and seeping up from little springs, the quick floods of heavy rains and the sprinklings of rain. If a reservoir has a dam to catch and hold it all and a smart gate to let it out when and if you need it, it will serve you well. If not, guess where the water goes? It runs off to here and there and nowhere, as do your ambitions and great notes and ideas and conversations and memories.

**CHAPTER 7**

# *Organizing Research*

Research is one of the writer's undertakings that benefits most from an organized approach, whether you are researching print media, from live sources or on computer. This chapter explains how to organize and target the information-gathering process and to make sure you get what you need while saving time, energy, paper, phone bills and miles on the odometer.

## THE BASICS OF ORGANIZING A WRITING PROJECT THAT INVOLVES RESEARCH, OR THE HELP OF OTHERS:

1. Think the whole thing through and list the operations that need to be done in the order they need to be done. What do you already have? What can you do yourself? And what must you get from others or elsewhere?

2. Think again, and add the steps you forgot to the list above.

3. If other people (such as a coauthor or assistant) are helping you with the project, decide what each person will do and put the name of the responsible parties next to each step on your list. Make sure everyone knows what he or she is supposed to do. For quick reference, put the name, address, e-mail address, phone and fax numbers of everyone working on the project on a single sheet and keep it handy.

4. Set up a time frame for the project, taking into account when the mission must be accomplished and how long each step may take. Allow more time than you estimate for each stage (*twice* your first guesstimate, or more, if you have a high "optimism quotient"). Make everyone involved aware of the time frame.

5. Do the things that need the most lead time first, or at least set them in motion (such as sending for or requesting information that may take awhile to receive).

6. Do, or set in motion, any steps that involve other people (to give them the maximum time to do their part, time to fit your request in and save overnight postage).

7. Check your time frame often to see where you are.

8. Continue with all the other steps on your plan, in order.

9. Follow up on steps five and six (above).

10. If time is tight now, concentrate on the things most important to the success of your mission and let some of the others go.

11. Continue down all the other steps in your plan until you are finished.

12. There is always some drama near the end. Always expect unforeseen problems, loose ends that take longer than you thought to wrap up or other delays of one kind or another. Take this into consideration when setting up time frames.

## CONSULT YOURSELF BEFORE THE SHELF

How many speeches have you heard where the speaker starts out by defining his subject straight from the dictionary? This is not usually the beginning of a stirring speech. Outside ideas, contributions and material are a great aid to good writing, no doubt about it, but be careful. To me, a speech, book or article created by gathering facts from others (the "authorities"), and then compiling them into a carefully homogenized finished product is sterile. Mere information passing is not the goal of a good writer, and getting people to read on isn't, either—but getting people to listen hard enough to change their lives for the better. And guess where most of that comes from? Directly from you, not statistics, polls and studies. These are great to reinforce and support what you want to say or provide a counterpoint to it, but it isn't the research's job to say it—it's yours. Your feelings, your passion and your convictions are what's going to fire the engine of your message.

So when you come up with an idea, subject or assignment, take a blank page and first write out everything *you* know about it. In other words, consult yourself before the shelf! Tap everything you know on the subject before you begin looking it up in the dictionary, the encyclopedia or on the Internet. Pull out all of your emotions, opinions and stories on the subject and see what you have. Then see what outside materials you might need. When you gather what "they" say before writing what you feel, you end up with a "they" book or article instead of your own. Remember that others can get the same thing from any public source, but no one else has what comes from you personally. Your own experience lends a subject more life and credibility than quoting Benjamin Franklin or Dr. Spock every other page.

Plus when you keep *you* in your writing, you will keep your interest in it, and readers will feel it.

## OTHER "IN-PERSON" RESEARCH

You can also research things by running them past other people. This gives you lots of credibility with both your readers and ultimately editors.

Direct one-on-one gathering is a premium writing resource. Any good material you can glean here saves time, helps you make and reinforce points and often germinates new ideas. And this is real-life nitty-gritty, not predigested, regurgitated ideas from secondary sources. So:

Ask . . .

Listen . . .

And write it down!

Just when you're sure you have everything lined up in order for the perfect essay, someone will, off the cuff, give you one or two new things even better than anything you have! And people love to be quoted. But this too must be written down, dated and filed, or you won't have it when you find a "fit."

---

**Greetings!**
    Don is tackling yet another of life's big dilemmas, **"HOW TO GIVE KIDS MONEY"**. From age 2 to 82 the transfer of money has perplexed us all at one time or another and we've all done some great things with great results and some dumb things with not so great results. We would love to hear **your stories, your advice, and your experiences, good and bad.** How DO you give your kids money? How much or do you pay for college? What about allowances? Do you pay your kids for grades? What about your married kids? Do you loan them money? Do you go into business with them? What about adult kids, married or not, living at home? Subtle ways kids drain the bank account? What about your grand kids, how or do you give them money? When is the magic time to no longer financially support your kids? How do you teach them to be financially responsible? What are your obligations to them? What are theirs to you? Etc., etc.

    We're wrapping up 6 years of collecting information and research on this subject and your input (we love solutions) would be appreciated. Fax your thoughts to us at **208-232-6286** or mail them to: **Don Aslett, Inc.**
        P.O. Box 700
        Pocatello, Idaho    83204
    To thank you for your efforts, Don will send you one of his latest books (autographed) so please include your name and mailing address.

---

*Sample "comment card"*

### Questionnaires and written solicitations

This is one of my favorite research techniques. It works well and costs little. Here is an example from one of my recent projects.

I printed up about three hundred of these and handed them out to people I thought had some brains and might be willing to help. Typically about two in twenty come back, but the material is usually rich. I keep all contributors' names and send them an acknowledgment, thank-you or even a free book eventually. I copy letters and filled-out forms from contributors to put in other relevant files and always keep the originals, too, in the main file for that questionnaire's subject.

## COMMENT CARDS

A variant on this approach. Most of us have access to a rich array of other people somewhere in our lives—in classes, presentations, seminars we are attending or giving, in meetings, at family reunions or on the job. In all of these and other places, we can collect good "front-lines" material on what we plan to write about. Many years ago I first made up a form for this purpose, calling it a "comment card." Something like this is easy to design and inexpensive to print. If you pass them out and then gather them up right on the spot (not later), you'll get about 85 percent of them back filled in, compared to about 15 percent if you send them out to people or wait till later to try to collect them.

These things are dynamite for four reasons:

1. They give you an idea of the real-life weight of subjects and concerns.
2. You often get leads to good secondary sources of information.
3. What is written here will jog your own brain and memory.
4. They alert people that you are writing a book, which on its own solicits comments and contributions. It includes other people in an exciting project.

Make cards or sheets like this simple and easy to fill out, so that, for instance, respondents only have to put an "X" or checkmark in a box, rather than provide essay answers. (But do provide a little space for those who really do want to do a little writing.) I always make mine 3" x 5" and print them on index card stock so they seem substantial and are easy to write on, handle and store. Best of all, they won't be rustled by the audience during your presentations, if you are speaking.

I've used these as evidence to support my conclusions, and they give me ideas for other books, media tours and interviews, too. The cards for *Is There Life After Housework?* are now fifteen to twenty years old, but still stored in two big boxes and still give me ideas. The little they cost in time and money has paid big dividends in the writing and sales of my books.

## SPONTANEOUS GROUP "RESEARCH DISCUSSIONS"

There is such a thing as group therapy for ideas and writing projects— or maybe we should call it "group enrichment." When I review where some of my best initial thoughts or anecdotes came from, it was often from a group discussion on the subject. One-on-one is always good, but there's nothing like bringing up the "big question" of your book in a group.

When people get going, they fuel each other, and as the discussion goes on, they try to outdo each other. This often brings forth some startling opinions and great stories. And believe it or not, after a group discussion, people will go home and think about something more than if you sent them a written request.

Group research discussions are usually free, too, and don't even have to be planned or scheduled. You just wait, like a panther in the shadows, until there is a lull at the water cooler, in the meeting, on the job or on a trip somewhere, and then politely toss out your question. (Needless to say, have a pen and notepad or recorder ready.)

One person (usually the most opinionated one) will lead off, his or her competitor will go next and then everyone in the group will toss their two cents in. You'll get some great off-the-cuff comments and analyses, so you need to capture what they say and how they say it. Just remember to tell it like you heard it. People structure their sentences differently and use different words when talking than writing—never forget this.

If you tell a group that you are going to call them together to discuss such and such, they may have preconceptions or misconceptions, but when you just guide them into a surprise "spill it all" situation, good stuff flows, and letting some of it flow into your book will make for livelier, better copy.

One of the best uses for a group is to help out with the always-tricky business of titling. A good title can be hard to come by, and this is one of the few areas in writing where the more input and ideas, from anyone or anywhere, the better. So explain the subject of your book or article, and get a group going on it!

## ORGANIZING INTERVIEWS

Interviewing is the more targeted way to gather "live material" for your writing project. Here are some pointers from the pros on the most effective ways to go about it.

> *I never transcribe a whole tape. As I'm interviewing someone, I start each side of each cassette on zero, then note where I am as the subject says something noteworthy: "124, story re how he started the company," or "325, stats re next year's budget" or "546, when bankruptcy fears haunted him." Then, when I sit down with my interview tapes, I just go to the key stuff and listen to those sections again, taking notes at the keyboard.*
>
> *Always test batteries, even fresh from a pack, before putting them into your recorder. Occasionally there is a "factory fresh" dead one. I carry a battery tester in my "interview kit," a small tool bag that also has extra tapes, batteries, note-taking equipment, a phone patch cord and a flashlight.*
>
> *You will need twice as many questions for a phone interview as an in-person chat. Phone conversations are much faster paced and to the point. Before settling in to do a telephone interview, disconnect call waiting. It's *70 on my phone—and yours.*
>
> *When you call someone to set up an interview, be ready to do the interview on the spot. Have some questions ready just in case the subject wants to talk now because she or he has to be out of town for the next week or two.*
>
> *—John Brady*

> *I never use a tape, though I tell the person I'm interviewing that they can tape our conversations if they want to. I like to make notes, because a tape makes people nervous. If I run into a spot that is unclear, I can always call them to unscramble it. I will always improve what they say somewhat, anyway.*
>
> *Promise people, and keep your promise, that you will send them not the whole manuscript but their own quote as you intend to use it so that they can call and complain or make changes.*

*I make notes in ballpoint pen on a legal tablet, or better yet, on a piece of 8½" x 11" paper folded in half. You don't want anything big or highly visible, just as you wouldn't wave a bed-sheet at a wild animal. To paraphrase Teddy Roosevelt, "Walk softly and carry a small pad."*

—*Frances Spatz Leighton*

*I don't ever use a tape recorder, because I relied on one once and it didn't work, and I ended up with nothing. So I take interview notes in longhand and my own shorthand, which I've developed over the years, on a letter-size tablet. I keep all of my original notes, even after I've typed them up in case a question should arise.*

*It's not a good idea to talk too much yourself when you're interviewing. At the end of an interview, I close my notebook and look at the person, and they usually give me one real good quote there at the end. And as soon as they leave, I write down how they looked, etc.*

—*Elaine Schimberg*

*I save my records of interviews for a year, because there is often someone who feels he has been misquoted. Then I can take out my copy and show him that if anything, I only made him look better.*

—*Seli Groves*

---

**One way of organizing interview material on computer when you've interviewed a number of people for the same project: First type it all up in a single document—each person's name, followed by everything they said. Then assign each person a number, and divide the material within their interview by topic with identifying subheads (such as "reasons to collect glass bottles" and "value of older bottles") above the topics and make a new document and put all of the answers to each of your interview questions together so you can pick the best, identifying the source of each quote with the person's code number.**

---

Researching the traditional way—in print media—and in all of the new ways on computers, both benefit greatly from an organized approach. It will enable you to find what you are after as quickly and conveniently as possible.

Exactly how do you do that?

Let's go right to the source, the research librarian of research librarians, Lois Horowitz, the author of *Knowing Where to Look.*

## The ABCs of efficient research, in print or online

The more things change, the more they stay the same. Nowhere does that saying apply more than to the art of research today. The heart of research, the material that answers your questions, remains the same whether it comes from magazine articles, books, encyclopedias, directories, government documents or someone's personal files.

But information is not just in print or on microfilm anymore. It's also on compact disk and on the Internet. As more and more people acquire computers with Internet access, the growing trend from print-only resources to online-only versions will accelerate.

Until the use of computers is universal and the Internet is a way of life, look for Internet access at your local library. The latest trend in libraries is to buy computers for public use. Of course, you will always be able to use the library's print collection—as long as there is one.

### BEFORE YOU BEGIN

Whether you do your research by computer, the printed page or a combination of both, there are ways to make it more efficient and satisfying.

Some things to remember as you embark on any hunt for information:

#### How much information do you need?

There is a fine line between not researching enough and not knowing when to stop. Consider the type of piece you are writing, how long it is supposed to be, the market for it and the interests of the reader you are appealing to. Then decide how deep you need to dig and how much information you need to gather.

Research is necessary to enrich, expand and develop information, but you don't want to end up a researcher instead of a writer. Don't let research add up a big bill for you, in time, excessive or unnecessary travel, phone charges, hired help and postage.

On the other hand, overkill is usually better than underkill. Having a lot to choose from is better than finding yourself short. Filling in the blanks takes time and mental muscle and can kill you when you are on a roll. Quickly leafing through and choosing the best of a dozen resources sure beats poring over and trying to extract something from a meager three or four.

So again, consider what you are writing and find the happy medium!

**Start early.**
Any type of research takes time, so allow for this—do it early.

**Remember "authority."**
We want what we get to be authoritative, something we and our readers can count on. Since the Internet, this issue has become even more significant because anyone with a computer can easily create a Web site without having his or her facts checked and post it for all the world to see. When looking for reliable information, consider

**1. Motivation:** Who has published the content on the site, and why? Both people and organizations can have biases, but individuals' agendas can be harder to uncover. Still, lobbyists, professional organizations, churches, companies and many other organizations have interests to protect, and careful writers will consider what they are. Try consulting U.S. government or university sites for objective information.

**2. Accountability:** Assess the consequences for the site's administrators if their information is faulty. *The New York Times* has more to lose by publishing inaccurate information online than the average Joe, so in general, Web counterparts to traditional media and other well-known institutions are more reliable than personal home pages. You may want to reserve judgment until you've checked several Web sites and compared information. When you cite a source, you'll not only be giving credit where it's due, but you'll also distinguish your opinions from someone else's.

**3. Timeliness:** Just because it's on the Web doesn't mean it's current. The constant work of updating a site is more than many people can manage. Look for a line at the bottom of the main page that says, "This page last updated on . . .," or analyze the content for clues to its age (dates or current events mentioned, passé cultural references). Because companies, governments and institutions have staffs to maintain sites, their information often is more current than that on individuals' pages.

**Start close to home.**
Before looking for the answer from someone across the country, look in your own backyard, whether it's a local library, a local research institution or simply people nearby. Local phone calls and interviews are easier on the wallet.

**It exists.**
The answer is somewhere. You just may have to dig a little deeper to find it.

**State your need.**
There's an art to asking a question. To give yourself the best chance of a useful answer, tell people exactly what you need rather than expressing it as a question that might elicit a yes or no answer. "I need to find an expert in cutting-edge pancreatic cancer research" is better than "Does this hospital conduct pancreatic cancer research?"

**Where is the information?**
In the BC era—Before Computers—my research plan involved a nine-step checklist representing the full spectrum of available research material, the idea being that the answer to just about any question could be found by using one or more of them.

These nine sources are

1. Books
2. Periodical articles
3. Encyclopedias, from the one-volume subject specialized to the thirty-plus volume general topic
4. Reference books (directories, dictionaries, bibliographies, etc.)
5. Government documents
6. Online databases
7. Microfilm/fiche
8. Original material (private papers, public records, etc.)
9. Experts and organizations

How has the Internet affected these nine steps? Let's take a look.

As you go through the steps, if you have used the Internet, you already know that information found there is more free-form than this nine-step plan. In the end, it's the answer or information that counts, not necessarily where you found it. Still, you can use the nine steps to help provide an organized approach to your research. The harder information is to find, the. more important a structured checklist becomes.

**1. Books:** Authors are still writing books, and people still want to read or use them for research. To find books by subject, you first must identify them. The multi-volume *Subject Guide to Books in Print* (SGBIP) was once the bible for identifying available books on a subject, mainly because it was so accessible. Now, SGBIP is online (usually via a library's subscription) as well as in book form. Plus, there are new ways to identify and find books. For example, try a subject, author or title search using one of the mega bookstore Web sites such as Amazon (http://www.amazon.com) or Barnes & Noble (http://www.bn.com). Their databases are huge and include many out-of-print titles.

To find almost everything that was ever printed on a subject, check the online catalog of a large public or academic library, including the Library of Congress. Most of their books are available via interlibrary loan. The Web sites of more than three thousand libraries in ninety countries are available through http://sunsite.berkeley.edu/libweb.

You may be surprised to know that as of this writing, there are hundreds of full-text books online and you can use a search engine to find them. (A search engine lets you do a subject search for useful Web sites.) Go to http://www.dogpile.com, type in the term "full text books" and see what you get—everything from *The Hungarian Revolt, October 23–November 4*, by Richard Lettis and William I. Morris (Simon & Schuster, 1961), Jack London's novels and *Little Women*, to *Natural Magick* (a sixteenth-century collection of books), the full text of more than three thousand books and pamphlets on Canadian history, and hundreds of works of classic fiction, popular fiction, short stories, drama, poetry, dictionaries, research and religious texts, not to mention the Bible and Shakespeare.

**2. Articles:** We used to find articles by subject through *Reader's Guide to Periodical Literature*, or one of the dozens of indexes to periodicals such as *Index Medicus*, *Philosopher's Index* and *Humanities Index* covering scholarly and specialized periodicals. Libraries are now purchasing network subscriptions to online periodical indexes, and card holders can access them via library computers or from their home computers.

You can still use the print versions, of course, but the online versions are easier to search (no more flipping through pages of different volumes). Also, most online indexes provide a free printout of the article, too (no more running to the stacks and photocopying the article).

Be sure to check http://igm.nlm.nih.gov, the Web site for the National Library of Medicine, where numerous health journals are indexed. Article abstracts are free online; full text is fee-based, but you can always photocopy them at your local medical school library.

While there is no single source to check on the Internet for periodical indexes, they appear as links in unexpected Web sites, so keep an eye open for them as you surf.

Also, remember that most online periodical indexes may go back only a few decades. You can pick up the trail in the print version if earlier articles serve your purpose.

**3. Encyclopedias:** Old as well as new encyclopedias can be useful in research. Most large libraries own encyclopedias published as far back as the Civil War or even earlier. Imagine the articles in them on scientific or medical subjects!

Online you'll find the currently published works. Check this Web site for links to several: http://infoplease.looksmart.com. Click on the word "encyclopedia." Most encyclopedias are fee-based and these can be accessed via your library's network subscription. Others, such as Britannica (http://www.britannica.com), are free, supported entirely by advertising.

**4. Reference books and directories:** Reference books such as almanacs and subject dictionaries usually found in a library's reference section contain snippets of information and facts. A good starting place online is http://infoplease.looksmart.com. Click on some of the research categories there such as "almanacs," where you'll find categories of information such as the Seven Wonders of the World, the forty richest Americans, a chronology of history, a list of U.S. associations with addresses and other typical almanac fare. For everything else, use a search engine that searches a dozen or more search engines simultaneously (called a meta search engine), such as Dogpile (http://www.dogpile .com). Be aware that there is much information that cannot be found through search engines since it is buried in databases where search engines do not penetrate, or behind the doors of a registered (fee or free) site such as *The New York Times.*

Published directories are great sources of addresses of anything from pet food manufacturers and funeral homes to lawyers. If you know the name of the organization you are looking for, type its name in Dogpile. If it has a Web site, chances are excellent it will show up this way. If not, search Yahoo (http://www.yahoo.com) by category. By typing in the word "dentists," for instance, you'll find the following (minus the descriptive annotations):

Bay Area [Calif.] Dentists Directory
  Top-Dentists [UK]
  National Dentists Directory

Association of Managed Care Dentists
American Independent Dentist's Association
American Association of Women Dentists
Internet Directories—Dentists

The potential for this kind of search is endless.

*No one person can know enough to write about the whole*
*breadth of the action in a novel without making some mis-*
*takes—but if you are paranoid and double- and triple-check*
*everything, you can keep the number of mistakes down. In one*
*of my novels, the action was taking place in a small town out-*
*side Madison, Wisconsin. After finding a sunset/sunrise table for*
*Madison on the Internet, I discovered that I'd forgot to consider*
*Daylight Savings Time.*

*The Internet really helps out here. You can find an incredible*
*number of things without leaving home or going to a library.*
*The other day, for example, I needed to know the length of a*
*human umbilical cord, and the Internet provided the answer:*
*two feet long.*

*—Don Donaldson*

**5. U.S. government documents:** The government is still the biggest
publisher in the country, issuing everything from pamphlets, books and
magazines to journals and position papers. Here you can uncover insider
trends; locate political contribution information; get the docket numbers
or case summaries and texts of opinions from most of the country's fed-
eral courts; declassified documents; investment abroad; even current jail
inmates in different cities by searching government Web sites at all levels.

How does one even begin to cover this wealth of information published
by governmental bodies? At Dogpile type in the city, county or state you
wish to research to narrow the hunt. At the national level, start with these
Web sites containing links to government agencies and their publications:

http://www.fedstats.gov
http://www.whitehouse.gov
http://fedlaw.gsa.gov
http://www.fedworld.gov
http://www.lib.lsu.edu/gov/fedgov.html
http://ciir2.cs.umass.edu/govbot
http://www-libraries.colorado.edu/ps/gov/us/federal.htm

**6. *Online databases:*** Online databases—public, not private—are now largely the Internet itself.

**7. *Microfilm/fiche:*** This category is probably the only one not represented on the Internet, except if you search the Web site of the major producer of microfilm collections, UMI/Bell & Howell, to see what's available. The enormous amount of material that was in microfilm before is still in large libraries. It represented just about everything ever published since the seventeenth century—books, magazines, newspapers, pamphlets, theater programs, political tracts, ephemera, journals, diaries and private papers. This is important for research in older publications and original material that will likely never be covered on the Internet.

There's a growing trend to move much of this information to CD-ROM, which will make the information easier to access. For example, the CD-ROM *American Journey: History in Your Hands* provides broad coverage of tribes and their common experiences via government documents such as treaties, eyewitness reports of battles and massacres, folktales, legal opinions and reports from the Board of Indian Commissioners.

**8. *Original material, private papers:*** The National Union Catalog of Manuscript Collections is a directory to unique personal collections in thousands of repositories nationwide such as the Thomas Edison papers in the Edison National Historic Site, West Orange, New Jersey. It is available at large libraries and online at http://lcweb.loc.gov/coll/nucmc/ (click on "RLIN AMC File Easy Search Form").

**9. *Experts and organizations:*** Experts are usually affiliated with companies, universities, think tanks and other organizations. Many of them have written books and articles. Look for them online through the directory search listed previously (in number four) or via a bookstore Web site such as Amazon. Another great source is expert Web sites such as Profnet (http://www.profnet.com), AllExperts.com (http://www.allexperts.com) or Experts.com (http://www.experts.com). These types of sites offer searchable databases, often vast, of experts on your topic and e-mail addresses where you can reach them. Because of the publicity opportunities and esteem given authorities on a subject, many knowledgeable people volunteer this type of service, or even pay to provide it.

A more informal kind of expert or organization you can tap into is a listserv, or e-mail list server. As you poke around on the Internet, you will discover groups or clubs that exchange information by e-mail—on certain kinds of court cases or copyright, for instance. If you subscribe to them (their Web site will give instructions—for some such groups you have to qualify), you will automatically be updated by e-mail on whatever the group's special interest is.

In your research hunt, don't give up. Poke around, ask questions, strike up a conversation with a librarian or someone in the know and place yourself in her hands. Learn what's out there and read the how-to-research guides such as *Find It Online: The Complete Guide to Online Research*, second edition, by Alan M. Schlein. No matter how much the format changes, there's an enormous amount of material available. There always has been, and there always will be.

---

**Research for angles as much as for information. You can find all the ordinary information about your subject like anyone else can, and this is all well and good. But it is how you paint, present or package your subject that counts. Take the subject of cleaning, for example—most people would find this to be "the removal of dirt." But you can look at it from many different angles: humor, health, safety, exercise, sociology, history, the environment, economics and even family and male/female relationships. It is digging up all this, and then picking well, that will make your writing about anything come alive.**

---

## ORGANIZING WHAT YOU'VE GATHERED

There are a number of ways to organize research. A No. 1 research rule . . . you don't have to use it all, but save it all!

1. File folders are a traditional way to keep certain types of information together so that it is not lost and is easy to find.

2. You can categorize the information on the computer and save it on a dedicated disk.

3. Designate a specific spot in your office where everything related to this subject is kept. It can be a drawer, a stacking tray or on a shelf. Place all research, books and everything you can find on the topic here.

4. When you're done with the current project, save all your background notes and information. A thorough job of research can open up other writing opportunities on the same subject—spin-off topics, articles or books. It may also give you the chance to approach the subject from another angle.

There is a time to shut down research and new incoming stuff, and organize and process what you've got!

**CHAPTER 8**

# *Organizing Your Market Attack*

This chapter will cover an area that often suffers from disorganization and the "hit or miss" approach—our efforts to market what we write. The central truth here is that the surest way to be published is to send publishers what they want and need, and to write things people want to read. *This* is the target and you can hit it if you pick a good subject and audience to address, and then proceed in a logical and orderly way from there.

## SELLING WHAT YOU WRITE

This is the part of authorship that many of us face too late—the selling of what we have written. Too often our egos and idealism can get in the way of what we are going to do with the finished product. Our or our family's loving a manuscript is not the same as the public's loving it. And until we get it in their hands, they can't love it.

Marketing starts with finding a publisher for your writing so it can get your work into the hands of buyers.

---

Beautiful and bold is isn't the same as sold!

---

### Your marketing plan

Whether or not your writing sells is mainly up to you, not luck or publishers or bookstores.

Your marketing plan should begin the day you think of a subject and jot your first two pages worth of material down, in great inspiration and enthusiasm. On the third page or so, you should stop and answer this big question:

**Who is going to buy this, and why?** No matter how much you love the subject or know about it, if you can't come up with a good answer here, I'd be real hesitant about going on to page four.

You can pick any old subject, spend a year researching it and possibly come up with a respectable end product, but in general a "good subject to write about" has three basic requirements:

1. Do you like it? (Are you passionate about it?)
2. Do you know it, professionally or otherwise?
3. Will it interest others? (Sell!)

Unfortunately, many of us may be experts in something that might not sell. Breeding emus, for example, might be a fascinating subject and you might be the world's foremost expert. Spending a decade doing a complete and perfect guidebook to it, however, may not be advisable if you are looking for best-seller numbers. It will have a very limited market.

If there are not enough people out there who need to know all the details of emu love life, you might, however, be able to turn this expertise "inside out" into a novel whose main character is an emu breeder.

A subject such as abortion, feminism, religion or racism—even if you are a true expert in it and have a passion for it, may not sell a bunch of books or a pile of magazines. Most people look to books and magazines to be entertained or to gain something or solve a problem—they don't, unfortunately, necessarily want to be challenged, lectured to or forced to think.

Analyzing your passion, knowledge and commitment to a subject, and its timeliness or marketability, is important. Here is one place I suggest you make a call to or visit a publishing professional to run your idea by him or her. This opinion might be free or it might cost a little, but it's better than working for four years on a manuscript and sending it to someone only to hear, "This is good, but it will never sell."

1. Strong expertise in a subject and the ability to help actively market it yourself is a good omen for a new book. Energetic marketing and promotion by the author have put many a book onto the best-seller lists.
2. Finding a new and unique angle or approach is critical, especially for popular subjects that have a lot of competition.

I managed to write a million-seller on the most lowly profession and one of the least popular subjects—cleaning—while others in the same field didn't make a dime putting out this type of book. **In my case my book succeeded because it was the first to bring the methods of the professionals to the home cleaning scene,** and because my humorous and visual style helped to lighten and sell a dreary subject.

> *Whatever you are doing or would like to do, see if there is competition for it. If there is, bells should go off in your mind and you should say hip, hip, hooray! It means there is a live heartbeat of a market out there. If there is no competition, that should be a red flag. It means someone else tried it and failed, the market is simply not there or the time is too soon for it.*
> —Rohn Engh

---

One big ingredient of publishability is talent, of course, but *almost equally important,* when it comes to actually being published, *is choice of subject*—what you choose as a vessel to pour all of your hard work and energy into.

Many talented people doom themselves by investing a vast amount of effort into some subject that is almost unpublishable, or very hard to get published.

On one hand, it is easiest to write about, and we may do the best job on a subject we really love. On the other hand, especially in the modern world of publishing, *"Will it sell?"* is a pretty critical question. It's most critical for books because they are such a big-time investment of time and money, and publishers weigh their subject matter so carefully. Magazine articles give you more leeway. There are so many magazines (including ones on the narrowest and most specialized imaginable subjects). And if you can make even the most off-the-wall subject funny or otherwise somehow more interesting, it might sell to a general-interest magazine.

What is the solution for this? List all the things you feel strongly enough to write enthusiastically about, and then do a "reality check" (with ordinary everyday people, or the specific audience or special-interest group you have in mind) to see which ones are most salable.

---

## THE "IT'S A JUNGLE OUT THERE" ATTITUDE TOWARD WRITING

I began writing as a totally ignorant author, unaware that there were many books out there besides the ones I used in school or saw in our little local bookstore or the public library of Pocatello, Idaho. Then, after I self-published my first book, I went to an ABA (American Bookseller's Convention, now called Book Expo). In four football field-size convention rooms at Chicago's McCormick Place, there must have been five miles of booths, all stuffed with hundreds of different books on thousands of different subjects. I have a pretty good imagination, but even at my best I could not comprehend that many books. (More than fifty thousand new ones a year, and that is just the commercially published ones. There are probably many more individually printed and self-published ones kicking around.)

It was pretty intimidating to say the least, and I was forty years old and a successful businessman, confident in my abilities. If you stood there and looked at all of that long enough, you could reduce yourself and all of your ambitions and dreams to a needle in the proverbial haystack.

The key thing to remember here is that the fact that there is a lot out there, doesn't make you less. It might put you in a bigger pool to swim with the bigger fish, but someone else's more or much doesn't depreciate the value of "mine." I learned later that of that convention I was so in awe of, with its thousands of books and promotions, the single book in my little two hundred-dollar booth outsold 90 percent of the books being featured by the top, giant publishers, and I was a janitor and a farmer from the boonies in Idaho.

If getting published were easy, if being a great heart surgeon were easy, if staying in perfect health until ninety were easy, if raising great kids were easy, then everyone would be doing it. And in the case of books, there would be not five but five hundred miles of booths worth of new books out there. Instead of worrying about how hard it might be to get published, worry about writing a book so good that publishers will beg you for it. **The thing many people don't realize is that most publishers are hungrier than you—they have a big company with an even bigger overhead to sustain**, and if they don't or can't find good new books and articles, they won't eat, either!

## RIGHT ON TARGET

Here is an approach that will do wonders for your marketing of what you write, even before you write it. When I first played basketball, after about a year of running, leaping and throwing the ball at the basket, my coach said to me, "Don, do you shoot at the basket?" "I sure do," I said. "Isn't that the whole idea of the game?" "It is," he said, "but I notice you don't always score with your shots. Try this: Instead of shooting in the general direction of the basket, or at the whole of the basket, start shooting for the **pinpoint center of the hoop.** Not the rim, but the exact center." I tried it, and it worked miracles.

In writing I suggest you do the same. Get *Writer's Market,* either in print or through its continually updated subscription service online at http://www.writersmarket.com, and read the sections that pertain to the type of writing you have in mind. Those packed paragraphs will give you not just the needs and interests, but the address, the editor's name, the magazine's circulation or number of books per year the book publisher publishes. Then it will tell you (the center of the basket) **who their audience is, exactly what they publish** for that audience and what they are looking for. One magazine may say, for example, that they reach an audience at the upper end of the income scale, ages thirty-five to fifty, whose main interest is seeing a better return on their investments. Another will tell you they only publish material suitable for an audience of women between eighteen and thirty and concentrate on glamour issues. Both the magazine and book publishers listed there will tell you what they want and don't want. It will soon become very clear to you that if you want to get published, you don't just fling your tablet into the air in their general direction. Find a goal and give it your best shot.

---

• Take the time to *aim*, rather than scatter shoot! Another place organization counts is in *not* sending submissions out blindly to any old place just because you have them finished and are in the mood to get out. Look before you leap. One of the biggest reasons for rejection is failure to find the right places to send that particular idea or piece of writing to. This calls for some research. This may sound like a waste, but you're *really* wasting your time if you don't do it.

*Research, research, research for markets. I use* Writer's Market, *scour the bookstores and keep my eyes and ears open for any new markets available.*

—*Mary Jo Rulnick*

• **If you find a magazine that sounds promising, but you've never seen or read it, go to the library and check it out.** ***Scan and sample a few copies.*** **You might also want to write for guidelines and sample copies. Sending an article to a publication you've never read is like bowling with the pins hidden.**

*To make market research easy for me, I subscribe to* Reader's Guide to Periodical Literature *(though it's around $260 a year) and don't buy any magazines not listed in it. I have it dating back to 1932, in bookshelves right in my office. With these you can look up a subject and see where and if it was done, has it been overdone, etc. Even the trends in that subject, you can tell from the article titles.*

*I also have copies of magazines I often refer to or write for, such as* Time, Fortune, *and* Motor Trend, *back to 1960, stacked up in order by year (only the top one gets dusty!). I have copies you can't get at libraries, or only on microfiche. This way I can research things right now, even in the middle of the night—the info is immediately available. Many of the subjects they are talking about today, they were talking about ten years ago.*

*I recommend going down to the annual book sale at the local library, usually about twice a year. You can get terrific reference books here for next to nothing, and save hundreds of dollars a year by having the info right there.*

—*Jim Joseph*

• **Take the time to find the easier places.** Some places are simply easier for beginners to "break in" to. Again, taking the time to read market guides thoughtfully to discover which these are will really pay off.

• Once you have an audience in mind, be sure to **shape or slant your manuscript to that audience** as you are writing. If the audience you have in mind for an article loves visuals, be sure your article includes them.

• Targeting includes submitting your manuscripts, queries and proposals in the form and format a publisher wants to see them in. See Recommended Books for guides to this for every type of submission.

**If you constantly keep in mind the person or persons you will be selling this article or book to—who and where and when—you will consistently write material that will be attractive, if not seductive, to that reader.**

*To stay on target while writing, I always choose an imaginary person or persons that I am talking to, all the way through. For my book* The Performing Artist's Handbook, *it was a string quartet in Cincinnati. All through the writing, when I had a question, I always asked myself, "What does Isobel need to know? Does Randy, the cellist, need to know this?"*

*For my book* The Bipolar Child, *it was a nineteen-year-old girl I know, and her parents. On my Web site, I had 175 messages a day from parents with bipolar children, so I really knew what they wanted to know.*

—Janice Papolos

## WRITING BIG CAN START WITH WRITING LITTLE

A book is often the first thing we think of writing, and then often comes the reasonable assumption that an article or two might be better, for starters. Good thinking. My first published work was an article for a technical magazine. I got twenty-five dollars for it, but it might as well have been twenty-five thousand, because it was instant reinforcement of my writing dreams. Writing for a newspaper or magazine forces us to learn to write concisely, which most of us need. Also, the turnaround time for articles (the writing, not necessarily the publication or payment) is short and fast. You have the chance to try out many different subjects, which is also good training. Few of us work on one article at a time. You can have any number of stories going at once—just make sure you keep that many separate files. And don't work up tight against deadlines. Allow plenty of time for them all to mature.

## A FEW POINTERS ON PROPOSALS

*When typing manuscripts and proposals, don't get fancy with font styles and sizes and special formatting of all kinds. Everyone today has a word processor that can do these things, so they're*

*not impressed. They just want to see how well you can put
words together in good old Times Roman or the like.*

—*Jean Loftus*

*Consider the marketing of books a business—using a professional
cover letter, which should be written and organized to grab an
editor's attention.*

—*Lynne Alpern*

*In my book proposal, I made a quick-reference chart for editors
showing the pros and cons of all existing books of the subject,
plus mine (which of course had more Xs in the right spot than
any of the others). This was a unique feature that helped sell
my book.*

—*Jean Loftus*

*You want to make your proposal package appear to be some-
thing special. You also want to make it easy for editors to keep
together and maybe slip into a take-home briefcase. Thus, every
project I ship is enclosed in a sealed plastic bag. That way the
material arrives virgin at the publisher, clean and easily read (at
least the title page) through the plastic. The sealing machine cost
about a hundred dollars, but I've had it for years. The plastic
bags I use for this are inexpensive and made to be sealed. Slip
your stuff into one, hold the open end under the sealer, and the
bag is heat sealed. What does the editor think? "Here's something special . . . and presented that way."*

*I also have a letterhead for every project, book or article. I
leave the upper right-hand corner blank, for illustrations or
other customizing elements. The letterhead for "You and Sports,"
for example, has a striking silhouette of people in action there.*

*I make sure that in my queries, you know right now what
the book or article is about, right in the first paragraph. I always
do multiple submissions and never include an SASE: If I don't
hear from them, I don't give a damn.*

*None of these tricks make up for poor writing. If the writing
is not good or great it won't sell!*

—*Jim Joseph*

## IF YOU'VE GOT IT, FLAUNT IT

Believe it or not, a remark we often hear from people who would like to be published is, "I've written many things but have never sent them anywhere." This is like saying "I'd like to meet a nice girl and get married," and then making it clear you never intend to go anywhere outside the walls of your home. At least aspiring actors and songwriters who want to be "discovered" have enough sense to make the scene, travel to the city or cities where the action is. A manuscript that *never* leaves the shelf or drawer is probably never going to published (if you're counting on posthumous discovery, forget it!)

---

**Marketing begins with getting you material *out there*.**

---

*I always tell people who want to sell their work that it's like a railroad track: one rail is talent, and the other marketing.*
—*Rohn Engh*

*I spend 30 percent of my time marketing my writing—speaking, networking, e-mailing and sending packages to prospects.*
—*Jean Lawrence*

## INVENTORYING YOUR WRITING CAPITAL

Now is a good time to start making and keeping a list of all of your writing plans and projects. Inventory your ideas by subject and topic, what you have written and what you want to write.

One of the most efficient ways to do this is on computer, where you can adjust, revise and expand things easily. Keeping lists of things like article and book ideas on computer makes it easy to just add new ideas right to them, instead of collecting piles of disorganized notes. A spreadsheet may be helpful in listing ideas in categories.

You can go beyond listing to writing a brief overview of the idea, plus markets it might appeal to, and publishers or publications you might submit it to. There is plenty of room to add outlines, tables of contents and research as it comes along, and to keep track of what stage you are in writing it, when it was sent out, when it was published and when you were paid.

• Once you have all of your ideas listed, review them regularly for the ones that have the most potential for advancing your writing career, and the ones that you just *like* the best.

• Since I'm a highly visual person, I like to not just list the book ideas I'm taking seriously, but bring them to life by doing a tiny cover sketch and brief description for each one, and put them all together in my own little illustrated "catalog" of my writing capital.

## POINTERS FROM THE PROS ON RECORDING SUBMISSIONS

*I have a loose-leaf binder for the correspondence on each project—letters, e-mails, faxes and so on, back and forth. The name of the project is on the binder and a red circle sticker on the active ones. I have nineteen binders right now, for instance, twelve active.*

*I make a list of the publishers I am submitting each project to (from LMP and International LMP) and the date, and put the submission letters themselves into the binder after it. I may make handwritten notes right on the letters, as needed. If an editor calls to discuss a submission, I type up notes on the call and put them in the binder.*

*—Jim Joseph*

*I file everything in a filing cabinet, with a different folder for each story. I also keep a master list of each assignment, with checkable categories for assignment date, due date, payment date and payment received.*

*—Kyle Minor*

*Index cards help me keep track of submissions. Each time I have a new article to submit, I research the markets and jot them down on an index card in the order I want to approach them. I place the article's name at the top of the card, then number the publications down the left-hand side. Beside each name, I write the editor's name and the payment. I write the date I mailed the article and when it was accepted or rejected.*

*—Mary Jo Rulnick*

*I have an Idea file on my computer (I have it in a Word file, but
it probably would work better in a spreadsheet). Every time I
send out an idea I note the name of the idea, then list the editors
and publications I sent it to with a date, and the response.
Example:*

|  | *Publication* | *Editor* | *Date sent* | *Response* |
|---|---|---|---|---|
| *Idea #1* | Glamour | *Smith* | *5/7* | *No* |
|  | Health | *Jones* | *5/9* | *Yes* |

—*Laurie Tarkan*

---

**There are computer programs designed to help you record market
information and send out and track your submissions, among
other things. These include The Working Writer and Ink Link,
which you can check out at http://dolphinsoftware.bc.ca and http://
www.companion.novalearn.com, respectively.**

---

## SEIZE THE IDEA (AND THE MOMENT!)

When you have a good idea for a book or article, don't wait to act on it.
Write it down and think it over. The tiniest hint may turn out to be the
map to a gold mine for you.

A friend of mine was a successful dentist. His daughter got married,
and at the reception, he noticed that she had received not one but three
new Crock-Pots (they were a rather sudden cooking rage). He didn't
notice any guide to cooking with them, though. The next day he
ambled to a couple of local bookstores to pick up a Crock-Pot cookbook for his daughter. He found none, and that intrigued him. So he
went to the big bookstore downtown and had the clerk check all their
computers to find one ... and came up with zero here, too. He had
found a need, and he didn't wait to fill it. When he got home he cleaned
out the garage, set up a desk and table, and quickly put together a
Crock-Pot cookbook. It sold millions! No more down in the mouth, for
him or us, if we learn to act on good ideas when they first hit. One
of the best things about writing is that it wakes you up and keeps
you awake.

## MANAGING MULTIPLE WRITING PROJECTS

You don't have to start just one writing project at a time; you can start on several, or even all of your writing ideas at once, if you want to. This will give you something to switch to when you get stalled or bored, and help deal with the waiting that is so much a part of the writing profession.

Once you submit something for consideration, it may be months before you hear from an editor. During this time you can work on another project, or a different phase of this one. Having multiple articles or books in different stages of development allows you to move from one to another and not waste time waiting for answers to your queries or proposals.

## REJECTION LEADS TO ... PERFECTION

You probably know people who have written a few things and gotten some of those mean, ugly, insensitive rejection letters back. This scares the heck out of many would-be writers and keeps them from trying again. Like, "If you go diving, you might be attacked by a shark," so you never go diving, no matter how much you want to.

If it makes you feel any better, many rejected submissions are never even read!

The longer you write, the fewer rejections you will get, but if you are writing and submitting anything at all, you'll get some rejections. That is no different than going to the parade and running into "No parking" signs all over the place. What do you do? Go home? Nope, you just keep driving and looking until there is a spot for you.

Your work could be a masterpiece, or a piece of junk, and either way, times and circumstances may affect whether it gets printed or shipped back. If the latter, so what, big deal. Most rejection letters are just form letters anyway. If you keep writing, you'll win. If you lay down and whine about it, or spend weeks showing your reject around to everyone to get their sympathy instead of sending your manuscript back out, revising it or writing something better, you're just wasting valuable time. Get back on the horse!

I took my first self-published book to a major local publisher in person, and this big wheel sat at his desk and frowned at my great book on cleaning toilets. A week or so later he turned me down. In essence his rejection said:

*Dear Mr. Aslett:*
*You have some good information here, but there are too many*
*cutesy asides [my humor] and too much of your own personality*
*in the manuscript. To sell, this book must be more serious and*
*factual, and the format will have to be changed entirely.*

*Signed,*
*Editor in chief*

I didn't take the humor or the personality out of the book, or change my idea of what kind of book it should be. I just looked for another publisher. Twenty years later it is still in print and has sold more than a million copies.

So don't let publishers or others determine your destiny. Most rejections have a reason, so listen and refocus if you need to. But *never quit!* A rejection should just inflame you to excellence, make you determined to show them how good you are, or can be. Even with millions of book sales under my belt, I still expect rejections, and as long as I keep writing, they are just motivators.

If you aren't willing to invest time, have patience and continually improve your writing, it will probably succeed in proportion to your effort. If it doesn't work, make it work. If a publisher ignores you or turns you down, resubmit it to others. None of us knows any secret formula, but we don't quit trying.

## POINTERS FROM THE PROS ON DEALING WITH REJECTION

*Sometimes the sheer enormity of effort for the return you get is*
*daunting. After an appropriate amount of sulking (two hours), I*
*redouble my efforts.*

*—Jean Lawrence*

*You can't freelance and be down too long after a rejection*
*because the rejections do come often, even for longtime*
*professionals. It's a cost of doing business. Learn what you can*
*from it and move on.*

*—Maxine Rock*

*We understand that a rejection often has nothing to do with the quality of the submission. Other business-oriented issues can prevail. And when a rejection is based on the work itself, we have never failed to learn from the experience.*

—*Clyde and Suzy Burleson*

*When I get a rejection, I allow myself to get mad as heck and even rage for a while. Then, I put the piece and the rejection away for a day or two—or as long as it takes—and then coldly analyze the rejection. If I see merit, I fix the piece and then re-market. If I don't agree with the rejection after my cooling-off period, then I simply re-market. Their loss!*

—*Kelly Boyer Sagert*

*I try not to send out anything I don't think is good. If I think it's good and they don't, then I can say to myself "more fool them" and try to resell it.*

—*Charles Mann*

*After many years as a professional writer, I assume I am going to be rejected and am surprised when a query is accepted. To ease rejections, I make a list of magazines before I send out the query and if it comes back, I send it to the next one in line.*

—*Ruth Winter*

*They say there's a buyer for every house on the market. Well the same is true for writing. You need to find the agent or editor for your writing. There's someone out there who will love your piece.*

—*Mary Jo Rulnick*

*I don't get discouraged when a proposal of mine happens to get rejected. That's because I usually have a good number of projects in various stages of development. When one gets turned down, I shrug it off. Sometimes, a turndown is a relief, in fact.*

—*George Sullivan*

## HOW TO HELP YOUR PUBLISHER SELL YOUR BOOK

One error writers make, especially when we plan to convince a publisher to publish our book, is assuming that it will be entirely that publisher's responsibility to distribute and sell the book because this is how they earn their money. This is the wrong attitude. You, the author, have a tremendous power to market your book, and to build in the marketing as you write it.

1. While I am writing a book, I have a separate file called "Marketing" and consistently feed it anything I pick up, hear, see or learn from others—things like sources of possible buyers, groups that might be interested in this subject and even the names of contacts in the field that might somehow help boost sales. This is important gold to mine as the book nears completion.

2. Who will be buying your book is the most important question when considering the format, size, illustrations and cover design of a book. Bear this in mind when making all of these decisions with the publisher.

3. Don't wait until you have a finished book in hand before contacting potential special marketing sources. Getting them enthusiastic about your book as it is developing builds a good platform for a more formal presentation later—you will not be hitting them cold turkey.

---

**Think marketing—evidence of audience demand, competition, key contacts—throughout the process, and you'll be many steps ahead of the game!**

# CHAPTER 9

# *Organizing the Writing Process Itself*

"It's what's up front that counts" applies more to writing than to any other profession. This means not just the raw material we have in our head to draw upon, but the organizing of it we do before we ever put pen to paper. Though the image of a writer pouring out totally spontaneous inspiration still persists, there is no doubt that the most likely way to ensure publication is to organize what you write.

Just about every form of writing—articles, nonfiction books, novels, speeches, plays, even essays and poetry—profits greatly from some kind of organization, which may also be called structure. This chapter will explain the different principles that can be used to organize both nonfiction and fiction, as well as the different ways to do it, physically.

---

If you put a project on paper unorganized, it will be a job, a fight, slow, even discouraging. But when things are in order, you will be the one giving the orders!

---

## ORGANIZING BEFORE YOU WRITE

### Preparation is priceless

We often underestimate the "setting up" of things in our anxiety to reach the end product. Let me give you an example of this from the world of home improvements, that carries over right into writing. The preparation before painting is generally a timetaker. No painting at all takes place for a few hours as we cover and drape everything we don't want painted, from the door hardware to the windows and counters.

When you are preparing like this, no paint is going on, and you can get nervous thinking you aren't getting anywhere because you aren't painting. (The same way you sometimes feel when you're outlining, or writing a synopsis.)

Preparation sometimes seems to go on forever, even to the point of impatience. But getting ready to paint or write has its rewards—big time—because when the stage is finally set, and everything is in place and ready to go, we can pick up the roller or spray gun (or pen) and really go.

> *Beginning writers tend to go to the writing too soon. The result is poor quality of copy, frustration, even writer's block.*
>
> *A plan or outline for your writing helps you organize your thoughts, allows your writing to flow more easily and helps you avoid rambling and repetition. It also gives your writing more depth.*
>
> —*Frank Thomas*

### Take the time to find the best angle on the subject

A photographer friend of mine did have a nice camera, but so did I, and his pictures were...just better, clearer, more dramatic, better composed. He chuckled when I expressed my disappointment about my own pictures compared to his. "Ho! You take as good or better pictures than I do," he said. "You just don't take as many, and then sort them down to the best. Film is the cheapest part of taking pictures. I don't take just one or two of the subject. I take five or six or even a dozen, and out of the bunch one or two are always superior."

Likewise, pen and paper are the cheapest part of writing. When you see a subject, before you start actually writing about it, jot down not one view or two but maybe a quick eight or ten angles on your idea. Then pare them down to the one that really works.

### Put the source before the chart!

Organize your raw material even *before* you organize a story or article. Have all of your research, notes, reference material, etc., organized and at hand before you start.

Once you have it sorted out, seeing what you have—the amount in each pile or on each subject—will help you see the general outline of your subject, or the "lay of the land." Making the table of contents, and the order from the separate by-subject piles, will not only give you super ideas, but also will have the material already organized to fit the chapters. It's a plain case of "horse before the cart," or in this case, "the source before the chart!"

## POINTERS FROM THE PROS ON PREPARING TO WRITE

*My most efficient organizing tool remains the good old legal-size file folder. Each file is marked with the name of the article and the editor's name. Everything goes in here: letters, contract, instructions from the editor, research material and so on. While preparing for an article, I pack my folder with newspaper clippings and anything else that seems relevant. Then, when I'm ready to write, I can spread everything out and have a sweeping view of what I want to include ... something that's not possible on a seventeen-inch computer screen.*

*—Maxine Rock*

*I find organization of any new project important in keeping the book on the subject and moving forward on schedule. By the time the contract is signed, I already know, from the outline and proposal, how the book breaks down into chapters. I first assign file drawer space to the new book, then start a new folder for each chapter. Into these folders go notes, clippings, information on sources and any other details pertaining to that chapter. When I'm ready to tackle each chapter, the materials for it are in one place.*

*In addition, I have a spiral notebook with a section assigned to each chapter. Here I keep a record of all interviews and published sources consulted. Later this can be valuable in double-checking facts or defending the work if questioned by editors or the publisher's fact checker. It also contains what I need to compile a bibliography.*

*Finally, I type on one summary sheet vertical columns for chapter numbers, title, projected chapter word length and actual length when finished. I paste this inside the front cover of the notebook, where I can check at a glance to see how the project is going and what remains to be done.*

*This all sounds rigid and binding. But I don't hesitate to adjust the plan when the book is in progress if new research uncovers relevant material that has story value and adds to the subject.*

—George Laycock

**Marking your references:**
*I just finished my eighteenth book. I tried keeping references on cards like we were taught back in school, but it didn't work for me. I found myself making notes in books, and underlining in books (I buy them). I ended up using Aigner precut index tabs, plus Post-it notes, to mark the location of material in books I'm consulting. I write the topic on the tab. This is almost like an outline: the tab is the overall heading, and the Post-its, the A-B-Cs. I got this idea from my daughter, a lawyer. For example, when doing an article on medical promotion, the tabs might read "Brochures," "Newsletters," "Ads."*

**Organizing expert sources:**
*I do a lot of medical writing, and I use an index card file for the names and phone numbers, etc., of experts I talk to. Many magazines will call and check your sources, and this way if a fact checker calls, I can easily locate what I need. I also use an index-card file for sources. On the card I put the person's name, address, title and so forth, and when I talked to them about what.*

*Don't forget those quotes. After time passes, you can forget what your sources said and what you did, so if you make a direct quote from someone, put in those quotation marks.*

*If the information I've gotten from someone is pretty technical, I'll send it to the interviewee afterward with a thank-you, and tell them not to argue about the writing, but to check that it is technically accurate. They are usually grateful for this, and helpful.*

—Elaine Schimberg

## GOOD WRITING IS CARVING, NOT WHITTLING!

Many would-be woodcarvers just whittle away, and by the end of the day or week, have a pile of shavings, and blisters, but no worthwhile result. Too many people write this way, too, just chipping away in hopes that something rare will result. Good organization will transform you from a whittler to a carver, so your work will add up to something in the end.

I took a group of Boy Scouts to Philmont Scout Ranch (a 137,000-acre high-adventure base in New Mexico) once for a twelve-day backpacking adventure. Around the campfire in the evening, away from TV, video games and books, there was plenty of time, so I took out my tools (a tiny saw and pocket knife) and went to work on a walking stick. Two days later I had a marvelous "snake stick"—a walking stick with a realistic-looking snake wrapped around it. The boys all cast envious glances at my stick and offered to buy it. I promised them that if they really wanted a stick like this, they could walk out of camp ten days from now with one as good as mine that they made themselves.

This blew their little minds, but they trusted me, their leader. What we embarked on was a process much like writing in that it was about 60 percent organizing (readying) and 40 percent creating (carving).

1. **Total commitment to your project** is the first step in organizing, so first I got a firm commitment out of them to make a stick.

2. Next we **researched for good material for our writing project**—combed the forest for branches or young trees of just the right length and diameter, with no forks or knots.

3. Now we **outlined the entire project**—sat down and drew the pattern of the snake wrapped around the stick.

4. Then they grabbed their knives, but I quickly made it clear that before we started carving any details we had to **rough out the form** of the snake first—write the rough draft. So now we took the little saw and cut along the lines we'd drawn, round and round the stick, just about ½ inch deep. Then we took a screwdriver and pried and chipped the wood in between away, leaving us the rough form of the serpent on the stick.

5. The boys were delighted and awed with how quickly getting ready like this put them on their way. Now they were ready to pick up their knives and complete it—**refine the draft and fill in details.** And as writing does with good preparation, their snake came alive on the stick.

6. They thought it was finished now, but that snake, like good writing, still needed the last step to set it off, to smooth and polish it, and get it the rest of the way to realism: **the edit**. I handed them a wood rasp and sandpaper and in minutes their snakes looked as if they were going to crawl right off their sticks.

On the tenth day we marched single file back into base camp, passing many other groups of boys with their leaders. All ten of mine had superb snake sticks, made by their own hand. They swelled with pride as all of the others stopped, gawked, and oohed and ahhed over their sticks: a real testimony to what a little getting ready and organizing can do, even if you have only average ability.

## WRITING IS THINKING

You may not see it that way, but your editor will. Writing must communicate, inform, describe—*have a point.* If all you produce are pretty words that circle around the topic like dust devils, you're going to have a hard time getting those words published.

Before pretty words comes structure. Structure is the framework into which you fit your sentences and paragraphs, as a house is built upon a frame, or a body upon a skeleton. Without structure, your writing is a jumble of board and brick; a spineless mass.

Manuscripts like this cross editors' desks every day. They may be neatly typed, or begin with a flashy lead that promises something exciting to follow. But about halfway through, the editor's hopes sag, just as the article or story is sagging.

What's wrong? Often pieces like this are little more than a random assortment of paragraphs. Others may have a problem with weight and balance, some elements overwhelming others of equal importance. Or the writer may be guilty of "trackback"—unintentionally presenting the same facts and ideas over again, albeit in a different way.

Organization—thinking your way through an article, or a chapter, and setting up a sound structure—is the way to prevent this, and make sure there are bones and muscle under the skin of your prose.

---

• You wouldn't start to build a nice new home without a blueprint. You need "specs" to end up with what you expect, because building an article or book is just like building a house, it takes some sort of master plan.

• Writing is like pouring cement—75 percent of the time and effort is in setting up the forms. What they are (how well thought out, and solid, straight or true) is what your finished sidewalk or patio will be like.

---

*I learned an incredible amount about organizing from doing my first book. The biggest thing I learned is that before you write the first word, you need to know what is going to be contained in the entire book. Otherwise, you end up doing a lot of extra work—repeating yourself, putting things into the manuscript in ten different places (and you won't notice the repetition).*

*A general idea of what you are going to write is not enough—you need to know exactly what you are going to write in a given chapter, or section, before you start it.*

*We're always so eager to start on something we may not want to be bothered to do this, but the amount of work it saves is monumental.*

—*Jean Loftus*

## THE BASICS OF A SATISFYING STRUCTURE

There are some exceptions, but by and large, good, publishable writing has to be *headed somewhere*. It has to start at a good place to start (and one that catches the reader's interest), follow a distinct and clearly marked path through the subject from there and have a clear-cut ending. This is true not just of nonfiction but of fiction, where this underlying framework is called the plot.

How do we decide what order to cover the parts, or different aspects of a subject, in? We can organize by the following:

• **Time, or chronological sequence.** Example: the different tribes of early Americans who inhabited a river valley, one by one, over time. You can even use reverse chronological order.

• **Start to finish.** Such as how to patch a hole in a sheetrock wall, step by step.

• **Need to know.** Bringing up, and developing, topics, as the reader needs to learn about and understand them, such as all the things he needs to know to prune a tree without hurting it, or to understand the tangled web of black and white race interactions in America.

• **Alphabetical order.** Scottish surnames, from A through Z.

• **Geographical.** The favorite perennial flowers in every part of the country (working your way from east to west, north to south or whatever—but not hopping all over from hither to yon).

• **Type of thing.** Such as an article, chapter or book on casseroles, or appetizers.

• **Popularity.** Pet snakes, from most to least popular, or commonly asked questions about something, by how often they're on someone's lips.

We have a wide choice of ways to organize, and any one of them is good (including others not mentioned here), as long as we pick one and **stick with it** all the way through. Don't switch organizing principles in midstream!

## SHORT-FORM OUTLINING

Just watch a good sculptor at work, or even a lumberjack with a chain saw making wooden bears out of tree trunks. They never worry about the details until the basic form is there. They always rough something out first, giving it the general form of what it is going to be. In writing this can be done by outlining, but there is a shorter and simpler way to do it, too. For a whole book, for example, this can just be a three- or four-sentence summary. For example, a complicated and long-researched book I did on how to give children money all started with this brief description of purpose and intent:

1. Money is a fact of life and central focus of every family, and it isn't going to go away—establish this.
2. Tell a bunch of disastrous kid/parent money stories that will remind and arouse readers to the fact that indeed we have a need here.
3. Come up with a variety of solutions to this problem.
4. Show the rewards of wise management, of giving kids money in the right way.

Once you put down a basic description of your subject and slant, not even a complete one, maybe, you have a frame to begin welding details to. And this is so simple. You don't have to struggle with outlines, or a too-big pile of ideas. Just bare-bones it down to the ABCs and watch how easy structuring can and will be from there.

### The speech outline method

When Carol is writing an article or chapter, she absorbs all the research and then makes something very much like a speech outline on a single sheet of paper. She writes each subtopic of the subject in bold type, and then under it puts all of the key thoughts on that subject in as few words as possible, or even her own form of shorthand. When she's done, she can just glance at this sheet as she writes and see the logical path through the subject, and everything she must be sure to cover.

## POINTERS FROM THE PROS ON OUTLINING

There is no one way to do an outline or "map" of the path you will be taking as you write. Here are some different ways of going about it.

*"Eyeballing" an outline:*
*Though I am a professional organizer, I found organizing my writing to be the hardest part of it. The way I do this now is: make a list of everything I want to cover in a book or article. Then I look at the list and organize it, put it in order. I can't do this in my head, I have to be able to see it. Once it's all on paper I can see that this topic should go in the same chapter as that one, and that topic must be discussed before that one.*

*Some people do the same thing by putting all of the topics they want to include in a book on index cards and then putting the cards in order.*

*This gives you an outline, or skeleton, of your book, and all you have to do is flesh it out.*

*—Deniece Schofield*

*Brainstorming an outline:*
*I have a big easel (like the one seminar leaders use) with a giant tablet on it and use this to free-associate on the article or book I'm working on. I jot the different sections that might be in the book on it, just anywhere. For example, if the topic is the pros and cons of writing at home I might jot "can make own schedule" and "very easy to goof off." First I write everything I can think of on or related to the subject, and then after I get it all down, I consider what should come first, second, etc. This is kind of a "mind map," a way of brainstorming by yourself, and it also helps you see what's missing.*

*I do use this same easel technique with articles, and it's even better for them because you can see the whole article at once rather than a chapter at a time, as you often have to do with books.*

*—Elaine Schimberg*

### The "pile" method:

*Computer files and scanners are all well and good, but I use the "pile" technique when actually working on something. When I'm working on an article, I pull all the materials I have about it out of my files, gather additional information from journals, books, etc., then arrange it all in piles grouped by some article-relevant criterion, on bookcase shelves I keep empty for this purpose.*

*Piles give you more information, faster, than any other method I know of. Even the process of making the piles helps you evaluate whether you've clustered concepts in a meaningful way. Think of all the information you can subsume just via positioning, all of which is lost in using a "file name" on a computer. There's the position of the pile itself, including which shelf it's on. Foundational stuff goes at the bottom, details at the top in my case. Whether I've put a pile on the left or right of the shelf tells me other things.*

*And of course, you can look at the sides of the piles and identify well-used references simply by color, texture or binding.*

*—Kenneth Green*

### Making a "balloon" outline:

*An informal method of outlining I use often is called the balloon outline. I take a page from a legal-size pad, put a working title for my piece on top, and then draw a large balloon like the dialogue balloons in a comic strip. Inside, I write the thought I've chosen for my lead. Then I draw a second balloon and draw a line down to it from the first balloon and further develop the lead that launches the article. In the third balloon I put the thought that follows that and so on down the page. I keep making and filling in balloons describing the flow of material I wish to write. Often I will end up with two, three or four pages before I get to my ending.*

*When I'm done, I have a road map of where I want to go. But it is by no means rigid. As I write I decide this should go higher or that lower. Or I may decide to introduce an entirely new thought or aspect along the way.*

*On larger assignments such as a book, I and my fellow members of the ASJA (American Society of Journalists and Authors)* go beyond the sketchy outline I've described. We go to the next step, fleshing out our outlines with our actual research notes. Each of us does it in our own way, but we generally come out with similar results.

In my own case I am a scissors and paste-up man. Again I go to a legal pad sheet and start with the working title. Then I flesh out my balloon by scissoring and pasting the appropriate notes directly onto the sheets. I do this page after page until I reach my ending. I end up with a completely filled-in outline covering maybe a dozen pages, all numbered at the top. If I need to get more detail or a special fact from my pile of research, I number that item in red pencil and key it to the same number in my research.

This preparation for writing may seem tedious at the time, but it pays off, and in the end it saves time.

—Frank Thomas


While researching an article, I take detailed notes during interviews and then I put them to the side. I allow my subconscious to arrange the material for me and to select the most powerful anecdote or resonating quote. I may peek at my notes, but then I write my rough draft from memory alone. I arrange, rearrange and tighten, and then very carefully check the veracity of my work. From time to time, I'll discover that I didn't include a poignant or relevant fact and so I'll weave that in. But working from memory in the early stage gifts me with a natural flow that I just can't force.

—Kelly Boyer Sagert


**Outlining software:**
Many word processing programs have some kind of outlining feature, and there is also special outlining software, such as More for Mac users. I'm sure you'll love More as much as I do— a good outliner is invaluable for creating nonfiction how-to manuals. I use it for to do lists, too. To try out an outliner you can go to a "shareware" site such as www.tucows.com and try out programs and then buy them if you like them.

—Ken Evoy

## When novel writing

In general, fiction writing is less "linear" than nonfiction, and many fiction writers prefer a looser form of outlining.

### Making the grand plan:

*I have almost never dealt with a subject that I had not been brooding about for years or even decades ... and the time has not been wasted because my understanding has had the chance to mature, and the subject has been illuminated in ways not previously apparent.*

*But one day, at the conclusion of such introspection and evaluation, I decide that of three or four potential subjects I will focus my attention on the one that seems the most viable at that time. I roll a sheet of paper into my machine, and below the date I type a brief statement of what my thinking was in selecting that subject, and I outline in chapter headings the entire book as I perceive it at that moment. Never do I get all the subheads right; never do I get more than one wrong. This then becomes my guide for the next three years, and with surprising accuracy I foresee at the time of making the decision the whole grand design and the interrelationship of the parts.*

—James A. Michener

### A flow chart for fiction:

*My "flow chart" is my bible when I'm writing. I make this up for myself, and it has the number and name of the chapter on the left, and a brief synopsis of the main events in that chapter, what happens in it, on the right. It also—a key ingredient—tells when the action in that chapter takes place—what day or days of the week, and the time of day. The events in one chapter, for example, may take up two days, just part of one day, or a week. If there is a time during which nothing happens, I note this on here, too: "Tuesday and Wednesday: no events."*

*I note the weather conditions and time of year when the action takes place on my flow chart, too, because it often has a bearing on the writing. In one of my novels, for example, the time of the sunset is important because the characters are trying to accomplish something before sunset.*

*A flow chart like this lets you see, plan and keep mindful of the whole time frame during which your story takes place. It also helps you keep your time sequence straight. You won't, for example, have things happen on a weekend that would have to happen on a business day or forget to consider weekends at all. Or if you say, "A week passed" somewhere, you won't forget to take it into account.*

*A flow chart also makes looking back to check on or find something in your plot much easier, and when a character says something, you can look at the flow and the time elapsed and say, "Is that true?"*

*—Don Donaldson*

**Scene-by-scene outlines:**
*In the novel I'm now writing, I started with a one-page overall synopsis and expanded this to pages and pages of scene-by-scene outline. It's a lot easier to go back and adjust an outline than a manuscript, and easier to find things in it, too.*

*I couldn't decide whether certain characters should be good or bad, or in between. So I wrote up three different scenarios for them, in outline form, so I could look at them in terms of the framework of the rest of the book. If you reach a crux or problem point in your book, work it through in outline form—it's much easier than doing it in the actual manuscript.*

*—Jean Loftus*

*We borrowed one of the most helpful organizers from many of the writers who do scripts for motion pictures and television. We develop a project scene by scene, outlining each one in short, terse sentences on 3" x 5" index cards. This allows us to deal with facts, structure, premise, character development and other elements in an easy, orderly manner.*

*—Clyde and Suzy Burleson*

**Outlining in your head:**
*I know that outlines are a good way to organize a story, but I don't always follow them slavishly. As I'm writing, I often think of things I know people would like to read about, and I put them in the story. Often these turn out to be the best parts of the story.*

*Sometimes a story has to be thought about for a while to get*

*it unified. When a story has become organized, grown to maturity, in my head, it is now time to write it.*
                                                      —*Anna Lee Waldo*

## ORGANIZING AS YOU WRITE

You never quit "organizing" to write, even when you are deep in the process of actually putting things down on paper. It is then that some of the biggest organizational challenges pop up.

### Bottom line basics

As you start, make sure you're aware of the physical organization called format. No publication market wants to see pages that are not double-spaced or consecutively numbered, from start to finish. This rule may seem too basic to even mention, but it is ignored more often than you would believe. As for format beyond that, you can consult one of the comprehensive guides to manuscript formatting listed in Recommended Books.

The most reliable way to get results (be published) is to find the "recipe" for what you're writing—query, proposal, article or whatever—and follow it. This is too large a subject to cover in detail here, and there are many fine books (see Recommended Books) that will tell you every last thing you need to know about it. But just to give you a quick idea:

• The recipe for a good query and book proposal is much the same: What the subject is, why it is exciting or important, what you have new or different to say about it, how you are going to develop it and why you are an excellent person to write about this subject.

• A newspaper story or column is built on the famous classic pattern of an inverted triangle: the most important things said first, followed by the more expendable (in case the article needs to be cut to fit).

• Magazine article: Title, a good one, lead, body (filled with anecdotes, quotes, research, and developed in an orderly way) and then a conclusion (often suggesting action).

### Organizing a book

The most businesslike way to write a book is to sell it *before* you write it. To do this you usually have to do a proposal, which is really just a sound plan for writing a book, written with a selling edge—with some copy at the very beginning and a sharp slant all the way through designed to convince publishers that this is going to be a book your audience can't live without.

So if you've done a proposal for your book, you already have an overall plan and detailed outline for writing it. The Recommended Books will give you some outstanding guides to preparing a proposal for either fiction or nonfiction, if you haven't done this yet.

> *My proposals are carefully constructed, and the finished book is usually very close to the proposal. It's not that some miracle happens as I'm writing, it's just that I thought it through well to begin with.*
>
> —*Janice Papolos*

### Chapter and terse

When writing a nonfiction book, you want to be sure to have clear-cut "beginning" and "ending" chapters, and these often have a somewhat inspirational or reflective tone. If all of the chapters can have a similar or parallel structure, it's usually a real plus.

As for length, the chapters don't have to be the same size (an occasional minichapter can be a nice break and a real emphasizer). But when they start creeping above forty-five manuscript pages, you will be in danger of losing the reader and his patience in a sea of never-ending copy. If you find this happening, restructure to avoid it—carve a new chapter out of the original somehow, on some logical basis.

### Keep your eye on the angle

Whether you're writing an article or a book chapter, keep your angle, "slant" or theme in mind always. You are not just writing about goldfish, but the best goldfish for a backyard pool; not just about horses, but what makes the Appaloosa so popular.

Straying from your intended subject, forgetting what your angle is supposed to be, and just wandering around the subject in general (or even getting *off* the subject) is one big reason manuscripts miss the mark. Your manuscript or query is very likely to be rejected, and the writing will have to be heavily edited or redone.

### Don't forget the "plot path"!

This is one of the most important parts of nonfiction, especially "how to" or informational writing. When you sit down to write, forget all *you* know about the subject, and put yourself in the reader's place. Remember, now and all the way through what you're writing, that for the most part all he knows is what you've told him. So start out by telling him what he needs to know to start, then what he needs next and so on. As you move along, you're building a foundation of knowledge for him, and then building steadily on that foundation—adding floors and walls and windows and whatever. Never forget—he doesn't know everything you have in your head. He knows only what you've told him so far. In fact, if you stop and study what you've covered so far, you're very likely to discover that you've forgotten a couple of the most important aspects (because to you, they're so obvious).

### Writing to fit

Most of us can come up with plenty of good stuff to put in our message or manuscript—including lots of stories, anecdotes and examples. This is some of our most valuable "ore," because from the days of Aesop's fables and earlier, it's been clear that stories bring a point home better than even the most brilliant logic.

Having lived a long and intense life, from the farm to the big city, from mopping floors to TV appearances and big business operations, I have real-life stories galore and am generous with them in my manuscripts. My editor agreed that there were some great stories, but how and where I used them was often questioned, especially in my early manuscripts: "Great story, but it doesn't fit here." I'd give a vivid account of my struggles with a sewer main break that threatened to engulf a whole building, for example, and she'd point out that it fit much better in the "customer relations" chapter than where I had it. There was nothing wrong with the story in itself—it really caught and held the reader's attention; it just didn't do anything to advance the argument where it was.

A good editor will catch and help fix an occasional problem like this, but if there are fifty stories that don't fit, your chapter or article is going to be disjointed and unfocused. So don't get so caught up in how neat a story is, and all of the fascinating details, that you forget to ask yourself: What is this story essentially *about*? Is it to the point here?

---

If you don't write things from the right angle (to fit the publication, or the writing project you have in mind, and for that matter the very spot in that writing project where it is supposed to go), you will miss

**the target and not be published.**

**Two of the most common sins of writing:**

• **We jump to a new subject without adequate transition. We made a great point, but we leave it without building a bridge to the next point or topic. We don't finish the job!**

• **We leave off the ending. You can't just ramble on about ideas and ideals. For an article, book chapter, essay or story to be satisfying, it has to have a wrapup, a finish, a conclusion.**

---

### Color can help you write

You can use color to turn a jumble of notes and ideas into a finished article, or to analyze a finished piece or chapter and discover what went wrong (see chapter ten). If you're writing a magazine article, for instance: Begin by putting all the thoughts and facts you want to present on paper. Now spread out these notes, grab some colored markers and start thinking. What is your capsule sentence? Express, in twenty words or less, what the major point of your article will be. Circle it in a bright color such as red and keep it in front of you as you proceed.

Go through your notes. What are the major elements needed to develop and bolster your capsule sentence? Choose a different color for each of these elements, then use markers to color code each idea and fact to the major element to which it relates.

Keeping your crimson capsule sentence in front of you at all times, write a snappy, attention-getting lead, then move quickly to your first major element. Exhaust all of the points within that color before you move on to the next major element. (Don't forget transitions.) Keep going until you've said it all. Glance back at your capsule sentence and write a solid finish.

Color coding helps you think, to look at the all-important structure instead of just words and sentences that all look the same on a white sheet of paper. You can even use color to start structuring your writing as you begin your research on a topic, color coding facts as you dig them up, seeing instantly how they relate to a project as a whole.

Color can help analyze markets, too. Whether you write fiction or nonfiction, you can use colored markers to dissect published pieces, to see what "formula" a given publication favors. How heavily are quotes and anecdotes used in an article? What amount of description versus action and dialogue appears in a short story? Mark each of these in a different color and the answer will be clear. You can also dissect articles, stories and chapters you enjoyed reading to see what made them so good.

### Computer tips for writing

Many of us writers use only a small percentage of our word processing software's (and computer's) capabilities. Most processing programs, for example, can not only produce a manuscript but also help you outline it, make an annotated table of contents for it, send out multiple submissions efficiently and more.

Read the manual, consult the "Help" menu, turn on the "Tips" feature of Microsoft Word, and talk to writers who use the same program. Learn as much as you can about what your equipment can do to help you, and the shortcuts it can offer.

• On a computer you can develop and revise outlines, plots and characters as the ideas occur, without accumulating a bunch of disorganized notes.

• Your word processing program probably has a provision for creating and recording the formats you want to use throughout your book. In Microsoft Word, you will find this under the "Format" menu. With this you can set up a style for your basic body copy, large heads, medium-size heads and small headings, then just highlight the copy in question and hit the button for that format and zoom—it's done.

• You can use the endless typefaces of a computer to good editorial advantage in the draft stages of a project. For example, you can call out all notes to your collaborator in unmissable **Chicago**, notes to the editor in Geneva, notes for the designer or illustrator in Courier, and underline places where you still have a question for yourself.

• When working on books, until you reach the stage of truly final manuscript, it is usually most convenient to make each chapter a separate document.

• If all of your files on a project are in one folder, Microsoft Word will list them alphabetically, by the first word of the title you gave each file. To get around this, and put the files you find yourself opening most often near the top, either add a blank space before the beginning of the title of these files, or add a few alphabet "cheat" letters at the start, such as "A-Zebra pattern variations," and "AA-Zebra pattern imitations." Likewise, you can add late-in-the-alphabet letters to the beginning of titles you want to drop down near the bottom of the list.

• If the number of documents on a complex and drawn-out project keeps growing, move the ones you are no longer using much into a second (or third, or fourth) folder on the subject, to get them out of your way. Keep only the files you are actively using now in the main folder.

• If you do a lot of cutting and pasting, reshuffling of copy and notes on computer, you can save document opening and closing time, and possibly confusion, by stacking all of the pieces to be relocated at the end of the document, under a clear heading, till you've worked your way all the way through the chapter.

• No book folder would be complete without a file for notes to yourself while working—everything from that weak point you noticed that needs shoring up to what parts could be cut if necessary to "I'll never take on a subject like this again!"

• To avoid the horror of accidentally making those brilliant new revisions to an old version: Give each new version of a chapter, article or whatever a distinctive new name, and to be really safe, get it out and away from your folder of current working files!

• Don't forget to spell-check!

*Don't sit down and try to write a book on brand-new software. Use a program you not just like but know and can navigate well.*

*Customize your desktop for maximum space to work and ease of operation. In Microsoft Word, for example, you can decide which are the most important buttons and put those only across the top of your screen. You just go under "Tools" to "Customize" and hit "Command" and check out what's in there. You can find gems in there that you will end up using all the time. I, for example, often use the binoculars, bullets, case changing, headers and footers, and sorting A–Z. When you find something you like, you just highlight it and drag it up to the toolbar. And you can move things around on the toolbar.*

*(If you go too far in this direction, however, you'll end up back in activities used to avoid getting around to writing a book!)*

—*Jean Loftus*

### #!~(*$%#!! that duplication!

You collect all the good stuff you can on a subject. When you finally go through and take out and write from this collected material, you keep out what you use and also keep the leftovers, the runners-up or not immediately needed stuff, just in case.

As time goes by, you get to wondering if you really did "go through" everything in the pile, and by now it may be piled together with new and fresh. Nothing is worse than having to do a second sorting for the used and unused!

Once you've plundered anything, X it with a pen or marker, make a big checkmark on it or staple it together on four sides. This way you can still save it in case some little fact is missed and needed, or some legal issue might require it being kept, but remove it well away from the new material! Trust me, mixing things up is not the way to advance and streamline your writing efforts.

### Haul the dead limbs away the day you cut them!

Likewise, all that we write isn't gold: some of it is dross, doesn't work, isn't any good. It may take awhile, but you will eventually come to see what is and ought to be scrap.

Then for anything that is for sure dead, sweep it up off the floor and off your desk or computer document and get rid of it. If you stack it around the good stuff, there will inevitably be confusion and time wasted. If you leave the leaves piled in the yard, they will get reblown around, and so will piles from writing. Haul the dead limbs away the day you cut them!

### Don't shut down too soon

We're so enthusiastic when we start, but on a long project like a book, this often diminishes as we get closer to the end, even to the point of carelessness. You are so tired of it, you just want to get it finished, out of the way. You have written, written and written on this subject, and you are sick, sick, *sick* of it now. You're now willing to toss anything in it, accept anything, just to get it over with and done.

Beware! This happens to all of us, and how we deal with it can make or break a manuscript. This should be a red alert. The "let's shut it down" urge comes when you are tired, in a hurry, out of patience or under deadline. But what still needs to be done, still needs to be done. There are usually loose ends to be tied up, last things to check, things that need to be improved, some paperwork that needs to be tended to and little missing pieces. Those last touches are often the difference between good and great.

### Organize to give credit where credit is due

Keep all sources that require permission or acknowledgment listed somehow so that you can give proper credit where credit is due when the time comes. Otherwise, you may forget, there will be some frenzied hunting at the end and some things you may never find! Add things that may need permission to your permissions list the minute you tuck them into the manuscript.

---

Pleased as you are to finally be done with a project—the final draft is in the mail—don't dismantle your working piles too soon (put your references and research away, return things you have borrowed for the project and so on ). In the editing and publishing process that follows, you're very likely to need to consult something here. Dejunk and disperse after your book is in your hands!

**CHAPTER 10**

# *Organizing After You Write*

If you didn't organize your manuscript before you wrote it—or tried to, but somehow you think you missed the mark—fear not, there are things that can be done to fix the situation. You can transform a wandering dissertation into a well-oiled machine, and this chapter will explain how.

## WHEN THE BLOOM IS OFF THE PROSE

Things are going well—words are flowing and then glowing, getting better with each hour or day, and in your mind the manuscript is nothing short of marvelous, unquestionably the best stuff you've ever done. Visions of royalties circle you, and you begin to rehearse your debuts on *Oprah*, CNN and *Larry King Live*.

Then one morning you pick up this priceless piece of copy and read it again, expecting it to knock off your socks. Instead you find yourself wanting to throw up, or throw it out. The examples you loved, quivered over as you smoothed them into the manuscript, now are stone cold dead. The manuscript seems stiff and wordy, there are things that don't seem to fit and some of it doesn't even make sense. First you wonder if someone sneaked in at night and rewrote it, then you start searching for the real draft, figuring this must have been the first draft. But no, it's the same piece of work that you drooled over for a month.

This will happen, and it might just be the contrast between an over-idealistic, subjective view and a foul, discouraged mood later. But somewhere along the line, that copy lost its luster, almost to the point that you want to start over. You feel discouraged, mad, disgusted.

This is a bad time for a writer, and it happens even after six bestsellers in a row. It happened again on my thirty-sixth book. When I sat down to read my "masterpiece," it was a disasterpiece. Since I'd been through this before, I put aside any thoughts of high jumps and waited awhile. A week later I read it again and saw that although a number of things could and should be better, there were also some parts well worth keeping and expanding on.

So give your work the "cold eye" first yourself. It is bound to get the cold eye from others eventually, and they might just kill it (reject it!). If you just wound it instead in some places, which will heal, both you and it will survive and will probably be a better book for the experience. (And you'll be a little humbler, too.)

---

**It's always best to do your "editing" readings on paper, rather than a computer screen. "Cold type" is still the best somehow for giving things that "cold eye"— seeing things as critically and analytically as we need to at this stage. (What we writers really need is a machine that prints a manuscript out in something that looks 100 percent like the pages the publisher will eventually deliver to us for proofing. If we could see now everything that suddenly, chillingly strikes us then, we could fix it now before it costs us money—those infamous "author's alteration charges."**

---

*People treat pieces of writing as if they were children; they bring them out in to the world with great pain and then they're afraid to do anything to them, to tinker. But I'll bet any writer who is good either cooks or took alarm clocks apart when they were kids.*

*—Carl Mills*

## BOUND OR BULK?

I am very much a tangible, have-it-in-hand person. And when it comes to organization, a pile of pages, even in order, doesn't do it for me. Anytime I have anything even close to completed, book or article, I print it out and bind the pages together, generally in a plastic spiral binding. Machines are available from office-supply stores that will punch and bind things up to full manuscript size. Most copy stores (and many offices) have binders that you can use if you don't want to invest in a binder yourself.

You can use a loose-leaf binder for the same purpose, but a real binding always makes me feel more committed.

When material is bound, it

1. Gives the psychological feeling that you have a book.
2. Keeps everything that goes with or to the book together so it is all neatly organized in one place.
3. Is easy to hand around, carry in your car, work on, etc., and it won't get out of order.
4. Is easy to work on: to find or jot things in, for you or anyone else who might have to review it. You don't have to sort or page through a big messy pile.

If I take a book to another stage and enter corrections and additions, I print out a fresh, new copy and bind it. Always leave room, when binding manuscripts like this, for notes, additions or rewrites. You can leave wide margins, or all the left-hand pages blank, some extra blank pages in the back or whatever.

## "DIAGRAM" TO DIAGNOSE

Unsatisfactory sentences, phrases and even paragraphs are easy to fix—a few minutes of reflection, quick tryouts of different wordings, a switch of a sentence or two, a glance at the thesaurus, if necessary, and we are usually home free. But there is a much more insidious problem that is not so simple to dispose of, and it has to do with our old friend structure. And article or book manuscript has some nice pieces in it here and there, but it seems to meander all over, pull in different directions and arrive nowhere. When a manuscript is muddled like this, we can feel it—we sense those conflicting strands, those different currents swirling below the surface. We just don't know what to do about it.

This is a perplexing problem, and after years of puzzling over it, my coauthor Carol found a way to "X-ray" a manuscript to see exactly what's going on in it, so it can be remedied. She calls it diagramming, and here is how to do it.

Take the manuscript, page by page, and scan each page quickly to see what it is about. Not what it was supposed be about, or even what the headings on the page, if any, say it's about, but what those paragraphs actually discuss.

Write that down as concisely as you can, and write nothing more until you reach the next topic or new thought, then jot that down. When you're doing this, note also all major subtopics of the topics discussed, and when necessary, as briefly as you can—what the transitions between topics are.

OK, this is a little tedious, but when you're done, you will have a clear X ray of what is actually in your manuscript (and you will understand why it doesn't work yet). Let's give an example here to help clarify this:

**Diagram of Article: "The Manx Cat"**
What a Manx is (1 page)
Where breed originated (1 paragraph)
Other popular breeds of cat (1½ pages)
Why many cats have stripes (⅔ page)
Manx Appreciation Society of America (1 paragraph)
Genetic problems of Manxes (¾ page)
The Manx personality (½ page)
The appeal of Manxes
The shame of abandoning cats (2 pages)
Breeding Manxes successfully (1 page)
What makes Manxes different: they have no tail, and move differently (2 paragraphs)

Hopefully you are enough of a structure detective now to see where this article has gone out of order, and off the tracks entirely! (Turn to page 285 to see where it goes awry.)

## COLOR CAN HELP YOU EDIT YOURSELF

You can also use color to get a clear, objective view of copy you're dissatisfied with but are not sure why. You can look over a magazine article, for example, and mark in red every point that ties in to your capsule sentence. Long stretches of copy with no red marks? That's a signal that you've digressed too much, gone too far off the mark. Get out the black pen and start deleting!

Find each of the major elements in your story, assign them a color and then use those colors to highlight the amount of space you've given to each. Are there six paragraphs circled in yellow and only a couple in orange? What does that tell you? You may have skimmed over that orange topic too quickly. Perhaps you need to do more research, get a few more quotes for it. Or the abundance of yellow may signal that you've rambled on too long about that topic. Would the piece as a whole be better if you cut some of that out? Color coding like this can also show when, and where, you've backtracked or leaped forward to another topic instead of continuing on the one at hand. It works equally well to analyze longer pieces such as book chapters. Again, just identify all of the major subtopics of a chapter, assign each a color and start coloring yourself a picture of exactly what you have filled your pages with.

When you have a heavily edited piece of copy with marks and lines going every which way, using different colors to show additions and switches in placement of paragraphs can cut down on confusion.

## OTHER WAYS TO SEE AND FIX STRUCTURE

### Try it, and then *look* at it

We tend to think of analyzing words on paper as a solely mental process, but the visual plays a big part and can really help us out here. If you think something might go somewhere else than where it is, move it there, and then eyeball it and the answer to whether it works will be clear. If you wonder if you should recast a sentence, type it out the new way, lay it next to the old, and the answer will be clear. Is this chapter in the right order? Eyeball the headings and subheads quickly, and you will know. Might something serve as the lead for your new chapter? Put it in place, and wonder no more. This even works when you have a pile of good "snippets" that need to be spliced together. Spread them out on a desktop or a big table, and how they can be fit together will become clear.

• When analyzing part of something (article or chapter), it helps to isolate it. Make temporary page breaks and print it out with no neighboring copy in sight. This will help you concentrate on the problem piece. You can even separate and print out all the subsections of a problem article or chapter this way to make analysis and reshuffling easier.

• If you're working over a manuscript and discover pieces that belong somewhere else, move them there, but don't distract yourself from what you were doing by trying to blend them in now. Just leave an extra line space between each of the "orphan" pieces and the discussion they belong in so you'll know later that you have to work them into the above.

• There are different ways of restructuring things, including the old cut and paste, and switching things around on computer. Before you start dissecting and reorganizing a chapter or article by any means, save a copy of it. This will give you the courage to be bolder, without fear of losing forever or rashly removing some precious piece.

## ORGANIZING RANDOM PIECES INTO A SATISFYING WHOLE

There are times when you may want to do this, and not just when your collaborator has handed you a draft that seems to be a giant jigsaw puzzle of prose. You may, for example, want to assemble your six years' worth of essays, or weekly columns, into a book. Some hints on how to go about this:

• In general, work from the known to the unknown. Put all of the pieces you can figure out what to do with together first, and then worry about what you have left.

• When trying to make chapters or whatever out of random essays, you can organize by any of the principles outlined in chapter nine. But you have two basic choices here—either putting like with like (all essays on the seasons, or family relations, together, for example), or creating more of a conscious variety, such as creating chapters on the different periods of your life, so you can have more variety in the subject matter within each chapter. The former method works well if you have a strong, solid amount of material to work with on each theme. If you don't, the gaps and weaker topics will be apparent. The latter method usually allows you more changes of pace within the chapter, and the randomness of the order can hide a multitude of sins (such as the fact that you never did say much about X, Y or Z!).

• Bear in mind that no matter how masterfully you fit pieces together, if they are by different authors, the final result will not have the same grip on the reader that a single-author, continuous narrative text has.

---

**When you are deep in a manuscript, shuffling, adjusting, moving and rethinking things to get them the way they ought to be, you will feel it: the music of finding the natural order of things!**

---

## DON'T LET REDO BECOME OVERDO!

Redo, or revision, is a major part of writing, and often the thing that makes or breaks a piece. Just don't let redo become overdo. There is a time to quit editing and improving and get on with it. Lots of good books have died because the author died before he finished all his revising and polishing. The more you work on something, the less you'll be "wowed" by it because you know the copy so well. Some books I was ready to toss after the eighth redo. Most copy needs a rough, a revised draft, an edit and then a finish. That's three redos.

## POINTERS FROM THE PROS ON REVISION

*Ray Long, the famous old-time editor of* Cosmopolitan, *always said, "Revise when you're tired." Going over a manuscript at the end of a hard day, you will be impatient with needless verbiage, and cutting will be easy. Polishing will be, too, surprisingly. I always rework first drafts in late evening.*
*—Keith Monroe*

*On the computer it's no longer a question of the old first draft, second draft, etc., because you are redrafting and doing partial rewrites constantly.*
*To avoid version confusion, when I do a new draft of a chapter, proposal or whatever, I change the name (such as to Gall Bladder article 3). Sometimes I name things for the editor they are intended for.*
*—Nicholas Bakalar*

*Write the first chapter the best you can, then keep on going through the book to the end, before you try to revise anything. You need time between writing and revision.*
*—Jean Loftus*

## "FREEZING" LEFTOVERS

The first blow to my confidence as a writer came when I got my first edited manuscript back. Carol must have had a 10' x 10' chopping block! Much of my "best" stuff was axed because it didn't work or wasn't needed where it was.

When we work on books, much good material I put in my drafts ends up out, but not gone. We keep all leftover and cut copy for another time and place. It may even be the catalyst for another book!

How do we do this? As Carol is editing the book, she drops any pruned-out pieces into computer files like the following:

Cuts—these are saved in case I want to review them, and argue about anything that got the axe.

Maybe copy—a notch above cuts, but not necessarily priceless pearls. Carol will scan them quickly near the end of the project, just in case.

Find a place for?—means pieces that didn't fit where they were, but are definitely worth trying to tuck into this book somewhere. She will do that before the manuscript is finalized.

Bits to fit—small pieces that belong somewhere else in this book, and Carol knows where, but doesn't want to take the time to place them right now.

Save for next book—copy that really belongs in a entirely different book, such as one on business management, teaching children to clean or clutter. Carol gives these to me at the end of each project so they can be refiled in the right hard drive or drawer.

You can use this principle to create your own categories for "freezing" leftovers.

## DELIVERED TO THE EDITOR DOESN'T MEAN DONE!

Publication for the most part is a drawn-out process, so don't let your organizational guard down the minute you turn in the "final."

• Don't try to read a manuscript, large or small, for more than one thing at once (for art ideas, for editing, for technical corrections, for proofing). One agenda will distract from the other, and you are sure to miss things.

• If you are checking two versions of a manuscript or proofs against each other, or against a third copy, the piles will always get mixed. Assume this and check back to fix it.

*When the editor sends you back the copyedited manuscript, don't read just the places that have been changed, and the queries. Read the whole thing through again, to catch any little*

*problems or oversights (yes, even copyeditors make them!) Don't get lazy now—read the book from cover to cover carefully. Check for consistency of all kinds (if the chapter titles have been changed, are they now the same both on the chapter and in the table of contents?) Don't assume others will do all of this. No one is as emotionally attached to your book as you are, or committed to it—no one will find more errors than you!*
*—Jean Loftus*

## ORGANIZING ART AND ILLUSTRATIONS

The whole process of producing a book or article that will be illustrated is usually longer and more complicated, and will profit greatly from good organization.

• Early on, as soon as you are aware of the need for an illustration, put a "slugline" in the manuscript at that spot, e.g., "Picture of reorganized closet goes here."

• You do sometimes want to have illustrations just for sheer graphic or "scene setting" effect, but in general, let illustrations do what words cannot to help the reader understand things.

• Artwork or photos should ideally appear right after or with the copy that mentions or explains them.

• After you have your photos or artwork assembled, you need to assign them all numbers and then key those numbers in to the text— the sluglines will now read something like "Illustration X goes here." When choosing a numbering system, try to pick something that can accommodate the fact that chapters or sections will almost inevitably change position in the book or illustrations will be cut or added. For this reason numbering illustrations by chapter ("16-1, 16-2," etc. ) is usually more manageable.

• Number illustrations on the back with labels, not in ballpoint pen.

• Provide all captions on a separate document, keyed to the illustration numbers. Don't forget any necessary credit lines.

• If your book has many illustrations, there is almost bound to be a mistake in the final unless you are very vigilant through the whole production process: pictures in the wrong place, upside down, "flipped" or with the wrong caption.

Most book publishers won't pay for art or illustrations, so be sure to make clear note of the fact that you own them. Don't let the artwork or photos themselves get lost at the publisher or printer. Get them back as soon as they are willing to release them and file them away neatly. You can always use them again someday in press kits, brochures, greeting cards or board games based on your manuscript, and maybe even your autobiography someday!

**CHAPTER 11**

# Time Management Tips for Writers

Once you start writing, the clock will tick as it always has, only you will hear the ticks better and worry about them more, because now you know how much more you can do with time than just watch it go by!

This chapter is a potpourri of tips on time management for writers. It includes ways to help you get started (even jump-start yourself when necessary), to keep going when you don't feel like it, to get the most done in the time available, to maximize the times when you're on a roll, to avoid wasted effort, to make the best use of your biorhythms and to accomplish more than one thing at a time. It even includes a little on organizing your life for writing, such as keeping personal habits and even the most innocuous addictions from sabotaging your output.

Here, too, you will learn the much-needed secrets of coping with the forces that make writing the most "procrastinatable" pastime around!

## "HOW DO YOU WRITE SO MUCH?"

What are the questions I am asked most often, now that people think of me as "rich and famous"?

1. "Do you still work at your regular job?"

In my case that job is cleaning, and managing a large professional cleaning company. And yes, I still do it, sometimes twelve hours a day. Plus I have a busy schedule at home and in the community, and of public appearances.

2. "How do you write so much?"

The answer to this is simple. It's not that I do more than most people, it's that I piddle less. It's a simple matter of replacement, at home or on a plane. People will spend hours, for example, catching up on the latest gossip or filling out a crossword puzzle. True, the latter is some exercise for the brain, but I can get more and better mental exercise from writing something that won't just be chucked in the wastebasket when it's done. When you use your time to write , you can sell your work and change lives with it, instead of just tossing it out like clutter.

## KNOW WHAT PART OF THE CLOCK YOU OWN

The more writing we do, the more aware we become that different parts of the job have different mental demands. For parts of the writing process we can be half awake or on autopilot and still make progress, and other times we have to think and analyze and compose with everything we have. Writing calls for gathering and listening, planning, roughing things, rewriting, sorting and filing—all of which will have different demands on your mental engines.

The most crucial time is when you really have to draw on your creative juices, see the whole scope and shape of a project, put together all those ideas and find words that don't just lie on the page, but sing. You are going to need 150 percent of your mental powers—no loafing here, folks. Everyone is sharper or duller at different times of day—so pay close attention and learn yours. Nothing is worse than trying to do high-demand work at a time of low energy and mental output. Once you've been writing awhile, you will come to know your own patterns—your highs and lows.

### The magic of early

My own patterns are so clear-cut it is scary. Early in the morning is when I write most and best—four A.M., and sometimes earlier. In the early morning, everyone else is usually in bed. The phones don't ring, the kids don't fuss or demand and no one is asking you to run errands. Best of all, it's dark out, so you won't be distracted by the weather, the neighbors or other exterior goings-on.

I know many people are convinced they are night people, but the mind is much sharper in the morning than at night. Many studies bear this out. I've seen people change their work time from night to morning and marvel at the difference. While going to college and running the cleaning business I created to pay my way, I had little time to study, and I would try to do it before going to sleep after cleaning buildings all day. A professor told me that thirty minutes in the morning would go further than three hours the night before. "Everyone knows that!" Well, I didn't, so I switched, and he was right.

Get up early to do your writing. Go to sleep earlier so you can!

Nine P.M. to midnight is generally dead brain time, anyway. We often waste it snacking on food and drinks we don't need, drowsing or watching TV. Go to bed at ten P.M. and get up at five A.M.; that's seven good hours of rest.

I get up early, get right to work and write until I lose my edge—generally about seven or eight A.M. I usually lie in bed with a pad and pencil from four to five A.M., then jump up to work at the typewriter from five to six. Until about ten A.M., I am dangerous with creativity. I can put out material that afterward I don't believe I actually did.

After that, I do the more mundane, or "flunky," work—process the daily paper flow, file, write letters, revise things I've already written, etc. After five P.M. I'm so worn down mentally I can't even decide what TV channel to watch or what I want to eat. That's when I shovel and dig and rake the yard or build something in my shop.

This schedule usually nets me six fresh, quality pages of written material a day—good stuff compared to the forced-out, dredged-up stuff we often do in the evening. That's six pages. Do that for a month and you'll have a 180-page book done. Using your mornings, you can be a published author before you know it. Another perk of this is that you'll go into the day from six A.M. on knowing you've already had a productive day!

Try writing in the morning for a month; I'll bet you'll not only put out better material, but more in a month than you usually do all year. And that is worth a little schedule adjustment.

---

**When is the best time of day for *you* to do mental work? Once you find it, the key now is to not fritter it away.**

---

*I do most of my work at night. I prefer to work from after dinner, around eight or nine, to two or three in the morning, sometimes later, when the world is quiet. Then I sleep in, spend the "day" with my husband, perhaps an early movie, have a nice dinner—and get back to work on "my time."*

—Elizabeth Pomada

## GETTING OVER THAT "STARTING" HURDLE

• We often find ourselves waiting for the "right mood" to get started. But the perfect time or conditions for writing only appear once in a while—are you going to waste the other twenty-six days in the month? Just get started, get moving, and your mood will change. Get moving; start writing and that will motivate you!

• It always helps to start with the part of a writing project you like, one that that delights, charms and tickles you.

• If you've already started on a project, leave things at the end of the day so that you can just pick up where you left off. If you don't have to dig out and rearrange everything, it's a lot easier to start.

## POINTERS FROM THE PROS ON STARTING RITUALS

*Some writers don't even know they have a starting ritual, but most of us have one, and I think it's important. Mine is sitting down at the desk, and while waiting for the PC to boot, turning on the radio or putting on some music. I light the day's first cigarette or drink coffee while reading notes for the task at hand, or scan the latest revision of whatever's to be worked on. A ritual beginning of a period of work ties a writer to the work.*

—Robert Sloan

*To jump-start a piece of writing, I usually begin with the line "This is just a draft." It takes the edge off the perfectionism that can slow a writer down.*

*I also think a few things, or even mutter them aloud. One, I will never finish this piece. Two, if I do finish the darn thing, it will never be published. Three, if it is published, no one will ever read it.*

*Having purged myself of all evil spirits thusly, I then proceed to write.*

—John Brady

*I write books exclusively, and beginning them is the hardest— probably because you know you are starting on a vast enterprise*

*that may take you a year or more. To help here I tell myself,
"You don't really have to write the book, just the outline of it. Or
just the outline of the first chapter." I carry this approach
through the whole book—telling myself, I only have to write a
thousand words of the first chapter, and the next time, not even
finish the chapter, but just eight hundred words more of it. This
helps to keep it from feeling like an endless tunnel that you enter
and never emerge from.*

—Nicholas Bakalar

*In each session of writing, when I quit for the day, I stop in mid-
sentence, when I know what the next few lines will be. The next
day those lines will come easily, and I've kick-started myself.*

—Keith Monroe

*Sometimes I use reverse psychology: No! You are not allowed
to write! (After all, who wants to drive more than a grounded
teenager, or an adult whose car is in the shop?) Eventually, I
want to write so badly that I know I won't stop—and so
then I start.*

—Kelly Boyer Sagert

### Get ready ahead

It's important to write when you are on the edge and hot. Spending half
the morning getting ready will mean many lost pages and writing
impulses.

Don't waste crisp, creative time fiddling around and setting up
things. What a way to ruin a good day! I never prepare in the morning.
At night I review, then lay out what I intend to write the next day.

When you get up, you'll be off and running instead of rummaging
around. Be ready *before* when you get up so you can hit the ground
writing. Like laying your clothes out the night before for faster dressing
in the morning, have things ready to pick up and go—your notes collected, references assembled, pencils sharpened and a blank sheet of
paper in the typewriter—if you still use one.

## QUIT STALLING BEFORE STARTING

A while ago, Carol and one of her assistant editors had fun recording a
classic part of the writing process.

## Checklist for Action

You've already

changed your T-shirt to a sweatshirt (or your sweatshirt to a T-shirt)

put on your house slippers

cleaned your glasses

reset your watch

loosened your belt

trimmed your nails

studied your profile

checked for gray hairs

washed your face

combed your hair

plucked your eyebrows

brushed your teeth (and put the cap back on tube and rolled tube up neatly)

made a snack

looked out the window

eaten your snack

brought in the milk or mail or paper

put the dishes away

weighed yourself

run out for cigarettes

cleaned the light switch

adjusted the lamp

thinned the correction fluid

emptied the wastebasket

chewed your pencil

filled the stapler

emptied the ashtray

played with paper clips

gone through your in box

checked and answered your e-mail

sharpened your pencils

emptied the pencil sharpener

selected an FM station

alphabetized your CD collection

dusted the top of the bookcase

looked through the junk mail

done last month's expense accounting

made that tune-up appointment
cleaned out your notebook
re-prioritized your old list
typed a new list
straightened the pictures on the wall
emptied your pockets
leafed through *Writer's Market*
read the captions under the pictures in the dictionary
read a few old *National Geographics*
matched all your socks
put all the hangers in the closet facing the same way
put a fresh box of baking soda in the fridge

**There's probably nothing left to do but write . . .**

If this list looks familiar, it's because we are all artists at stretching out the start of something, when we want to. We can call this dawdling, piddling or my favorite—dinging—but under any name it is a real time waster.

If you want to see a quick increase in your productivity, just make sure all your time on a writing project is working time. Most people hunt, daydream, scratch their heads, shuffle things around, pick things up and put them down again, etc., for at least a third of each hour they "write."

---

**Reorganizing your piles or filing can sometimes help you get started, but beware—even organizing can be an avoidance activity!**

---

## ON MINUTES AND MARATHONS

For ten years now I've collected material and written bits and pieces for a book I call *How to Savor the Moment*. My box of material on it finally maxed out, and it felt like time to break it down into chapters. So I took it with me on the plane to Hawaii. On the five-hour flight, I skipped the movie and outlined an attack on that ten years' worth of prime notes. For the next thirty days, including Saturdays and Sundays, I got up at 3:30 A.M. and wrote till my energy and inspiration left or church started. I wrote in about eight-hour sieges and didn't let breakfast or the bathroom interrupt my momentum. By the thirty-first day, the entire draft was done. I doubt I'll ever do anything like this again, but it worked and felt good, really good!

Lately, I've had only snatches of time before, during or after life's main events of making a living and being a good parent, spouse and neighbor. But when time pops up, I always have three or four partial book manuscripts, articles or poems with me, and I tear into them. It's amazing how this adds up.

You'll seldom get marathon writing spaces if you have a job, a yard, kids, relatives or neighbors. If you have any other talents or serious hobbies (such as music, carpentry or a sport), you get even less time for your writing. So you need to write whenever you get the chance, or you'll be forever starting.

---

**Any time is a good time to write—one sentence, one idea recorded right when it comes to you, consistently, beats taking off a whole year to do nothing but write!**

**To make the most of time fragments, dive into your project as though you have only fifteen or twenty minutes to work on it. Keep a feeling of urgency so when fifteen minutes turns into thirty or sixty, you'll have done more than you hoped for.**

---

*Don't think you can't get started on something because you'll never be able to finish it in the time you have available right now. Start it anyway. An hour here and a half-hour there will really add up, by way of precious pages that get you closer to the goal.*

*—Kirk Polking*

## HOW TO WRITE FORTY BOOKS AT ONCE

When I tell people I've written more than thirty books they are amazed, but when I tell them we have at least forty more in the works and on the way, they give me a look of total disbelief (as many people are struggling along on a single book). Don't be awed or impressed or for a minute think doing this is difficult. It isn't. It's just a mechanical process, and you could easily do forty or four hundred books or articles at the same time. The process is really a no-brainer.

OK, you start forty books or articles over a few years' time, and you have a drawer, box or file for each one. Every day things will come your way for some of your topics, so you make notes or clip the item, and toss it in the box or file it fits. Some days you'll come across two or three items, others (such as when you return from a trip or seminar), you may have twenty or thirty. In minutes these can be tossed in the files or boxes. I don't meddle with a box until it gets pretty full or I am inspired to transform it into a rough draft—I just keep feeding the boxes.

Let me give you an example here. My wife and I raised six children, and all of them are strong, moral and productive adults. In spite of these now forty-year-old successes, I, like all parents, struggled with some aspects of the process. The one thing I felt a little failure on was how I taught or administered money handling with them. So the idea popped into my head to do an article on how to give a kid money.

I quickly wrote down my feelings about this and noted some of the bumps and heartaches I'd had, and some of the things I'd heard from other parents about their money struggles with kids. I labeled a box and tossed all this in it.

Three days later I asked the trust officer at my bank about giving kids money. He lit up like a gasolined campfire. "Don, that is one of the biggest problems in banking." And he proceeded to relate several whats, whys, whens and hows, and gave me a brochure about the subject. He told me of a recent incident where a youngster, age thirty, inherited $500,000 and blew it in a year—great material, confirming my belief that giving kids money is a problem whether they're two or sixty. I tossed all of this in my box at home, knowing now that this might have the makings of a book, not just an article.

A few days later at church a dozen parents were talking about having co-signed loans for their kids when they were newly married, in college or buying a nice car. Eleven of the twelve regretted it because they ended up making the payments or getting the car back. Bingo, more beautiful material! I jotted it down, and tossed it in the "Kids and money" file that evening.

A week later, during a day of negotiations with a lawyer, an accountant and a couple buying a business, I mentioned during lunch my "book" on kids and money. Both the lawyer and the accountant leaped to dominate the conversation with numerous disaster stories, both agreeing that the subject of kids and parents and money was a grave one. I wrote on menus, a pad and napkins what they said and tossed the gems in the box that evening!

A week later I was speaking at a seminar to some engineers and intentionally steered the conversation to kids and money, and boy did I strike gold. One fellow said his sixteen-year-old daughter inherited seven thousand dollars from her grandma, and it about ruined her. She let her studies go, saying, "Hey Dad, don't worry. I have money." I wrote down this and all the other comments and tossed them in the box.

Later that month I was speaking in New York City at the National Mother of the Year Convention and was seated at a table with the likes of the famous Marriotts and Sellecks. I remained quiet in the midst of such well-known guests until one of them asked me, "What book are you working on now, Don?"

*"How to Give a Kid Money."* Pow! A fistfight almost broke out at the table. I learned that seldom do husband and wife agree on this matter, and if the marriage splits up, the poor side usually drains the richer spouse's wallet—more trouble. Great conversation, strong opinions from strong people, perfect material for a book. I subtly wrote it all down, and when I returned home, several pages went in that box, now growing nicely! Oh, and on the way home, I saw a kids and money article in the airline magazine, and I tore it out and boxed it, too.

After four years, my "Kids and money book" box was heaped with pure, documented, real-life material. The book was more than half done. All I had to do was spread the information out on the floor, organize it into chapters and add to and expand on what I had—a simple process!

How much time had I spent on this book? Little.

How much money had I spent on it? Zero.

I think you get the idea by now that this is a simple process of closure on your daily exposure! I've been doing this same thing for all of my book ideas for days, months and years. It takes no work. Just keep your eyes and mind open and grab everything that comes along.

I've done all this while busy with the ordinary life of making a living, traveling, visiting and going to church. I don't stop and take hours to write anything; I just jot little notes, tear out pages and collect brochures as I'm doing other productive things. The later stages of production—the mechanical side, do take some time and money if you are self-publishing a book, but the basic act of writing doesn't. So don't ever use the "no time, no money" excuse to not write!

---

**There isn't a single second in your life when you can't be in some way advancing your desire to write!**

---

## DEADLINES ARE DEADLY

I hate deadlines—I hate the word when I hear it because I know it means trouble and gross inefficiency. Eighty percent of those who work to deadlines are late with their deliveries. They let deadlines become their master organizer and set their inner clocks to beat deadlines.

In writing, organize yourself to stay as far away from deadlines as you can. Anything cut close is cut wrong. If something is due mid-February, the deadline mind will automatically ask what the exact deadline day is and then structure a schedule to meet it. This is a road to pure misery for everyone involved. Deadline people working with other deadline mentalities learn to lie to each other to compensate for those last-minute emergencies that will always occur to threaten the deadline. Well-organized, good managers never use deadlines. If it is due mid-February, smart, efficient people will have it done mid-January. Once you learn that now beats later about 99 percent of the time, you are going to be ahead of most of the other strugglers who are always scheduling things, then rescheduling them and rescheduling them again.

Eliminate *deadlines* from your vocabulary and you'll have an advantage over most writers. If you want something done well, and easily, then do it months before the deadline, or even before the deadline is set. Deadline thinking is bad news. Good writing is something you just don't push and hurry, and when running behind, you cannot make a mood or instantly call up creativity. Writing is more emotional, if not spiritual, than it is mechanical, and even preparing to write has to be done creatively, a long time beforehand.

### The sure way to beat deadlines

How do we get in trouble with deadlines? Let's look at a diagram of how the average person's schedule looks to him right now. Let's look six months ahead, say from January through June.

JAN   FEB   MARCH   APRIL   MAY   JUNE   JULY

Busy times          Open time (Oh boy!)     Project due

The time ahead always looks freer than the time at hand, so we don't even think about squeezing that project we know has to be done in now—instead we target "open time" right before a project is due.

That may seem logical, but that big block of busy—all of the demands in front of you right now—will move with you down the line. New demands and opportunities will crop up as well. If you wait till later, you won't have any more time or opportunity than you do now.

Productive people always have a completely full immediate schedule. This is the secret of "Ask a busy person if you want something to get done," because they do things now, while they are busy, not later, when they imagine some open time will appear. Open time is never open when you get there. Even if you spot a future blank in your time schedule and put writing off till then, that opening has almost always dematerialized by the time you get to it. Life goes on during that whole six months, plus we always carry a big load of "wish I could get tos" with us. There is a very good chance that you will be even busier during that "open time" than you are now!

So crowd that writing in now, find some time now and get started now. And don't worry, that open time later will fill with better stuff than the delayed load you've been carrying. This style of doing will double your output and cut your deadline stress in half.

You'll always be busier later than you are now! You have choices and options now; you won't later.

Most people's approach:

| **Now/today** | **Later** | **Right before it's due** |
|---|---|---|
| You get an idea or assignment, and schedule it. | Prepare for it. | *Do* it. |

The smart approach:

| **Now/today** | **Later** | **Before it's due** |
|---|---|---|
| Get an idea or assignment and start doing it. | Finish it. | Free time (and time to improve what you've done)! |

One big cause of deadline problems is promising by hopes rather than fears: You tell an editor or client what you suspect they would like to hear rather than the truth about how long something will take, as you know it. Trying to please someone by being unrealistic like this will only ultimately displease them!

Don't try to shove everything aside for a deadline. Guilt over neglected obligations to your family, spouse or yourself will end up eroding some of the time you "stole" for writing. Make time for the things important to you, such as birthdays, anniversaries, favorite holidays and exercise, and you'll go back to your work relieved and refreshed. If there is no joy in your life, it will show in the manuscript.

## PERSPECTIVES FROM THE PROS ON DEADLINES

*I need a specific deadline or else I can think of a lot of things to do other than write, and I do meet deadlines. One time I didn't. I called the editor of a major woman's magazine to explain why my article would be late. I said: "My brother-in-law just died, my husband had an operation, and I had an operation." She said, "That's too bad. When can I expect the article?"*
*—Ruth Winter*

*I write more than a dozen columns a week, and I've never missed one. How do I accomplish that? As soon as I finish one column, I start putting information on the next one in that series into the computer. I'm continually feeding the computer for the next series of columns, and sometimes for ones farther off yet. I do a little on each column every day.*
*—Seli Groves*

*Deadlines: You have to respect them. Publishers don't need any more writers who are going to be six or eight months late with their book. The kind of writers they need are on time. Deadlines are not incidental, but part of your professional responsibility. Forget the attitude: "I'll write a good book and deliver it in my own good time."*

> *Some people do actually write themselves out a schedule. I keep my eye on the clock, but not in a systematic way. As the deadline approaches, I speed up my pace to get the job done on time.*
>
> —Nicholas Bakalar

> *Meeting deadlines on a complex project always requires a small degree of pure luck. If it becomes clear that we are possibly going to miss a deadline, we notify those involved as early as we can, explain why we will be late and agree on a new date.*
>
> —Clyde and Suzy Burleson

## FEELING PERKY OR MURKY?

An area we seldom hear about when it comes to writing may just be the single most important factor in organizing yourself to start and continue writing. And it is totally personal. It is the need to be rested and feeling good. There is no way you can continually produce good material when you are feeling bad physically. Maybe you'll create a wisp or two of good stuff now and then, but not consistently. So take a look at your lifestyle for things that blur your focus and reduce your output. Writing is hard if you're stuffed with food; dimmed by drugs; or suffering from a hangover, indigestion, headaches or exhaustion. Make sure you get enough rest, and remember that each morning is shaped by the night before. Eat less and better. Consider dumping any unhealthy habits you have (they're probably expensive, too).

## EXERCISE JOGS YOUR MIND

We must exercise to keep healthy and give us the strength and stamina a writer needs. But exercise takes time, and we're always tempted to skip it when we're deeply immersed in a project or working on a deadline.

In the time you waste complaining about lack of time for exercise, however, you could be walking or jogging around the block. And often you can do other things at the same time, such as review your master plan and refire your ambitions, think of how your characters will interact with each other, figure out whom to call for those World Series statistics or decide what magazine would be interested in the historical background of the muzzle-loader. You can even read while riding a stationary bike.

Busy as you may be, don't skip exercise. It doesn't just tune up your body; it lifts your spirits and recharges your mind as well.

## A CLEAR MIND MEANS A CLEAR PATH

Clear thinking requires a clear mind and a clear path. Sure, conditions can't be perfect for writing with several kids leaping around or the phone ringing constantly, but there is plenty of mental clutter you *can* shed—such as grudges, resentments, pettiness and trivia—to make room for the wonderful world of writing. You can't write well when you're caught up in fury about your ex or the neighbor's dog. Things like this are a big liability.

Take a deep breath and allow yourself to drift for a few minutes, then get to work. If that doesn't do it, try channeling all this passion into your writing.

Being fresh and unfettered is a great way to work. Your might and mind melt into your manuscripts instead of fighting all those other things gnawing away at your life.

> *I have some little techniques that help me zero in on the fact that I am working, and concentrate. I always start out my writing day with a cup of coffee or hot chocolate in hand. I may not even drink it, but it helps me start. And I put a supply of some little treat I really like into a plastic bag, and bring it with me. It might be peanuts, or peppermints, or whatever turns you on. I'm only allowed to eat this while doing things connected with my book, only while I'm working. I eat them very slowly, sometimes just a half peanut at a time. This is a way of not just rewarding myself, but of reinforcing the fact that this is work time.*
>
> *—Frances Spatz Leighton*

## DRESS SIMPLE, DRESS QUICK

Home workers can dress casually, so take advantage of this. When writing, dress simply so you can dress quickly. Getting too gussied up may give you the urge to leave the keyboard and get out and be seen!

Don't let things go too far the other way, however. Do your hair every so often, wear a favorite shirt, splash on some cologne or do whatever little thing it takes to keep you feeling good about yourself. How we feel about ourselves will show in our writing.

> *[When writing] I customarily wear loose Bermuda shorts, very loose T-shirt or sport shirt, loose socks and floppy sandals. I have grown to feel wonderfully at ease in that uniform; it restricts me at no point and leaves my arms and hands free to move easily.*
> —James A. Michener

## DON'T SABOTAGE YOURSELF

I was impressed the first time I heard the expression "He shot himself in the foot," meaning we are often our own worst enemy. We writers are guilty of doing this, too—self-sabotage, you might say, such as when we

- start a book, and buy a new 36"-screen TV on the same day.
- work around a blaring radio or TV.
- buy so much writing equipment that we have to use all our writing time and money to pay for it, and have no time to use it.
- get too many "second opinions" on our work.
- take a second job when we are about to start a novel.
- get a puppy in need of house-training two weeks before a manuscript is due.
- think we can do full-fledged writing with only half the attention.
- hurry through to the end just to be finished.
- always wait for a better time, place or mood.
- don't bother to back up our writing regularly.

Check out of sabotage lodge!

## BEWARE OF THE NEW MYTH IN WRITING: "MY TOOLS WILL TAKE OVER"

Don't believe that automation will pick up any slack you leave in your writing. Tools don't take over anything in the judgment or ambition court. If anything, they can make you lazy and careless. Tools can expedite mechanics but cannot, will not, make value decisions as to your time use or the quality of the material you gather. Often you can finish a task in longhand while you wait for that new miracle computer program to boot up.

## FIGHTING DROWSINESS

Losing your wits to drowsiness is one of the worst of all organizational blunders. Trying to caffeine yourself up to continue when you're feeling tired is really dumb. If you find yourself nodding at the keyboard, don't just try to find a quick fix. Find the cause and fix it! Are you having trouble sleeping at night (from drinking too much coffee or pop all day, or from lack of exercise)? Are you going to bed too late? Reading the latest hot novel until two A.M. is not going to help you start on yours the next morning at nine.

Are you eating too much during or right before your writing time, especially sweet or starchy foods? Is the room too warm? Or, a very real possibility, are you simply bored with the topic you're working on?

If you feel sleepy and can't seem to shake it, try a quick walk around the house or the block. Take a short rest or nap if you must (often just fifteen or twenty minutes will do it), rather than drinking three more cups of coffee. Caffeine won't kick in till later, anyway—probably about the time you're really trying to go to sleep.

If all else fails and you really must keep going, chewing will usually wake you up. Raw carrots, apples, salt-free popcorn or hard pretzels or sugar-free gum are some of the less fattening ways to take advantage of this technique. Sucking on a cough drop, lollipop or hard candy can help, too.

### Drowsiness in a bottle

In the enforced isolation of mental work, we are often extra-aware of physical ailments of all kinds, from headaches to toothaches to muscle cramps. For many of these, thanks to the endless shelves of over-the-counter remedies and our doctors' busy prescription pads, we can take things to ease the pain or reduce the discomfort. But often, after we take them, we find ourselves battling a different enemy—drowsiness. Antihistamines, for instance, even the "nondrowsy" formulas, can really sneak up on you.

If the condition afflicting you is not serious and the job at hand requires 100 percent alertness or an especially long day, you might want to think before you pop that pill. If you really need your full mental powers, or the job must be done today, working with an ache might be better than giving up early because you couldn't stay awake.

What about that other kind of bottle, the kind long associated, rightly or wrongly, with writers: alcoholic beverages? What is the truth here? A drink or two at the end of the day can sometimes help you write more fluently or turn out a long-overdue or hard-to-write letter. But it's no good for the long haul. Drinking easily leads to more drinking: After a drink or two your judgment about whether to take another drink has already been impaired. And doing long stretches of hard mental work with a headache or sour stomach gets old.

## SOMETIMES YOU HAVE TO SLOG

> *The great composer does not set to work because he is inspired,*
> *but becomes inspired because he is working.*
> —*Ernest Newman*

Some things are a joy and a pleasure to do, but others (yes, even in this glorious odyssey of writing) are just plain tough. Sometimes to finish them, you just have to keep picking your discouraged, disheartened self up off the floor and throw yourself back at them—keep putting one foot in front of the other and ticking things off your to do list till they are done.

We all have an inner voice that is all too ready to tell us, "Give up, you just can't do this!" Replace that voice with one that reminds you of *why* you are doing this and of the skills and strengths you have that will make it possible.

## WHEN YOU FEEL "ADRIFT"

Our goals in writing are often so abstract and far removed in time, we can sometimes feel detached or adrift. When this unsettling feeling hits you, the antidote is to make things more concrete and specific, more clearly related to the end result you're after. Some ways to recenter yourself:

- Redo your to do list, or make one if you haven't yet. Get very specific about what you need to do today (and tomorrow and the next day) to move yourself closer to your goal.
- Sort through, neaten and reorganize your piles on this project.
- Think about what you *do* have finished or accomplished.
- Remind yourself of why you're doing this—the big picture.

## DON'T CONSTANTLY COMPARE YOURSELF TO OTHERS

Our constant comparison of ours with theirs is a big wet blanket in life. I'll bet we could cure this hangup in a hurry if we just once could see all of the top writers' drafts, rejects and failures. We live our own short-comings, so we see them; but we seldom see others' shortfalls, so their show seems perfect right out of the chute.

When my company first contracted to clean in Las Vegas, one of the clients insisted we see a spectacular Vegas show. From an audience view it was spectacular—the lighting, sound effects and fireworks were astonishing, breathtaking. The dazzling routines, colorful clothing and lack of it certainly made their point.

For months the visual and mental impact of that show stuck with me. Then we were invited by that hotel to bid on their maintenance ser-vice. They took us through the whole building, every part. And there, backstage, were the props and outfits we'd seen onstage, and now we were seeing them up close—no fanfare, just hanging on pegs, frayed, faded, sweat-stained, patched and soiled. The finished writing of others can be impressive, but you don't know everything that went into it behind the scenes. Your own is of value just by being yours.

Some of us won't do something because someone else can do it better. That's like not eating because someone else isn't hungry. The purpose of writing, and for that matter most things, is not competition. We seem to get carried away with comparisons and measurements and ratings. Sure some pocketknives and watches are better, but they all cut or tell time, regardless of their guts or glitter. When it comes to writing I'd place "fitting" above "fine" any day. Quit wasting time rubberneck-ing at other writers and do your own thing!

## HANDLING A LOW AFTER A HIGH

You need to be prepared for those times in your writing when you seem to be stalled. The flood of thoughts and ideas turns into a trickle, or even seems to dry up entirely. The more determined you are to keep going, the more you labor and strain at writing. I've done some of the most inspired writing in my life during some incredibly busy times. Then came a four-day weekend; I was thrilled to know that in the com-ing week, I would have four full, unscheduled available days with noth-ing going on at home or my office. I looked at that fun, challenging and potentially profitable pile of writing to do and just got goosebumps.

I was on a high—unstoppable! I had absolutely no obstacles. I was in perfect health, business was booming and all the kids and grandkids were doing well. So into the week I went, with visions of great writing output and grandeur.

I got into that long, lovely clear space, and the longer I wrote, the worse my copy became. I reread what I'd written in the first two days, and it all looked like junk. I found myself forcing out copy the next day, getting out about two lines in two whole hours (when I usually would have put out at least a half dozen pages of good stuff). I felt drowsy, though I'd had plenty of sleep the night before. I switched topics, shuffled research and tried again to write, but the results were still awful. I took it home and kept working on it on the couch in front of the TV, and then in bed. I got almost zero finished, but I kept plugging away at ideas and notes.

After three days of total discouragement and very few completed pages, on the fourth day I read some of my rough notes. I found a couple gems in there that got me going again! The bottom line is I didn't walk away from it. I managed to do *something*. Even when things were slow and sparse, I had some good ideas, some things to latch onto a few days later when the inspiration came back.

I just don't believe in laying the pencil down when I feel like lying down. Take a break? Why? A break might just make things worse. Why get away from it if it's what you want to do? A good writer plows when it's cold or they will beg during the harvest when they have nothing on the page.

## KEEPING A GRIP ON THE "GIFT OF GAB"

Talk, the other form of communication, is invaluable—to cement relationships, form bonds, convey thoughts, share feelings, gain alliances. But if we do it too much of it we not only waste time, but run a real risk of using up our "sap," talking away our writing impulses and ideas.

In an office, you may be able to spend a good part of the day talking and socializing and still get by. When you're trying to write, when all that counts is what is on the paper at the end of the day, and how good it is, this won't work. After the talking we writers do have to do, after the interviewing and polling and consulting or whatever, comes the time when it's just us and the page.

It's so much more fun (and easier!) to talk than write that we may even welcome interrupters with their idle chatter. Fight the impulse!

Don't talk during keyboard time, even about your writing business. Make calls that need to be made for your writing projects before or after your writing is done for the day. Only *writing* is going to get it written.

## DON'T CHEAT AT THE COMPUTER

Thinking that you're writing just because you're at the computer is about as foolish as thinking you're working just because you're in the office. Don't get caught up in the five thousand other features of our amazing machines. This means no dallying with computer games, Internet wandering or writing notes to all and sundry in e-mail. Stick with word processing during your writing time! OK, you're allowed to check e-mail if there is something you need for your writing on there, but forget the other thirty-two messages for now.

> *Every writer will have a personal list of "most-opened reference books" (mine are* The Kentucky Encyclopedia, Bartlett's Familiar Quotations, Roget's Thesaurus, *and* The American Heritage Dictionary*), and I believe they ought to exist as hard copies. More information is, of course, available on the Internet, but anything that takes a writer away from the work is not helpful. Nine times out of ten what I'm looking for can be found much quicker in a book, with fewer distractions than my favorite URLs offer.*
> —*Robert Sloan*

---

**When you enjoy writing, you tend to take every opportunity to express yourself—on greeting cards, in letters, surveys of opinion, and chat rooms on the Net. Until you finish that long-dreamed-of manuscript, try to channel your creativity here!**

---

## DON'T WASTE WAITING TIME

Waiting—we do a lot of it today, in all areas of our lives. We writers wait for the computer to boot up, for things to print out, for our calls be returned and while people have us on hold. Don't lose down time —use it!

*When I'm waiting to connect to a Web site, I use the waiting time to file papers, organize my folders or toss unwanted paper-work away.*

—*Mary Jo Rulnick*

Always think ahead for possible waiting time, and be ready for it. When lines and backups are unavoidable, always have something to read with you, or something to write. You can write notes and short pieces when traveling, and in meetings, read and clip magazine articles, review the mail, and write letters or first drafts, create characters or weave plots, while waiting anywhere.

Don't sit in traffic, for instance, and just rage. Traffic is a fact of life today, and there's nothing more pointless and unproductive than being angry because of it. Always travel with a tape recorder or notebook so you can record your thoughts as you wait. You can also listen to books on tape, or tapes on writing that may help you work out problems you're dealing with, such as developing a plot and characters for a steamy romance novel, how to write a book proposal, approach an editor or find a literary agent.

*I never go to an appointment, fly on an airplane or wait in a line that I don't have professional reading with me. By reading over forty magazines, newsletters and e-zines a month, I keep sharp on industry trends and marketing opportunities.*

—*Marilyn Ross*

## DO IT RIGHT THE FIRST TIME

Doing things right the first time (which does not necessarily mean writing a perfect first draft) is a real timesaver, and it applies to every aspect of writing. For example:

1. Keeping the names and addresses, etc., of contacts and resources well filed and up to date (so you don't have to search for them, or call to find out).
2. Having the purpose and scope of the article or book clearly in mind before you start, so you can slant it correctly.
3. Knowing the market for an article or book before you start.
4. Identifying the right place to go for the information you need.

5. Getting the editor's name straight when you copy it from the market guide!

## KEEP YOUR EYE ON THE "As"

We can always find all kinds of small, dead-end projects to work on, but getting a lot done is not the same as getting the most important things done. If you start work by jumping right into the hardest task for the day (whether it's making that intimidating phone call, or getting rid of all the repetition in chapter two), you'll get bigger and better results and feel better, too.

Often things we've dreaded, dodged and evaded forever take less than half an hour when we finally face up to them.

---

*Find your own answer. You know what keeps you from getting things done. You know the areas in which you're most likely to get into trouble. Nobody has to tell you that. Just admit your weaknesses, and create a system for getting around them.*

*—Art Spikol*

**CHAPTER 12**

# *"Just a Minute": Outwitting Interruptions*

We'd like to think of this whole book as an antidote to interruptions, the big ones like never getting around to writing, or stopping once you start, and the scores of little ones we fight every day. Whenever you're not writing, you're being interrupted!

The best-laid plans can and will be interrupted. We're settling down to write when suddenly there comes an unforeseen emergency—a friend calls from a phone booth near her disabled vehicle, desperately seeking a ride. This will take at least two hours, and it wasn't even on today's to do list!

If there is anything that could be called a miracle in writing, it is momentum. Getting on a roll, when things are flowing, and then keeping on it, gives us a real edge in writing. This is why, of all planning, our plans for avoiding or minimizing interruptions are the key to keeping the ballpoint ink flowing and the keyboard tapping.

## CONTROLLING THE MASS OF "OTHER"

When we work in an office downtown, we are in a special environment carefully created and sealed off from the rest of reality. Everything from the furnishings to the decor to what everyone is wearing says: Office! Focus! Paperwork! We have assistants and screening systems of all kinds to filter out anything that doesn't contribute to the job of the hour.

At home, except for our little niche of "office" (if we are lucky enough to have one), we are in the land of "other"—where every other mundane detail of daily life is likely to rear its head (if not shriek!) for attention. And we are there—so we see it, and feel it, and there is no escape from it. And often no one else to "delegate" it to. This is the essential challenge of working at home.

• Don't leave your office any more than you absolutely need to, till your writing is done. You can easily lose five or ten extra minutes on every trip because you notice the African violet needs watering, or the dryer or washer has just completed its cycle. All those minutes add up!

• Decide how much time you are willing to devote to extraneous matters during your writing time, and then keep track of it and **stick to it**. If your writing regimen calls for writing six hours a day, make that seven (so you have one hour to devote to the hardest-to-ignore interruptions). If something else crops up, forget it. Or put it on the list for tomorrow.

> *If you work at home, people don't see why you can't receive furniture deliveries for them, and the like. They don't realize you are no more free than someone who goes off to an office. This is true of not just neighbors and spouses but aging parents, growing children and friends.*
>
> *You must be firm about this and say, "This is my office." I live in a co-op, and if the super rings the bell and asks should he plant the holly tree in the front or the back, I say plant it wherever you want, and close the door.*
>
> —Nicholas Bakalar

> *I dislike rewriting and editing. No matter how important the project, I'll seize on any reason to walk away from it. That's why there's a small box of dog biscuits on my desk. My four big canines can be an unwelcome intrusion sometimes, and a biscuit usually distracts them. If the doggy treats are here, I don't have an excuse to go to the kitchen, where I might decide I'd rather do dishes. (That's how much I hate rewriting!)*
>
> *Not leaving the keyboard is probably why I use an enormous insulated coffee cup (fewer trips for refills).*
>
> —Robert Sloan

## THE UNEXPECTED SOURCE OF MANY INTERRUPTIONS

Granted, there are some interruptions we just can't do anything about, since we don't control all lives or the weather. But before you toss your hands in the air as many beginning writers do, blaming "them":

your uncaring spouse
the noisy, demanding kids
an unbending boss
your interfering mother-in-law or other relative
the UPS man, the TV . . .

If we had room we could list several hundred sources of interruptions. But surprise . . . 75 percent of them have one source, which is none of the above . . . it is you! Yes, you yourself engineer and are responsible for about three quarters of your own interruptions. You plan them and pull them off quite efficiently, too. You aren't the victim; you are the cause! A few points on minimizing interruptions:

1. If you do things early, interruptions are reduced to almost zero. About three quarters of interruptions are the result of past neglect or bad timing.

2. Many interruptions can be foreseen. If you sit down to write when you have something on the stove, have six call-backs waiting, when you're thirsty, irritated, the dog is whining to be fed or walked, or you need to hit the bathroom, you're a goner, because you will be forced to stop and do something as soon as you get rolling. Before you start writing, take care of all the little "to dos" in sight or get them out of sight!

3. If you have a cell phone hooked to your belt while you write, you deserve to be interrupted.

---

**If you are an interruptable person you will be interrupted many times. Anyone—or anything—can find you.**

---

## IF YOU ARE INTERRUPTED

Does that mean progress stopped? It better not or you'll never get much writing done. If you must deal with something:

1. Do it without breaking stride, if at all possible. Take the phone call, but before committing yourself to picking up your stranded friend, determine the best time to stop your work in progress. And then stop mid-sentence so you can get right back into it when you return.

2. Don't put it off till later (later is the reason it's bugging you now). You will only be busier later.

3. Crowd it in! Don't give it two hours—do it at top speed, at the same time as something else, delegate it, anything, but get it done as quick as you

can. Then shorten lunch and skip breaks to make up for whatever time you do lose.

4. There is nothing wrong with writing in small (five, ten or fifteen minute) segments, if necessary. I've learned to be supereffective with this. Just keep out of the deep doctrine of the matter—save that to do in a private place with plenty of time.

## HOW TO MINIMIZE INTERRUPTIONS

### Uninvited visitors

Because most of us writers work at home, people figure they can come, stop and visit any hour of the day or night, and we'll just sit back and accommodate them. The fact that you're home must mean that you're off work, free. Would they ever think of stopping into a class at school, walking right up to the teacher and starting in, "How are things, Mrs. Penwick? How is the grading curve this year?" Never! Would they walk into an operating room and stop the doctor and ask, "Well, Harry, how many hernias have you handled this year?" Would they flag down Andretti in his race car and ask him what kind of gas mileage he gets? Inconceivable. Yet people will drive down your driveway or show up at your door any day for a casual visit, come into your office and expect you to stop writing to chew the fat.

We teach people to respect our property, so why not our person, or our time? Remember that when you are writing, you are occupied, just as if you were in a meeting, sleeping, eating, in the bathroom or speaking to an audience. People don't automatically have the right to walk in and interrupt you—so don't let them.

• **Say "I'm working."** People know and honor that boundary of "working." I learned early that when I told people "I am writing," that was an invitation to nose in and around you, "because writing is just a fun, flippant little hobby." Not so, and let them know it. I never say that I'm writing anymore!

• **Let people know your working hours.** Establish regular working hours at home and make them known to all.

• **Let people know that you hate to be interrupted.** Make it clear that every interruption costs you money. Or use whatever explanation suits you, but get them to think twice about bothering you.

• **Don't have a couch in your office, or any extra chairs!**

• **If people do come during your working hours**, act busy. Be crisp and businesslike—don't stop what you're doing and don't make eye contact. This will send a stronger message than anything you could say.

Don't invite them into your house or office—greet them at the door and close it as soon as you can. If they are already in your house, keep edging yourself, and them, toward the door.

If it's a true friend, or someone you really like, smile, look at the time, and say, "I'll take a five-minute break, so talk fast!"

### Guests

Count on it, company will come while you are writing, and not always at the time you have planned, either, often in the middle of your best concentration. And not only do they come, often they stay, and bring their curious children. Most of them haven't a clue that writing is real work and you aren't free to wait on them.

The solution? Turn their invasion into a resource. There are always subjects that need input, so put people to work helping you. Besides, it gives them something more interesting and productive to do than just chitchat. The big secret here is to be prepared—have some pages printed out with questions about some topic you are researching, and ask them to write answers. This will get them jabbering among themselves, and you can walk away and go work on your own. It works . . . and they'll be careful about coming back to visit.

### The phone: a writer's friend and foe

If you are serious about becoming a writer, you have to make one decision first:

**Are you going to control the phone, or is the phone going to control you?**

Many more people choose the second than the first. Phones are a big source of interruptions (unwelcome most of the time), so do what you have to do to control them. Use any gadget or means that helps field interference from "any fool with thirty-five cents," or friends with cell phones who have nothing to do but call you.

"Bargain" rates have created the illusion that using the phone freely is not just necessary but almost free. Nothing could be further from the truth. It isn't the out of pocket cost of a phone that is the problem—although that can be considerable. It's the time it takes and interruptions it creates, the constant exchange of trivia because it is so convenient. The average "trivia" phone call takes at least fifteen minutes, and enough of those in a year add up to enough time to write a whole book. When a year is over, would you rather have a book, or a lot of dull yakking and fumbling around with a phone?

If you're not convinced yet, try this: keep track of the last twenty calls you make or take. Many are not necessary, and expensive, too.

We do have some phone obligations, when it comes to the safety of children and the like, but when you're writing and on a roll, a single interruption can cost you a whole page or more, or lose you a great thought.

• Get away from phones when you write. I do most of my writing away from a telephone, and that is one reason I sometimes get three or four books out a year.

• It only takes a second to unplug a phone or turn off the ringer, and what I don't know usually won't hurt me. If it's important, they will call back.

• You can take it off the hook, too—they'll get a busy signal and know you are home and busy . . . and that's good for your writing career.

• Let it ring: Many of us still have a phobia about phones—if it rings, we must answer it. Wrong! If they care, they will call back, and if it is an emergency, they will get the message to you somehow. I've watched people sprint to the phone while stark naked, or with their mouths full of food. Why? Let it ring—your writing is more important.

• If you own a cell phone, keep it a safe distance from your writing area.

• Have a second line, and answer only this when writing. Give the number only to those who don't abuse the privilege. When you get more serious about your writing, don't hesitate to get a separate, private line and keep the number to yourself. This way you can be reached in any true emergency, and you can call right when you want to and not worry about the family tying up the line. As an alternative, try caller ID.

• Control the conversation: Tell the caller up front how long you have to talk, and don't go more than a minute or two over that.

• If necessary, add a reminder: "Before we hang up, I need to mention one last thing."

• Speak up: Don't apologize or give detailed reasons. Just say "I've got to go now" and hang up.

• Use an answering machine or voice mail, and don't listen to the messages until your day's writing is done. Put your answering machine in a different room, if it's the type that broadcasts the messages. Once you hear it, it will distract you even if you don't do anything about what you hear.

• Reroute your calls and have someone else handle them.

• If you know that any important calls might be coming in, contact the person yourself before settling down in front of the computer.

• Have clearly established "phone times"—times in the day or days in the week—and let all your business contacts know what they are. Do all your phone business then, take and receive calls.

• Don't call when you should write, because it's more fun, and less lonely.

• Almost half of all calls on the phone lines today are sales calls. Tell solicitors you're busy and can't talk, wish them good luck elsewhere and hang up without further discussion.

## Food and drink

Food and drink distract and delay the best of writers. Don't let food and drink get in the way of writing.

**Don't do big dinners** when you're writing. If you go out to dinner, after all those drinks and calories, you can kiss good-bye getting anything done afterward. Stopping to have a big formal lunch or supper at home can have the same effect—make you drowsy and "loggy"—so make meals quick and lean when you're writing. You might even find, as I do, that fasting helps you do better writing.

As for coffee, my opinion of it is almost anti-American, but it is pro-writer, so here goes. In short, less coffee means more writing. The main things that speed us up are avoiding interruptions, feeling and sleeping good, no mess around us and not wasting time. Constant "coffeeing" violates every one of these. Coffee takes time to make and ready, always takes up a hand and space, and is always spilling and dripping. It's also a double-barreled interrupter: the more coffee, the more trips to the bathroom. Then when it really kicks in later, it keeps you from falling asleep. All that caffeine doesn't do any long-range good for you, either.

It's been estimated that the average American spends *seventeen months* of his life drinking coffee and soft drinks. How many stories could you produce in that time?

Between meals, try to keep food, drinks and snacks out of your writing area. Eat and drink and then get it out of the room, out of your mind, and get on with it. Let your concentration be channeled to the writing.

---

**Liquid is a big-time menace to keyboards, so make it a rigid rule: No beverages on the same surface as a keyboard, computer or important papers.**

---

## DON'T LET YOUR TRAVEL TIME BE INTERRUPTED

I travel a lot, and seldom strike up a conversation en route anymore, in airports, on planes and the like. I quickly put in earplugs and go to a corner to work. I always spread papers to create a "busy" image. That gives the message, and hardly any passenger, even those intrigued by the cartoons and paragraphs spread around me, will dare say a word.

Motels, too, can have no end of interruptions, or none—it depends on you. I only give my hotel number to two people—my operations manager and my wife. Everyone else has to go through one of these two to get to me. And 95 percent of the time, these two can and will be able to handle the needs of a would-be interrupter. I put the "do not disturb" sign on the door for the maids, or tell them before I start writing that they can skip my room because I cleaned it myself. They are happy then, and I don't get a peek or knock. I also grab some bananas and wheat bread and a couple of bottles of apple juice, so I can eat fast and healthy, without breaking my stride.

## WRITING DESPITE SETBACKS

Often we start, committed and prepared, but then . . . along comes the unexpected. Setbacks—losses, deaths, injuries, health or finance problems—take a toll of mind and body. How can we keep going on our writing plans and efforts in spite of these?

Often we think setbacks are deaths, great financial losses, a serious health problem, a community or county catastrophe, or Mother Nature beating us up a bit. These do come, for sure, and they can come right in the middle of our best chapter or our long-awaited book tour. Things like this can distract and test us, for sure, but look out for those positive "setbacks," too.

Such as about the time you are into the same great chapter with the same super commitment, a rich uncle dies and leaves you a bundle, or you fall in love and your focus switches from the page to the prince or princess. Or your spouse gets a big promotion at work and you have to interrupt everything for months to move and reestablish your life, and the kids in new schools. Or you get an offer for a full summer tour with the university you helped . . . I think you get the idea.

Setbacks—happenings that come along and take your mind, money and body off the writing job—are inevitable. We all have accidents and family members that get sick or die, or health problems that suddenly sneak up on us. If you aren't really rooted in your writing, setbacks, even minor ones, can clip off your writing like a sharp sword. This is a difficult call sometimes, as to what to do while you mend and mourn. Do you stop everything and earn the money for that unexpected big expense, and then pick up the pen again?

I can tell you from many personal experiences of my own—some of them merely emotional strains, some deep wounds and some of them beyond grief—there is no point in stopping and waiting for it to be over with, because some things will never be over with. Many hurts never heal completely—the mind doesn't relinquish things easily.

Often during truly trying times (after the loss of the great love of your life, or some other traumatic loss or disappointment), writing, burying yourself in work, is a great escape, the only answer, because when you're writing you don't have to think about "it" for a while, and you don't care enough about living right then to do much else, anyway. And if you write when you feel miserable, you will have the fruits of that writing to enjoy someday when you *do* feel like resuming living.

Much or even most of the time, we can't do anything about the unfortunate happening, but I've found that some of my best writing has come forth from the extremes, times of setback or elation in life. "Wake-up calls" stir our emotions and cause us to make mental leaps, adjustments and changes in direction that we would never make on our own. There is not one single reason to stop writing when the unforeseen strikes. In fact it usually gives us a bigger or better reason to do it.

---

**When it comes to the jolts and bumps and even tragedies of life, we writers have one consolation no one else has (except possibly saints). For us, the more awful something is, the more likely it is to yield good "grist" for the writer's mill.**

---

### Share your experience

Life events such as divorce, the death of a loved one or a health crisis usually require a lot of our attention, but they are also just the types of things that many other people need help in handling.

If you keep a journal and write about your experience from an emotional standpoint, not only will you benefit from this outlet, but later you may be able to turn this experience into an in-depth and meaningful article that may help others in a similar situation. Keeping chronological notes on what has happened, how you are feeling, the people you've dealt with, the challenges you've had to face and the help you have received will give a powerful picture of firsthand experience to help enlighten others.

Topics such as "How to Find the Best Lawyer," "How to Avoid Losing Your Identity in a Relationship," "Surviving the Grieving Process," "How to Recover From a House Fire," "What to Do in an Earthquake" and "What You Should Know About Patient's Rights," are enhanced by firsthand experience.

## HOW TO KEEP COMPUTER PROBLEMS FROM RUINING A DAY'S OUTPUT

You have a proposal or article due tomorrow and a thunderstorm knocks out your electricity for the night. Or your computer picked this particular moment to go down. When we're in a hurry is always when something breaks, crashes, quits, malfunctions. Breakdowns, and all the panic and desperation that goes with them, can really throw a kink into our progress.

How can you minimize "breakdown stress"?

1. Calm yourself. Don't assume that "the computer is down" means the end of life as we know it.

2. Turn the computer off, breathe deeply and restart it to see if it works. This is always the first thing to do. Chances are the computer will fix itself.

3. If that doesn't work, make a "pilot's checkover" of everything one more time: Check all the switches and plugs and connections, and look the whole thing over again carefully. Make sure it's dead before you launch into any fixing. Have you accidentally hit some button that is making the machine work differently, so it seems to be broken?

4. Check out the computer's built-in "Help" program if you can, or call your computer company's technical support department—keep the number handy. Just be sure you have something to do while on hold. Record any messages your computer displayed in its final moments verbatim.

5. Ask a knowledgeable friend or colleague with a similar machine if

they've ever had this happen. Many an amateur computer whiz knows at least half as much as the tech support line and is closer and cheaper (free!).

6. If none of those things does it, go to plan B—find a temporary alternative and use it to keep the job moving. Don't stop and carry the ailing machine personally to the "hospital" right now. Some possibilities include:

• Call a friend whose electricity has not gone down, or who has a functional and compatible computer, and ask to do your work on it. If you've saved everything on well-labeled disks, you should be able to finish the job without a problem.

• Libraries and some colleges have computers for public use.

• Many copy shops, such as Kinko's, have computers and printers that you can use for a small fee.

• Keep a typewriter on hand for moments such as this. As primitive as they may seem at this point, typewriters are pretty practical if your computer is suddenly rendered inoperable, and you are eager to keep writing or are under a deadline.

• Check with a secretarial service. Often local secretaries offer freelance secretarial services—they will type, make copies, collate and some can even do simple editing. They are usually reliable and their charges are reasonable. (Or call the person you used to use to type your copy before you discovered how easily you could do your own on computer.)

We often lose our tempers, our bearings and a full day of writing when something breaks. Don't do it!

## TO HELP PREVENT "BREAKDOWN" OR "DOWNTIME" STRESS:

• Save your manuscripts often on a floppy or Zip disk, and print each draft so you have a hard copy in hand and not everything is in the computer. Optimize often. Get a good virus protection system (for your e-mail, too) and update it regularly. Get a "toolbox" program such as Norton's Utilities, which will enable you to undo some computer kinks yourself.

• Consider a duplicate of machines you'd be lost without, such as answering machine, fax, printer, mouse. If the one you're using quits, you can just take the other one out of its box and plug it in. And put the broken one on the shelf until a handy time to have it repaired. With two hard drives, you can write in the one, and copy to the other. And stop worrying so much about whether you have a backup.

• If you are installing a new computer or accessory, and counting on using it immediately, bear in mind that there will almost inevitably be some unforeseen hitch or hangup, such as a missing adapter, a battery that needs to be charged for twelve hours or the like. So look ahead, read those instructions ahead and try to prevent this!

• Be sure you have enough, or an extra, of key supplies like paper, and printer and copier toner. Keep an eye on what's on hand and anticipate needs so you aren't forced to head off on wild paper chases.

• If your computer is threatened by frequent thunderstorms (always when you're on a roll!), you might consider investing in a Universal Power Source. This is a battery pack that can run your computer for up to thirty minutes when the power goes off, or you decide it's prudent to unplug! It will also protect your computer from damaging "hard shut-downs" caused by tiny interruptions in your power supply.

## FENDING OFF THE FAMILY

*My children are grown and I'd been thinking of going back to work full time. In fact I'd mailed my resume out to several businesses already. My family was very supportive and encouraging about my plan. Their support suddenly turned to annoyance, however, when I started writing at home instead.*

*When I actually got started, every fifteen or twenty minutes, my husband or one of my children would burst into the room with, "Where's this," or "Where's that?" I tried to explain that I was working, and they were on their own. My protests were in vain. After about three hours of continuous interruptions, I had a little meeting with everyone, and tried to explain the importance of what I was doing. They all stared at me like I was crazy. I went back to my computer, and in about forty-five minutes my husband came in and said, "Aren't you about done?"*

—*Martha Jacob*

If a man is working at home, daddy can usually go to his desk and do his work. But if you, a woman, are trying to write at home, your family may still see you in the role of housewife or housekeeper. Even in the twenty-first century, you may not be "working" unless you're vacuuming or making dinner. The worst thing is, it can make you feel like you're doing something bad by trying to stick to your writing.

When young, we might be foolish enough to think people are only jealous of competing people. But people can be jealous of abstractions, too—they want your attention, and don't like the fact that you are not available to them. Even cats will come sit on the most important pile of papers—they have an unerring instinct for this!

Possible solutions:

1. Try to work while everyone is away or asleep.

2. Explain to the family that just because you're in the house doesn't mean you're not at work. And just because you're at the computer, doesn't mean you're playing! Make them understand that the work you're doing is important. Show them what you're doing, and explain it.

3. Put your foot down, and set guidelines, or make strict rules for everyone to follow.

4. Lock your door, take the phone off the hook, ignore everyone.

5. Work somewhere else if necessary (see chapter five on setting up an outside office).

6. Make "deadline dinners" that are quick and easy. The next time you make stew or lasagna, make extra and put it in the freezer. Or maybe this is the night to order pizza, or give your son the chance to try his culinary wings.

8. Make the most of those priceless moments, or even days or weeks, when the pressure is off—the rest of the family has gone camping, or to the casino, and the house isn't getting messed, no one is waiting for a clean shirt, and you don't have to humor anyone or worry about their schedule. Get to the keyboard and write, write, write!

> *If you work at home, it's a confined area, like living in a small submarine. You have to become efficient. When my wife and I are both home, both working on different things, if we have something urgent we feel we must ask the other party, we simply say, "Can you talk?" If the other party is deeply entrenched in their writing (and stopping would mean having to work your way back into it again, and maybe losing your train of thought), we simply say "No," and the other party knows that means no, with no hard feelings.*
>
> *—Rohn Engh*

## WRITING WITH CHILDREN

Children are a wonderful excuse to delay our writing. But in reality, not a few famous female writers have written best-sellers as little rug rats played at their feet.

One philosophy is to outlast them one way or another. Either go to bed later than they do or get up earlier than they do in order to get a few extra hours of peaceful writing time. But even when they are up, they don't usually require constant attention. There are ways of keeping them occupied while you work. Let them play nearby as you write, which gives them the comforting feeling of being with you. Give them special toys that you save for the times when you are working. If you are fortunate to have more than one computer, then allow them to play computer games that do not distract you too much. Or even give them a child's writing software package so that they can "be a writer like Mom or Dad."

Nice as it is to have the little ones around, having them out of the house for a while does seem to clear the brain cells. If you really have to concentrate, send the kids to a neighbor's to watch a movie, or get someone to take them to the newest children's movie or the county fair. If you depend on baby-sitters for your writing time, no matter how good or faithful a baby-sitter you have, line up a backup baby-sitter!

### Pointers from the pros on writing with kids

*I know that when the kids start coming home in midafternoon, the disruptions will become so frequent that I'll lose my flow and energy and become frustrated. So I plan my heaviest writing and concentration during the quiet hours after everyone leaves and before they return. It's real tempting to do errands, rest, clean house or talk on the phone during my quiet blocks, but to produce, I must resist these temptations. No going out to lunch or watching the soaps, either.*

—*Sandra Phillips*

*"WRITER AT WORK" is the sign on my closed door at home. My family has instructions not to bother me unless it's an emergency. I take breaks to answer any questions and let them know I'm alive.*

—*Terra Koerpel*

*It's hard to hold a baby on your lap and type—they want to hit keys, too. Kids or grandkids are the same, and playpens seem to be out now. When the kids were young, I wrote smaller things, such as articles, fillers and greeting cards, that didn't require as much concentration.*

*I used to tell the children: Don't come to me unless you're bleeding, and sometimes they were. Dead silence is as worrisome as cries of pain. It means some child is checking to see how much toilet paper the toilet bowl will hold.*

*I got the kids to take me seriously, so that they knew this was my work, and respected it. (It helps for you to take it seriously first.) I'd say, "John's dad is a doctor, that's his work; Kelsey's mom is a teacher; and writing is mine."*

*I often set a timer and say something like, "If you let me alone to work on this for the next fifty minutes (this sounds better than an hour), we'll go mail it and then go get some ice cream," or "I must keep typing until eight o' clock, and then we'll play Candyland." Some might call this bribery, but I call it incentive. Put the timer where they can't reach it.*

*I may ask them to be quiet until I finish something. Once my son asked, "How is the chapter coming?" and when it became clear that I wasn't actually working on it, he became pretty upset.*

*I keep toys such as Legos and children's books in my office that kids can use, but they have to put anything they use back.*
                                                    *—Elaine Schimberg*

*When I'm writing I often get my daughter occupied with home-work or her Barbie collection. Or I ask her to draw me a picture for what I'm writing (if suitable). As they get older, you can give them a writing assignment of their own. Get them involved, so they understand!*
                                                    *—Hollis Stevenson*

## HOME "IMPROVEMENTS"

Tradespeople, salespeople and repair people (and the Census man) will inevitably come while you are working, not when you would have been doing household things anyway. As soon as you sit down to work, they will arrive, and it's bound to get you distracted or caught up in something else, even if you don't indulge in any idle chatter. And if someone is there working on something, you will be drawn into it, guaranteed.

• Whenever possible, make appointments for repair people and the like at other times of day than your working time.

• Try to make more than one appointment for the same day, if possible, if you are going to be disrupted anyway.

• Don't choose this time to break in new people. Stick with those you trust, who know how you like things and who you don't have to watch over.

• Always try to pin down *when* they are coming, so you can plan around it. If they won't say exactly when, at least make them specify morning or afternoon.

• Limit what you talk about. Keep it short, sweet and focused on the business at hand.

• Don't let an ambitious spirit flow over beyond your current writing project into everything else. Be careful how much you set up, stir up and commit to during heavy deadline times. It will inevitably take longer than the "hour" or whatever they say, and it may be hard to get back to the keyboard afterward. Few home improvements are a simple, one-time thing. One estimate may lead to a second, then further shopping around, thinking and rethinking, then further sales calls and visits. And then negotiations, time to move everything out of the way so people can work, the need to watch and monitor the work in progress, and aggravation about things that were done wrong or need to be redone. If you don't really need it now, stay out of it!

> *As for the problem of tradespeople interrupting your writing (someone is tearing out a wall as I write this), the general solution is to develop a habit of sort of going into a tunnel to write, but with one ear open for screams, if you have children. . . .*
>
> *Before the repair people start, tell them, "This is where I'll be if you need me." And while they are there, do mindless things like cleaning out files, sharpening pencils, updating the Rolodex, retyping things that need to be retyped, paying bills, etc.—things that don't require a lot of focus. If they're going to turn off the electricity, be sure they tell you ahead so you can save everything.*
>
> *—Elaine Schimberg*

---

A simple, often overlooked interruption-stopper: Just say "no" or "not right now." And mean it!

---

## BLAME THE MESSENGER

Errands are another time waster and focus shifter. If they don't end up killing the whole day, they can change your mode and mood and make it harder to settle down and write when you do get home. To minimize the time errands take:

• Don't go to town on writing days, at least not before you write.

• Do errands on the way to or from business appointments, or when you have to go out for some other reason anyway. Or plan all your errands for the same day.

• Write all of your objectives down before you go, so you can do them in the most efficient order.

• Don't do errands at peak times—don't go to the bank at lunchtime, for instance, and stay out of the supermarket when there'll be six carts at every register. Don't go to get your license renewed on the last day of the month (or if you do, bring a lot of work with you!).

• If you're on deadline, have things delivered instead of going after them.

• You don't have to run every errand that comes up. You can sub-errand it, maybe, find another place or way to do it, or a friend or neighbor already going there. Be generous with your own offers to help others when you happen to be "running" somewhere anyway. This earns you plenty of return favors for the future.

### Fighting the fidget factor

Writing has a high fidget factor for some of us. We feel an almost constant need to get a cup of coffee, chew a piece of gum, go get a snack. If you are plagued by this, try to make the breaks fewer and healthier: stretch or do a couple of calisthenics, walk around the outside of the house, use small barbells to do a little arm exercise. And make that decaf coffee or mint tea, sugarless gum and an apple instead of Oreos.

I get up and wash my hands and face when I need a break. I learned from the movie *The Hustler*. Remember when Fast Eddie (Paul Newman) was completely dominating the world's best, Minnesota Fats (Jackie Gleason), in a marathon series of pool games? They took a break, and Minnesota shaved, cleaned up, washed his hands, slapped on some shaving lotion and then came back and ruled the table. I get up every two hours or so and wash my face and hands . . . it works!

### If you can't get something out of your mind:
Anger and agitation are some of the worst interrupters. If you can't put something out of your mind after a real effort to do so, stop and do something about it. Make that call, write that letter, make that too-long-put-off appointment . . . and then put it out of your mind, and get back to work. Or make a list of nagging chores that you will do once you're done writing for today, or finished with this urgent project.

### Hiding out to write
There is a time to be out and about, and a time to hide. If it's necessary to evade interruptions, go for it.

More than one chapter in my books has been written after I spotted visitors coming down the lane and sprinted to the high sagebrush in back of the house and laid there with the wood ticks and wrote, rather than go through the same conversation for the sixth time with the same people who are cruising around town with nothing else to do.

If writing time at home is constantly being interrupted:

• Hide out at home by not answering the phone or door.

• As noted earlier, you can go somewhere else to write.

• A vacation alone for a while, even a day or two, can be a good hideout.

• There are writer's retreats located all over the country where there are no phones and no visitors, so you can write to your heart's content for a weekend or an entire summer.

• Keep your hideouts to yourself. Tell only one important contact, in case of an emergency.

---

*Whenever I have endured or accomplished some difficult task such as watching television, going out socially or sleeping, I always look forward to rewarding myself with the small pleasure of getting back to my typewriter and writing something. This enables me to store up enough strength to endure until the next interruption.*

*—Isaac Asimov*

**CHAPTER 13**

# *Keeping Your Office Clutter-Free*

What is clutter? In short, it's all that stuff you aren't using, don't really want, don't need, don't enjoy and don't have room for!

Clutter consumes at least 40 percent of our household cleaning and maintenance time, and more than we would care to admit of our writing time. We writers don't need to have anything—and this includes everything from long-outdated drafts to personal habits—in the way. Clear thinking comes from a clear path. Any clutter that surrounds you is taking its toll—you cannot write well distracted.

## SOME COMMON SPECIES OF WRITER'S CLUTTER

piles from past completed projects
piles of old papers of any kind
unkempt and uncurrent files
unfiled notes
excess copies
computer space filled with no longer needed or obsolete things
too many magazines and books
undone guilt-trip things—such as unanswered letters or never-
    filled-out questionnaires
manuals to machines and software programs we no longer use
    (or own!)
paperless paperweights
drafts, drafts, drafts
entire sections of newspaper saved to clip something from
old office equipment and accessories, such as unused monitors,
    printers and keyboards

extra or broken office furniture

old *Publishers Weekly*s

unlabeled videos and audiotapes

diskettes full of largely obsolete data, often unlabeled

tangled electrical cords snaking everywhere

used padded mailers and other envelopes kept to recycle (but we
always use a new one instead)

stuck-together stamps

outdated or worn-out office supplies

old Rolodexes and address books

All of those jokes and signs that say, "A clean desk is the sign of a sick mind" or, "This is my mess; I worked hard to get it this way" are no joke for anyone trying to be a productive and efficient writer. You can try to convince yourself that you may not be neat or well organized, but that you know where everything is. This is like saying you didn't bother to note exactly where you parked your car in the ten thousand-car airport parking lot, but you know where it is. It's somewhere in that lot.

Decide now that mess and clutter will never enter your writing domain. If you do, you'll be way ahead of those who settle for the assumption that a mess just comes with paperwork of any kind. If you can operate in a mess, you'll be able to operate far better without a mess.

## WHY DECLUTTER?

---

*The evils of clutter, in brief:* It is ugly, takes up space, causes confusion and loss of control and confidence, taxes others, makes you late, makes you hunt, distracts you, depresses you, makes you carry excess baggage and keeps you in bondage.

---

We may be satisfied, content in our cluttered surroundings. But whether we admit it or not, our productivity is affected.

- Clutter hogs the space we need for new and necessary things and our room to operate.
- Clutter slows us down and distracts us. How often have you started the day by looking for some paper or document lost in it all?
- In the midst of a mess, it's all too easy to make mistakes.

- If there is too much paper around, one of your clippings, photos, roughs or priceless notes will get lost—count on it!
- Papers left out get defaced and damaged.

Our goal is to write, not fight papers. Resolve now that you won't have to hunt for something, stumble over even one thing, shuffle or sort through even one pile. If you have a sudden inspiration and want to get it down, you shouldn't have to wade through clutter to do so.

## THE FIRST PRINCIPLE OF OFFICE DECLUTTERING

Following this rule will eliminate at least 60 percent of office clutter.

At any active workstation (on and around your desk, on tables and counters, on or in nearby shelves and cabinets and so on), keep only active stuff, nothing passive. This means that the things you need, use and are into all the time should be near you. The things that you might use, use only occasionally or might possibly need someday should be out of the way.

For example, the big center drawer in your desk should contain the tools you use daily, or at least frequently. The three-hole punch and the laminating machine should be kept in another place. You shouldn't have to paw through the seldom needed to find the needed. It's worth taking some time up front to shape up and organize or reorganize things, to separate the immediate from the someday stuff. Those piles of untapped (but important) magazines shouldn't be underfoot; keep them up somewhere out of the line of fire. Anything for later should be a little ways away.

When you're finished with something, the peelings of the fruit that went into the copy should be moved out of the area, not just laid aside. If a doctor left all the removed gallstones, tonsils and kidneys behind in the surgery room after he finished, think what the place would be like to operate in before long. The same principle applies to your writing. Keep only *active* material in your immediate area, or in anything you carry with you.

A good parallel here is the average bulletin board in an office, home or anywhere. At any given time at least half of what's on it is obsolete. It was all important once, but time passed and suddenly things are taking up space and doing no good. But no one seems to remove the old when it becomes old. This is the key to keeping your writing space useful: Don't let the past crowd out the present or the future.

A lot of office clutter, too, is things we're hoping to do later. There is no later with paper. The inflow of paper today, especially for a writer, is tremendous. Either you deal with it daily, or it will bury you and your aspiring writing career.

## A FOUR-STEP SYSTEM OF CLUTTER CONTROL

You don't need elaborate tools or organizers to keep a clutter-free office. All you need is to deal with things *now*, before they turn into trash.

We all organize differently, but hearing how others do things might give you an idea or a system to adopt or adapt. Mine is simple.

Sort all papers and other items, old or new, into four categories:

**1. Out** (trash or recycle): If you're through with it for good; it is broken, outdated or an unnecessary duplicate; you don't really like it (even if it was a gift); it's too big or too little, unused or unusable or just plain old trash, it should go out, right now, with no hesitations or regrets. Trash it or give it to someone who might actually use it.

If I have any lingering doubts that I might be getting rid of something good or worthwhile (which seldom happens), I know I can probably replace it quickly and inexpensively. If in doubt, it goes out. I've learned that if I can't decide now, it's only tougher to decide later. So out with it, out, out!

**2. Route:** You'd be amazed how many papers, tools, gadgets, articles of clothing, etc., that belong to others drift into our office space. These things may be good, but they belong somewhere else. So gather them up and route them, send them to where they belong, now, not later. The longer you leave things like this around, the more likely they will keep hibernating with you.

Into this category, too, falls the passive stuff of our own we mentioned earlier—things that may be worth keeping, but we don't need to have right around us. Move them to where you can still get them but they are not in the way. A tray or box on a shelf or in some other room is better than in a desk drawer or underfoot.

**3. Doubt:** This often crops up with old and new stuff. Things that are obviously useful to us or that should be routed to someone else are easy to take care of immediately. The useful stuff goes into our files or right onto the page we are working on now! However, in every pile there seems to be at least one thing that is potentially good, useful or important, but we can't deal with it right now or process it quickly, or we don't quite know what to do with it. It may be a letter, a message or a magazine with a couple of potentially interesting articles. Things like this I strip down (toss the envelope they came in and any unnecessary parts), and carry with me in my big briefcase until I find a few minutes to deal with them, the solution comes to me or I realize where they belong. It's amazing how when you carry something with you how you will find the time and the place for it. You have to, or you'll be carrying a bale of paper around before long.

You can also put your doubt items into a box or tray. But make an unbendable rule: Every single thing in this box will be resolved or dealt with by the end of the week or some other set time. And honor it, or you'll be back to piles and stacks.

**4. Sprout:** This category goes right to the heart of writing. These are the things that are going to help you get where you're going with your writing, and they go into those files and boxes that you feed daily. Make a place for the things that really help advance your writing: article, story, song and book ideas; notes and ideas for talks and presentations you are going to give; information on important new contacts; whatever you glean out of the daily flow of mail, phone calls and conversations, all goes into sprout (your active files). Good writers build the areas they want to write about.

## THE THREE STAGES OF CLUTTER CONTROL

Clutter is controlled in three stages:

- **Up front:** Before you even get it (see pages 207–208).
- **During:** While you are working, continue to pare down. Sweep up the sawdust and get rid of the scraps as you build the cabinet, not after it is all done.
- **After:** When something is complete, do a final sweep of the area.

Keep your office ready for writing:

1. When things are over and done with, bury or cremate them.
2. Condense and reduce things whenever you can.
3. Pitch anything outdated.
4. If you don't want it, get rid of it now. If that brochure that just arrived is for a conference you'd never attend, trash it now. Don't lay it on a pile to get rid of later.

5. Don't let others dump clutter on you. If your neighbor is always bringing you off-the-point articles from the Internet, for example, thank her sincerely for her thoughtfulness and dump them as soon as she's out of sight.

6. Don't get more and bigger storage devices rather than dejunk!

## Dejunking a desk

Your desk is the headquarters or heart of your office, yet it is a constant battle to keep it from being buried in papers and other clutter. To dejunk a desk:

• Clear the top. Your desktop is a work area, an action area—not a storage area. So get everything off here you can that you are not working on *right now*. Make sure you have uncrowded room to lay out notes, outlines or proposals. It'll make you feel more efficient, too.

• Keep urgent ongoing matters in clearly marked file folders stored all together and upright so they take up just one little area of the top. If you happen to be an "in sight" person like me, keep your hot projects in individual boxes or trays—no stacks. I like plastic boxes because I can see everything in them, not just the top page.

• Relocate any machines you don't really need to have right here. And make sure the ones you keep on there are conveniently placed.

• If you do want a few niceties here (family pictures or crystal paperweights), OK—but try to keep the number down.

• As for those desk drawers, often filled with forgotten or unnecessary things, empty them all out, and only put back in what you really need and want. Assign drawers a single purpose whenever possible.

## Clearing a paper backlog

Despite the onset of the "paperless age," with electronic records and publications online, the paper piles in our offices continue to grow.

The main cause of paper buildup is the decision to sort or organize later. But with paper there is no later, there's just more and more buildup. Paper keeps multiplying like two mice on a honeymoon. It never stops, so we must figure out a way to reduce if not eliminate the piles we already have and develop a system to prevent piles from stacking up in the future.

Use downtime, when deep concentration or full creativity are just too much to muster the energy for, to plunge into the files and piles.

• Much of what is stacked up—like schedules, names, addresses, good article starts, great titles and cut chapters—can be stored on disk, which takes up a fraction of the space. Remember, though, to label in detail what you have saved on each disk.

We also tend to make copies of everything we send out, which can eventually get very bulky. To cut down this bulk, make a master copy of a manuscript you send out and refer to this copy in your records. Ask publishers to discard a manuscript if it is rejected. This eliminates stacks of wrinkled, dog-eared manuscripts not fit to send out again.

If you save all your correspondence and manuscripts on labeled disks, you will have an accurate record of your writing. And you can make notes on the disks to help keep track of their contents. This is much more efficient use of space than numerous file cabinets or piles of paper.

• Cut through the clutter carefully. Fight the urge to throw the whole pile away lock, stock and barrel. Go through each piece; you're bound to find surprises. It won't take as long as you think. The older the paperwork, the quicker you can get through it because the reason you kept it often doesn't apply anymore. And few of us, fortunately, want to keep things that are wrinkled or defaced from our previous neglect.

• Go through each batch of paper, review it and either trash it or file it appropriately. You need to look things over, sort them, evaluate them and then deal with them, not restack them. You could make a pile of things "to read later," but be careful not to put anything on this pile that you just don't know what to do with right now. This might help reduce the clutter, but you'll have to make another pass through this pile in order to eliminate it.

• If the task seems overwhelming, devote a specific amount of time to it, like two hours per day for one week or a half day every day until it's finished. At this rate, it won't be long until you start to see some improvement. Order will start to come with empty spaces appearing where piles once had been.

• If you have a really big backlog, this technique will help keep you from feeling overwhelmed: Go through it all really fast, starting with the biggest and bulkiest things and those that can most obviously be discarded. This will reduce the mass and your discouragement. Taking a closer look at five or even fifteen boxes of stuff is a lot less demoralizing than a whole roomful. The older the paper piles, the better this works, and the quicker you can sort through them.

• You can go through clutter anywhere, so take a couple of the "to read" or "to review" piles with you on that business trip, vacation or to lunch. It's surprising how fast carried piles disappear. You can review a report or read a magazine article while traveling, waiting for your entrée or sitting by the sea.

• Mail is a constant concern. If left unopened, it multiplies and causes mental anguish. Set a goal to open, review and sort the mail each day. Try to make an immediate decision on each piece of mail to prevent piles to decide on later. This approach cleans the slate for each day's new batch of mail and eliminates clutter and office overload.

• Develop a new pattern of dealing with paperwork in the future, otherwise the reprieve will be short-lived, the piles will grow again and you'll end up spending more of your precious time fixing the same problem.

> *I don't happen to believe that a messy desk is a sign of creativity. And I've always thought that any work you don't like to do yourself, you should get someone else to do. Every Wednesday afternoon or whatever, I have high school kids come in and file things for me, put them away, exactly where I tell them to. So my office stays pretty clean.*
>
> —Rohn Engh

## OFF-SITE STORAGE

Once you've sorted, organized and detrashed everything, what should you do with the files and piles that you don't need regularly, but want to keep? Items like paid bills, research for a project you're not currently working on, old published articles, clips or business records need safe storage away from your office.

If they are worth keeping, then they are worth storing properly to eliminate the possibility of damage from water, rodents or age. These records should be repackaged in containers that are sturdy and stackable. Inexpensive plastic bins are perfect for this, and they come in all sizes. Identify them on all sides, date them if necessary and place them on shelves off the floor in a dry, well-lighted area.

Old client, research or writing files can be stored in a file cabinet or cardboard office storage boxes in a dry basement or garage if they can't be discarded. Go through each file first and throw away things you don't need to save.

Clean out your storage areas periodically to keep them neat and detrashed.

## MAKING THE INVISIBLE VISIBLE

Clutter quickly becomes invisible. We get so used to the things that have surrounded us for years that often we no longer realize they are there. Every time we're in the office, we look right at the Puerto Rico phone book we picked up on our visit ten years ago and the 1983 list of Kiwanis members we keep just in case we want to look something up, and we don't even see them. Look around your office the way you do when someone important is coming to visit; plenty of invisible clutter will suddenly become visible, and then you can attack it.

### Books

They come out at night and breed on the shelves so we all have lots of them, especially us writers. I once boasted a fine library, mainly to impress people, but I keep only the truly useful now (plus a set of my own titles to show off, of course!).

Most of us don't have enough room to shelve all of our books, so we have piles and boxes as well as shelf upon shelf of them. The way to make our books fit the shelves is to get rid of the ones that we don't really want or need or are obsolete. Just because it's a book doesn't mean we have to keep it forever.

Books were once scarce and almost sacred, like Bibles. If you marred or damaged one, in the library or at school, you were in trouble. Today, with more than fifty thousand new books hitting the market each year, some of them not worth cracking, we should be able to look at them more realistically. Books can be expensive, but they can be bought, checked out or replaced easily.

My favorite books have a place of honor and are generously written in. Many of the rest, after I read or use them, I give away, clip up or tear or photocopy things out of. I keep only what I need and file it. And books I didn't ask for—ones that people passing through give me to read, for example—are quickly scanned and recycled.

Use your own judgment here, but keep only the books that you'll use, cherish or even abuse if you need to. Donate other books to a local library or nursing home to make room for new and better books.

## REMEMBER: THE MENTAL FOLLOWS THE PHYSICAL

*I may make a mess when I work, but I always tidy up as soon as I'm done. Starting work at a messy, disorganized work top makes me feel defeated, unenergetic—it's like starting the day with dishes in the sink.*

*—Seli Groves*

Getting organized to write is both a mental and physical process. The good news here is that when the physical things are in order, the mental aspect comes much more easily. Keeping the place clean and getting rid of junk and clutter can actually help you write!

The condition of your writing space, small as it may be, directly affects not just your mood and attitude, but those of others who enter that space. I know that some people imagine the writer as a sloppy, unshaven person humped over (or lost in) a pile of trash—empty food wrappers, half-filled coffee cups, three days' worth of sardine cans and TV dinner tins, resources spread randomly and unidentified all over the place. But the writing process can get trashy only if you let it!

• Have a good-size garbage can, or more than one if you need it.

• It's particularly important to have a work area somewhere in your office that is clean and clear of stacked-up files and miscellaneous papers. Move out everything not needed for what you are working on now to a tickler file, your project piles elsewhere or the files proper. Things you're finished with should be dejunked and moved to storage.

• Be a neat office keeper. You will have a feeling of peace and control that carries over into your writing. Neaten your work area at the end of the day so it will be fresh and inviting the next morning. Before quitting, refile things that need to be refiled, trash any trash, neaten your tools and papers, wipe the fingerprints off your desk and put tomorrow's to do list on your desk.

• Polish up your place every so often—dust, vacuum, clean the monitor and keys, replace scattered references, clean the windows, etc.

---

**Why Carol likes a clean office: As an editor, there is often enough chaos right in the copy I'm working on—I don't want any in my surroundings!**

---

## CORD CLUTTER

When the cords in your office (phone, computer, printer, copier, fax machine, etc.) begin to resemble a snake breeding station:

- Replace unnecessarily long cords with shorter ones, or at least reel up the slack and use a twist-tie to tie it into a neat coil.
- Eliminate any cords no longer needed.
- Tie or tape wires together into a single bundle to give the dust bunnies fewer places to hide. Velcro strips are handy for this.
- Use a power strip or surge protector to consolidate cords into one neater—and safer—group.
- Enclose all the wires from a computer in the plastic cylinder of a special unit available at office-supply stores for just this purpose.

## CUT CLUTTER AT THE SOURCE!

One of the best ways to reduce clutter is to cut it at the source; go on the offensive to *prevent* and *avoid* it. The less that gets into your office, the less you'll have to dispose of later. Consider the following common causes of office overflow:

**Indecision:** We can't decide which of something to get, so we get one of each.

**Lack of goals and direction:** We're not sure which way to go, so we prepare for everything and anything.

**Ego, vanity:** We buy expensive things we don't really need, and then we have to pay for and maintain them.

**Depression:** We shop and buy more to make ourselves feel good.

**Irresistible marketing:** We buy things we don't need or already have because we like the ads.

**Upgrade fever:** We get the urge to have faster, more powerful, newer, bigger and fancier products when what we are using is often fine for our writing purposes.

**Compulsive shopping:** Don't shop for recreation. Just buy what you need, then get back home and write.

**Compulsive keeping** (many a file, office, storage area and entire house have been crammed full by this): Ask yourself, "What's the worst thing that could happen if I get rid of this?" Then get rid of it.

**Subscriptions:** We subscribe to periodicals we're no longer interested in or never get around to reading.

**Mailing lists:** These generate a constant flow of what ends up as more paper clutter. To get off unwanted mailing lists, write to the Mail Preference Service of the Direct Marketing Association, 11 W. Forty-second St., P.O. Box 3861, New York, NY 10163-3861.

**Organizations:** If you are no longer committed to them, quit. Organizations can really churn out the paper!

**Conventions and seminars:** Here we can gather many shopping bags full of papers, posters, folders, brochures, binders and novelties that we may never look at again. Don't take things just because they're there or free. If you go, take less—only what you really want! And dump that seminar stuff right away if three days with "the master" didn't do anything for you.

**Classes:** Many of us writers still have every note we ever took in college, plus reams of stuff from any classes or workshops since. When the class is finished, weed before you stack or store.

**Freebies:** For some reason we just can't resist anything free, whether we really want or need it, or not. Resist! Don't even pick up that ballpoint pen shaped like a banana, the free sample section of a book you'll never read or the CD-ROM of an Internet program you'll never switch to.

## SOME CLUTTER-PREVENTION MEASURES

• Keep new paper piles at bay by setting a regular time to pare papers, refile things and the like—such as the first fifteen minutes of each day or the first hour every Friday.

• Never save any more of something than you have to—save the article, not the whole magazine!

• Remember that it's much easier to eliminate things *before* they get into your systems (in boxes, filing cabinets) than to try and find the time to thin them down later. At least 60 percent of filed papers, for example, are never referenced again; so take a hard look and make sure you need to save or record something before you do it.

• If you save something to read, and you haven't read it (or even touched it) in two months, you should probably just get rid of it.

• Don't bring unrelated stuff into your writing area. Things like sports and hobby gear can easily take over!

• When you're finished with something, don't put it down—put it away!

---

**The rewards of decluttering, in brief: You'll have less tension, make fewer apologies, be able to find things, have room to do and grow, save time, save money, be free and be able to pass up future clutter.**

**CHAPTER 14**

# *The Second Step to Success: Don't Stop!*

Believe it or not, keeping moving in writing is even more important than getting started. Many would-be writers do finally manage to overcome that first big hurdle of getting started, but then they never get published because they don't keep going.

Remember, consistency is what counts! Ideas alone are worth little; the world is full of them. Contacts and breaks and all those glamorous big-time things are way down on the list of reaching your target, too. Consistency is what will do it. Application and persistence are the most important ingredients in success, even more so than talent and genius. Some of the most highly published authors in the world, whose books and articles we see everywhere, are not necessarily artists of the English or any other language. They are good, workmanlike writers who are organized and determined.

The bottom line of getting organized to get published: Get started and don't stop.

> *The only difference between me and anyone else in the world who wants to write and be published (but hasn't yet) is that I sit down and see it through to the finish. You have to start to start, and finish, to finish.*
>
> *—Janice Papolos*

## THE SIMPLE SECRET: PUTTING IN ENOUGH TIME

High accomplishment: Seldom is it talent, skill, luck or equipment, much of it is a matter of putting in enough time. Many of us keep our childhood attention span. We fiddle with something for a few minutes, and if the rewards don't start rolling in, we drop it. But real production means serious time on the job. I'm asked hundreds of times a year, "How do you get so much done?" I'd like to say, "I'm a magician. Presto, it's done," but the real answer is just plain time on the job. I sit down at the typewriter at four A.M. and don't get up until three in the afternoon, stay on the research trail, bang out those pages and structure those stories. It's amazing how much of a time management expert this will make you, just doing, working and thinking, swinging the pick, wielding the pen or the pencil—how good an organizer you'll become and how much will get done!

If you ask someone what they did today, they'll often tell you about the article or essay they were working on but for some reason didn't finish. When you total up the time they were actually on this project during an eight-hour span, they really only worked two hours; the other six they were around, not on the job. With so many attractive— and distractive—things going on, especially around home, we can easily jump from one activity to another. We remain with some for so short a time that by the end of the day we've really spent no time at all on what we worked on all day.

You've got to put in the hours to get your manuscript done, period. The chief difference between success and failure lies in the single element of staying power. It takes a long time to get psyched up and ready to write sometimes, so why not keep at it for ten hours for a change?

- Regular application beats the best rally of "once in a while."
- If you got an amazing and wonderful amount done yesterday, don't fall into the trap of feeling you can or should do less than usual today because of it.

## THE BULLY CALLED WRITER'S BLOCK

Who is he? That tough customer who moves in in the middle of a writing project and talks you out of keeping on the job. He scares you into blankness, idleness—you run instead of write for the next hour, week, month or year, convincing yourself that this bully people have nicknamed writer's block is a real stopper.

Guess what, would-be great writers—this bully exists only in your imagination! Yes, you made him up from all the stories and conversations you've heard about him from other writers. There are times in writing when you have to stop for a few minutes, or maybe longer, and rethink, regroup or redo something. But that is exactly the same as getting off the right road in your car. You don't just sit there until the right road appears, do you? No way. You just keep the motor running while you make a call, reread the map or ask a native, and then you are back on your way. **Never turn off your writing motor** when you get stalled or stymied. This is just one of the hills on a writer's journey—it may slow you down, but it shouldn't stop you.

In fact it is generally this stage of writing that forces you to come up with something better than you originally thought you had going.

> *When I first worked for an advertising agency, I was assigned to write commercials. My mind was blank. My boss advised, "Write twenty of these, as fast as you can. Never mind how poor they seem. Keep writing. Your brain will warm up. The commercials will improve." They did.*
>
> *I applied the same technique in other areas. When I was stuck for a catchy headline on an ad, or a title for a magazine article, I sat down with pad and pencil, and sometimes a glass of wine, and didn't move until I'd jotted at least twenty headlines or titles. In the second half-hour, some good ones came.*
>
> *Often I couldn't seem to write a particular paragraph (usually the lead) for an article or ad. Instead of waiting for inspiration, I made myself scribble versions of the graph, no matter how weak. This act always got me going.*
>
> —Keith Monroe

> *To give myself positive feedback and help keep myself going, I always look at that "word count" feature of my software. It gives me such a sense of accomplishment to see that count go from three hundred to three thousand to five thousand, and then twenty thousand. It's thrilling to see that you are actually writing something, and it is growing. When I hit a lull, I give part of my manuscript to someone I trust to get feedback. Whatever they say, good or bad, usually stirs me into action again.*
>
> —Jean Loftus

---

**A few stretches or a brisk walk is often all you need to break the cycle of "no inspiration."**

---

## HAVING TROUBLE KEEPING GOING?

Just so you know that you aren't an exception here, most us are better starters than we are finishers. We are just more aware of the times when we drop the ball and don't always notice how many times others do. Even things that were once burning us up with excitement will slip into semiconsciousness, inactivity, even complete dormancy, so don't think you're alone in this.

You will be on fire with enthusiasm, then the next morning or a few days later when you start on it suddenly, it is all just ho-hum writing again. But lying on the beach, going to concerts, driving new Lexuses, even having erotic experiences can get mundane on you, too. Even the best foods don't taste good at certain times or when you've had enough of them. And sustaining writing can be tougher than sustaining activities of other kinds (and this includes the Lexus and sex). There is a simple explanation for this and if you are aware of it, you won't be as likely to fold up when some of your writing seems to be inching toward boring.

In these modern days we've become dependent on, even addicted to, immediate rewards, fast returns on investment and prizes and bonuses for being anything above average. Everything is fast, even our food: a microwave makes us wait only seconds for things that once took hours. We are a push-button, instant-results society, and we love it.

When writing, on the other hand, we won't be rewarded after every sentence or patted on the back after every paragraph, even if we are absolutely brilliant! Nobody else knows what is in those pages of rough draft except you, and few want to know or will even listen if you read it to them. You can't be a spoiled child *and* a good writer—you just need to grunt, grimace and get on with it, day after day, week after week, month after month and yes, year after year.

It's kind of like the old-time miners' view of the mother lode. Those poor grizzled old fellows picked and chiseled into the mountainsides and streams for years, knowing that if and when they finally finished— found the mother lode—it would all be worth it. Likewise, we suffer for our manuscripts and grow while producing them.

Personally, I love the excitement of one big payment coming at the end instead of the little payments of praise and encouragement along the way. Once you view writing as a long wait with a sure reward, you'll be on the way to mastering the second virtue of a good writer—staying power.

Someone once asked my coauthor Carol, "How do you get your strokes in the intense but often invisible profession of editing and writing?" Her answer was that you have to give them to yourself—you know when you've done something well in this arena.

Here are a couple of helps:

1. Pick a subject that you're passionate about. I'm always careful to pick a subject to write about that I am 180 percent interested in. I love the subject, and want to see it in print. The more I work on it, the more committed and energetic I get. Then it is not work, but fun, a more attractive way to spend my time than playing, eating, romancing, spectatoring . . . anything. When you pick something to write on that is a "job," or a little iffy, you will constantly have to beat on yourself to keep up the work.

2. Quit listening to everyone else's appraisal or opinion of your ideas, or your writing. Most people don't write books because they are lazy, not because they lack talent. You are constantly surrounded by people more talented than you, and probably more interesting, too. But they aren't writing, are they? Why? They prefer to talk and analyze things to death, and when and if you listen, you start running in their rut and won't write as much or as well.

3. You need to see and be convinced that you are progressing, so I spiral bind even my rough drafts book-style, to make them look and feel more like the book they will someday be. There is something about having a tangible product in your hands that makes you want to work on it further.

4. Many people wait until they are finished with a book to find a title for it, but you should work on the title the whole time that you work on the book itself. If your book will not be self-published, the publisher will have the final say on the title. But a good title will help sell your book to a publisher in the first place. And if it's strong enough, the publisher will use it, and it will give your book a leg up on the competition. Meanwhile, it helps make your book a reality. Even if its publication is two or three years away, you will really believe it's coming.

5. Reflect on the time, money and bragging you've put into your book or article so far. This will make you determined to stick with it, no matter what. Pride is a great prodder.

*When I finish the first page, I tell myself happily, "Great, I've made a start." I have a page down in writing (even though I may rewrite it a half-dozen times eventually). Then I move ahead, focusing only on the first fifty pages of a three hundred-page manuscript. When I reach page 50, I cheer, "One-sixth of the pages done already,"—not moan, "Still five-sixths of the way to go."*

*At page 101, I tell myself eagerly, "Over one-third finished." At page 151, triumphantly, "I'm past the halfway mark; all downhill now." It makes all the difference when you accentuate the positive.*

—*Samm Sinclair Baker*

## ON A ROLL!

Just the opposite of the feared "block" is being "on a roll," when thoughts and ideas just seem to fly into your head and hands. This will happen as much or more than the "stall" times, and again the advice is, "Don't stop." Once you're really going, making great headway, don't stop—to answer phones, take a break, eat, make coffee or go to bed, even if "it's time." There are times to ignore the clock, meals, nags, even tired muscles and just keep going. When the spirit is willing, your imagination expanded, creativity pouring out—keep moving. Momentum creates momentum—the more you do, the more you feel like doing. It becomes self-feeding, and the results will be some of your best material ever. So one of the secrets of getting published is . . . don't stop for anything after you get started. Not because the computer broke down, company came, the cat coughed, it's my birthday, we are remodeling or going on vacation. Don't let life functions derail your writing. Make writing a part of it all, and a priority.

---

**When you're on a roll, don't stop until you droop or drop. Don't stop to crow and brag, or to admire what you've already done. Don't stop to read your press, bow for applause, evaluate your progress or look at yourself in the mirror. When things are falling into place, you feel like you could go on forever, *do* it. Keep going and increase your speed. Don't just make hay when the sun shines; make hay as long as there is grass!**

---

## DON'T GET LOCKED IN

Sometimes it's surprising how fast you can exhaust an idea that you first thought would take a whole chapter. The worst thing you can do when this happens is keep beating on that idea, squeezing it, fighting it to bring it to where you want it. This is a total waste of time. Smart writers don't labor long on something infertile. When the sails go limp, "jump ship" to another project, or a different part of this one. A wind of an idea will come up later, sometimes, but it is a waste of good time and energy to try to row the schooner all the way to your destination. Everything you write about will have several avenues or facets. Sticking with one aspect to the point of frustration makes writing really "unfun," and very few of us will continue to write when it isn't fun.

I generally have at least ten file folders for each book I am working on. Any time I reach a stall point, and I don't mean just a tough spot, but a case of simply running out of information and ideas, in the file and in my brain, I skip another chapter or go to the Art file and doodle and sketch awhile. Or I pick up the Marketing file and dream and scheme of how I will do it. After an hour or so of things like this, I'm usually rearmed with a new idea that has popped up all by itself.

---

**You can work on more than one book, article or story at a time. In fact, often a multiproject agenda is better because you can switch manuscripts when you need a change, or go dry.**

---

## FORGET ABOUT "THE BIG BREAK"

We always hear about that one great record-breaking feat, master move on the market or chance encounter with an editor—a single event that made a name or a best-seller for someone. This is often referred to as "the big break." Lottery winners, ace pilots and speedway drivers, too, are suddenly somebody all because they did something newsworthy. We hear this enough that we start looking for the big moment or the break that will make us and our writing career. This is why so many people live disappointed lives. Never mentioned in the headlines are the rest of the facts:

1. The lottery player spent ten thousand dollars on tickets before he won that million; and ten million other lottery players got nothing.

2. The pilot learned discipline and nerve milking cows and cutting trees as a teenager. He had years of flight training, flew seventy missions and was wounded three times and shot down twice prior to his big day. He was a good pilot before he shot down six enemy planes. That one act just made him visible.

3. The race car driver lost 167 races, he was burned over 30 percent of his body once and his passion for racing has cost him his life savings and three marriages so far. That one big win didn't begin to cover the costs.

Don't be deceived by big breaks; they seldom come. Don't waste your precious time and emotions gambling and praying and waiting for a big magical event to put you on top of *The New York Times* bestseller list. Don't live for the big light that is going to come on some day and make you rich, famous, admired and happy forever. That will only happen if you pick up many little sticks for a long time and build a big bright fire. Most accomplishment is the result of a lot of small or even tiny things added up over time. Don't save yourself for the spectacular, for the headlines. Score soundly in every game instead of dreaming of that one forty-point night. Accomplishment always has a history, and consistency is what counts.

---

**Persist! Sustain! Endure! Continue! Stick to it! Keep at it! It's hard to become a great or successful writer without it, partner: staying power.**

**CHAPTER 15**

# Dealing With the Downpour:
# Office Management

Being the creative types we writers are, we may tend to neglect or be uninterested in the everyday mundanities of office work. But creativity isn't much comfort when you can't find that contract you really need or miss a prime publishing opportunity because you lost track of things.

This chapter is a short course in office management to help you deal with the daily, weekly and monthly inflow and outflow in an orderly fashion and make sure that things that need doing get done. It will also show you how to keep yourself from being swiftly buried in papers (something we all need to know today).

Why organize?

1. To be able to find things.
2. To be able to use and enjoy them.
3. To make your writing time more productive.

## HUNTING REALLY HURTS YOU!

Having something but not knowing where it is—exactly, instantly—is almost as bad as not having it at all.

Whether you are writing or getting ready to write, "the hunt" is a true curse because of the time it wastes and the emotional anxiety it creates. When we can't find something, it becomes an obsession; we will go to any trouble and expense to find it. And what you don't find will bother you forever, even after the book is out or the article is on the stands.

Hunting really hurts you! When you break stride or thought to find something, it cuts the efficiency of the writing process tremendously. If you are a hunter, now is the time to repent, regroup and find a better way of keeping track. It's easy to begin the course of correction, because there is usually only one person to change or redo—*you*. You have full control of what comes in, what is kept and where and how it is kept, and how easy it will be to retrieve!

Forget the old method of piling things and then trying to remember where they are. In the good old days, before the paper glut, we may have had the mental and physical room to do that. Today, forget it! The average person handles at least three hundred sheets of paper a day, and once you become a writer, up that to four hundred or five hundred or more. If you don't believe me, just make a list of the pages you read, handle and process in the course of a day: not just manuscripts in all stages but newspapers, magazines, junk mail, real mail, advertising fliers and brochures, catalogs, memos, faxes, photocopies, computer printouts, bills and bill enclosures, instructions, etc. Let all this go for three or four days, and you will be buried.

The easiest way to put an end to hunting is to discipline yourself to process and file everything immediately! Now it is fresh, handy and efficient. Dealing with it now eliminates future fumbling and hunting.

The average executive today, according to *Forbes ASAP*, wastes 150 hours a year—almost one month—searching for lost information. The *Wall Street Journal* says it's more like six weeks a year we spend retrieving misplaced information from messy desks and files. Americans as a whole waste more than nine million hours each day looking for lost and misplaced articles.

## FILE IT, DON'T PILE IT

A pile isn't a place; a pile is a pile, and it invites other things to be piled on top of it. Piles are treated casually, and they tip and get scattered. Out of sight, out of mind really applies here. Anything piled will only get more piled on it and ignored longer.

Sort everything by subject (or whatever), then

• Put it in boxes or trays somewhere in sight, if you are the "in sight" type, like me. For me, out is active; seeing the pile or box helps me keep it in mind and get to it. A pile can be converted to a file in two seconds with the right box or tray. Once there, the stuff has some structure, an actual garage wherein to be parked and protected. This tiny thing will make a huge difference. Cardboard boxes are generally free, and plastic trays are inexpensive.

• Put it in file cabinets or well-labeled drawers (see the following and chapters five and six).

• Put it in an in-between state, for new and very active things, in well-marked file folders set in something on or near your desktop. Later these will go to the file cabinet or wherever. I keep the folders for my hottest and most current projects right on my desk until they reach the point of filing in a file cabinet. I mark files like this with big, bold letters on the front, never the tab. This way I can identify a file across a ballfield.

• Think twice before you file it—at least 60 percent of filed papers are never referenced again.

• Rather than placing notes and papers in a pile of things to file, file them now. Have file folders handy, along with markers or labels or whatever you use. If your files are in a different room or more than a swivel of the chair from the cabinet, then I suggest opening mail or sorting other newly arrived papers next to a pile of file folders and labeling and inserting the fileables as you go. At least then your "to be filed" pile is ready to go. And if you need a critical document, it's more efficient to flip through file folders than piles of paper.

• Never pile little things, especially; put them right in a file folder. Have a convenient folder to drop your daily notes, telephone information and anything you want to keep. When you need it later, bingo, it's right there.

## ORGANIZERS FOR PAPER

When looking over the wide array of attractive and ingenious organizers now available, remember that a better sorter or container is not going to make you get to things any sooner. *You* have to do that.

Unmanaged in boxes and desktop organizers can easily become "aging bins." Make it a point to review and act on their contents regularly.

### Some inexpensive paper organizers for the home office:

• Stationery boxes and shallow cardboard boxes
• The cardboard trays from cases of canned goods
• The tops of photocopy paper boxes
• Sweater box-size or larger, plastic containers

• Gallon-size zipper plastic bags
• The Avon boxes used to ship large orders

### Files

We work daily in my office on my latest books in process, as well as the forty-plus that are coming, and many magazine articles. So we keep all this in my active files, and each book has a separate file drawer. Needless to say we have lots of full-height file cabinets. We put a picture of a book's cover on the front of its drawer so we don't have to take the time to read the label, although we do label the drawers as well. Everything related to that book goes in its drawer—the original roughs, the copies we send to editors, their changes, etc. We keep copies of the finished book in there, too, with any corrections noted.

Although we may keep things like contracts, royalty statements, correspondence, cover designs, artwork and clippings of reviews of the book and the like in marked file folders, we don't worry about an elaborate filing system inside the drawer because once we get the right drawer, we can find anything we want in minutes.

Almost daily I toss new pages and ideas into those drawers. These are often handwritten, and filing them takes only seconds.

Instant access is the bottom line here—lots of drawers. We have drawers even for out-of-print or failure books because we will end up drawing something from them sometime. I bought twenty used five-drawer file cabinets for $160. I painted them and ended up paying a total of $400 for one hundred roomy and smooth-sliding drawers. Sure they take up room, but for us writers, the more resources and records at hand, the better!

## MORE FILING POINTERS FROM THE PROS

*When filing or storing things, always ask yourself: If I wanted to find this, where would I look, or what word would I think of?*
                                        —Deniece Schofield

*When I think of a new idea, I jot it down on an index card. I keep all of these cards in a 3" x 5" card file for easy reference. I keep individual articles, research or outlines in separate file folders, and file them in file boxes. The boxes are labeled fiction,*

*nonfiction, essays, children, whatever. My husband built shelves
in my office closet to hold these boxes, making use of every bit of
space available.*

*—Mary Jo Rulnick*

*I have three large alphabetized lateral files for my main files, but
when I'm working on something, I don't like to have the things
related to it buried in file cabinets. When organizing my initial
research materials, I like to use alphabetized accordion files,
preferably the ones with pockets.*

*I often have ten or so of these in use at once, as my research
expands and expands, as research does. This way everything I
gather is immediately filed under the appropriate heading.*

*I also use the boxes and racks that hold hanging files to orga-
nize materials for books in progress. I may have five or six of
these around my office at one time, on top of my desk or a nearby work table.*

*—Dian Buchman*

*A favorite organizing device of mine might be called the "inner
file folder." I use it to divide the contents of a file folder (containing a book chapter, research notes, newspaper clippings or
whatever), into smaller subsections. I take a sheet of 8½" x 11"
paper from the "recycle" bin and fold it in half, with the used
side inside and the fold on the left. Then I identify this new "file
folder" on the front and it's ready to slip related data into. For
example, my current book in progress has a lengthy chapter on
irony, and its file contains a number of inner folders marked
"Sarcasm," "Hyperbole," "Paradox," "Puns," etc.*

*While my own writing projects are nonfiction, this "inner
file" method could prove equally useful for fiction writers storing
notes on characters, research facts for historical novels and so on.
It's also great for organizing expenses at tax time.*

*—Sheila Davis*

*I am sitting surrounded by more than four hundred neatly
shelved, identical, computer-labeled boxes. They constitute my
filing system. The system lines the shelved walls of two offices
and a hallway. These boxes are 12¼" wide, 9¼" long and 4"*

*high, and made of sturdy white corrugated stock. When assembled (a ten-second job), they have a lid. Purchased in lots of fifty from a box or packaging supply store, they are less than a dollar.*

*When I undertake a writing project, I use these to make up a "project box." I rubber cement a thirty to thirty-six point computer-made title on the box's four sides (so I can store the box length or widthwise) and that project is "boxed."*

*Into the box goes all the project's notes, art, tapes, drafts, the works. When I'm working on that project, instead of rummaging a file drawer, I move the box from its stack to my desk and every scrap of information I've assembled is there, readily at hand.*

*The "project box" system has many advantages over filing cabinets and their drawers. First, there's no way for anything to slip out of the file, everything's boxed. Second, art lies flat, not standing vertically as in a file drawer, so it doesn't buckle, fold or get damaged. But the biggest advantage of these boxes is that they are portable, which file drawers and their bulky folders are not.*

*Yes, some projects, notably book projects, need more than one box. But if the lot is properly labeled (#1, #2, etc.) there's no hassle. Scan the stacks, pull the proper box and your writing is under way.*

—*Jim Joseph*

*I keep a binder for each book as I'm working on it (later I add a publicity binder). I start the binder with several sheets that look like this:*

| Date | Contact | Phone # | E-mail | Address | Notes |
|------|---------|---------|--------|---------|-------|
|      |         |         |        |         |       |
|      |         |         |        |         |       |
|      |         |         |        |         |       |
|      |         |         |        |         |       |

*This allows me to keep track of everyone I speak with and keeps all interviews on plain display. I never have to hunt for anyone's information. All outlines of chapters, correspondence, letters from*

*editors and the complete paper trail go in this "Master Binder."*
*(It makes for a nice history of the evolution of the book, too.)*
—Janice Papolos

*Some people shy away from computers and are just as effective*
*using a manual filing system. They can find things in a flash*
*because of the way they filed them. Others will find a computer*
*filing system the most effective. The most important thing to*
*remember here is that **none of these systems works if you don't.***
*You have to choose a method that works for you and then **use** it.*
*After you set up your system, then stay on top of it—**keep up***
***with it**. Make this a priority at a set time every day or week.*
*You also need to be selective in what you keep. Don't keep*
*everything. You'll save a ton of time if you determine whether*
*an item has value up front, rather than automatically stashing*
*everything away and then trying to sift through it all later.*
*Create a set of questions about information you may want to*
*keep and then ask those questions on each item before you*
*file it."*
—Dave Hermansen

### How to find lost papers

Most of us have spent many hours searching for lost or misplaced papers that are urgently needed now—notes for that meeting we have in twenty minutes or the article we are trying to answer the fact checker's questions about. Setting things up so that you simply don't make mistakes is far better, but if you have made a blunder, the following list may help undo it.

### Where lost papers are most likely to be:

• Accidentally clipped to the back of something else you've handled recently.

• Mistakenly placed in that file on another subject you consulted recently.

• Stuck inside a book or magazine you've recently read. (How many important papers have been lost forever after being stuffed inside an old magazine?)

• In the wrong "current" pile on your desk.

• In the copier.

• Accidentally included in some package you put together to mail to someone today (open it up and check, if it's still on the premises).

• (Gasp!) In the garbage can. Never empty the garbage can until you're all finished with the current project.

• Carried off by a recent visitor. People come into your office and sit down by your desk, often placing the stuff they're carrying on top of your stuff. When they leave, they inadvertently pick up your vital material. (The dangers of a cluttered desktop!)

• In the file or other place they actually belong, where you never even looked!

Some rules that will do much to prevent lost papers:

• Don't lay things from the file down anywhere when you're done with them other than right back where they came from!

• Don't pile papers from different projects on top of each other!

## COLOR ME ORGANIZED

Color adds spice to life, and it can be a big help in organizing things in the office, too. A few ideas include:

• The old office strategy of using different color carbons for different years can be adapted to the color of the year for all or most of the printed materials you produce: file folders, appointment forms, media appearance record sheets, whatever.

• A red or other brightly colored folder can be used for the things you need to look at or take care of right away, those rush items.

• Color can be used on lists for quick visual identification of different categories of to dos: for example, red for top priority, orange for errands, green for research, blue for R&D, brown for maintenance tasks.

• You can use file folders of different colors for your current book and article files for quick visual identification.

• Colored flags or self-stick removable notes can be used to call out places in the manuscript for different people's attention (yellow for the editor, gray for the designer, etc.).

• You can use different colors to identify things to or from different freelancers or collaborators.

• Colored envelopes can be used for different things—travel confirmations, forms, bills—so you don't have to stop to read them; you will know immediately what's inside.

• On a list of outstanding accounts, you can highlight receivables thirty days overdue in one color, sixty days overdue in another, etc.

• Bulletin boards can be divided into sections by color.

• See chapters nine and ten for using color to help organize your writing itself.

> *I use different color file folders so I can say, "Where is the orange folder?" instead of "Where is the file for the article on pumpkin-growing?"*
>
> *In the old cut-and-paste days, I typed every draft on a different color of paper, and when things like this were pasted together, it made for quite a colorful sight!*
>
> —Elaine Schimberg

## CALENDARS AND APPOINTMENT BOOKS

There are all kinds of aids and systems available today to help us organize and keep track of the traffic in our lives: from books and binders to computerized and electronic planners, such as Lotus Organizer and the PalmPilots (see page 227). Just remember that we are all different, and can all have our way of keeping track of time and to dos. You don't have to follow any expert's system, and you don't want to end up spending more time filling out a day planner than actually doing the things you want to get done. Some prepackaged planning systems are not only expensive, but so complex that unless you are ultra-organized, you may find it hard to keep up with all of the categories.

So choose the planning system most practical for your purposes, and the one that fits your own organizational style. For you it may be lists and calendars on the computer. I find that combining the monthly calendar and appointment book into one and carrying it with me, all the time, is the best arrangement. All upcoming events and appointment times, etc., are recorded here. The details on upcoming events and appointments I keep in easy-to-find files.

> *For me the beauty of a planner is consolidation. I have everything I need in one portable place—a virtual office away from home. In my planner I keep my calendar and address directory,*

*both my business and personal to do and action lists, my goals,*
*the magazine articles I want to read, cut from the magazine and*
*hole-punched so they fit in the planner, even my favorite quotes*
*(for when I need some inspiration, or need to sound profound).*
—*Dave Hermansen*

### A few pointers on calendars and planners

• If you use a published planner, make sure it has enough space and flexibility in the parts of its systems most important to you.

• We can have daily planners for detailing daily activities, weekly planners for our short-term goals and the more forward-looking parts of planners (such as quarterly or yearly objectives) for our longer-term goals. Just remember that these **lists need to be reviewed regularly and related to each other for maximum effectiveness**.

• To do lists are always helpful, but unless you work the things that need to be done into your schedule, they will remain nothing more than lists.

• On calendars: distinguish clearly between tentative and confirmed dates. And put personal, family and writing obligations all on one calendar to prevent conflicts from being unrecognized until it is too late.

• Remember that calendars won't organize you unless you look at them!

### Addresses

Contacts are among the most vital resources of our trade. When you can't find or have outdated information for someone, you can waste a lot of time and energy trying to locate that person.

Most people (and that includes us writers) keep addresses all over the place—in our day planner, on envelopes on our desk, on business cards, on a computer and in our wallet or purse. We need to pool all addresses that relate to our writing in one place, and carry them with us everywhere, so that we can find them instantly. Having to stop to get an address somewhere (even a well-organized place), or worse yet, having to wait for it, is an interruption we don't need and can avoid. Making a quick call or writing a quick note the moment the impulse strikes us is important.

There are all kinds of electronic address books now, as well as bound or loose-leaf ones, and new versions of the Rolodex. Many writers like to keep their addresses in a day planner or PalmPilot. Putting names and addresses in your computer enables you to design your own address directory and print it out in small enough type that it will fit into your planner. Whatever you use, be sure to include e-mail addresses, and make sure there is room for changes, updates and new entries. And enter those changes, updates and new entries the minute you become aware of them.

At least once a year, go through your address directory and bring it up to speed!

### PalmPilots

This more versatile little sister of the laptop is described by the manufacturer as "a . . . handheld computer with the soul of an organizer." It can organize all of your business and personal information for you, balance your checkbook, keep track of your to do list, the list of office supplies you need—even the grocery list.

A PalmPilot can be a big advantage for those who travel. You can take your office with you anywhere in a device that weighs only a few ounces: your year's calendar, your address book and all of your lists. You can have up to eight megabytes of data stored—notes, resources, references, interviews. You can plug in your own modem to a PalmPilot, or turn it into a cell phone, scanner or pager. You can use it to do correspondence, send and receive e-mail, and take notes. You use a stylus to inscribe them onto a small screen, and the Pilot will type them up. The microphone can also enter voice data as text. There's even a fold-up, detachable keyboard that fits in your pocket.

The best thing about PalmPilots is that all the information that you store or enter into them can be transferred to your computer at the push of a button. Likewise, you can download all of your notes on a project from your computer to the Pilot.

It even has an alarm! You can set it to go off anytime, say fifteen minutes before the critical luncheon, or just before the author you're waiting for will be on *The Today Show*. The alarm can be set even months in advance—any appointment you put on the internal calendar can have the alarm set to remind you days ahead of time or just before it happens. If you have a recurring appointment, the alarm will remind you each time (great to prompt you for meetings, conference calls and flights). It can also be used as a timer to move from one project or subject to another, which is ideal for recording billable time.

PalmPilots cost around $300. You can learn more about them at http://www.palm.com.

**Databases**

A database enables you to record key data and call it up in all kinds of ways. Once you enter data into a database, you can manipulate it and turn it back out in many different formats, which can save you a great deal of time and busy work.

When you enter the data into a database, each element you want to be able to sort by (such as name, address, phone number or fax number) is added and identified as a separate cell. This enables you to sort and find things not just alphabetically, for instance, but by first last names, state, city or whatever.

My general manager puts all of the information on my speaking engagements and other public appearances into a database as soon as they are set up: where; when; who; how many people will attend; phone, fax and address of both the contact person and the place where I'll be appearing; where I'll stay; my flight numbers; and my fees and expenses. This makes it easy to eventually generate an invoice—everything is already in the database. Documents can be merged with a database to personalize them.

With a database you can easily print labels or find all the checks you entered this week—the computer will even calculate the total for the deposit slip for you. A database can be used for bills, invoices and statements too; you can tell it, for instance, to find all overdue outstanding invoices and print late notices for those customers. You can enter all of your e-mails into a database and use it to call up all of those relating to a particular subject.

You can find databases where software is sold, including mail-order catalogs and computer stores.

## HANDLING THE MAIL STREAM

We all get plenty of mail today, a high percentage of which is junk, and once we start writing we will only get more (hopefully the quality will improve along with the quantity!). Snail mail, the current label for the old faithful U.S. Postal Service, is not the only player in the game now—faxes and the speedy delivery services, from FedEx to Airborne, are newer ways to accumulate a guilt pile. You can't escape from all of this incoming information—all you can do is process it intelligently.

### Organizing correspondence

I value the written word about twenty times more than the spoken word. Asking or reporting something verbally is always weak to me. But once it is written down, it is documented forever (if you make copies and save them).

I love doing business via correspondence, because I have a tangible piece of evidence that eliminates confusion and uncertainty. People forget or misconstrue what you say, but what you write is on the record.

#### *Outgoing*

When I write letters, I keep several copies, one in each file it applies to and wherever it might be needed. This keeps me from having to move things around and ending up wondering where I put them. I also send a copy to any person who might have an interest in or be connected with the subject or project at hand. Copies are cheap, and they can eliminate many calls and follow-ups later.

One-time, dead-end letters I keep in an inventory file for three or four years and review these from time to time for ones that I am still waiting for or interested in a reply to. These I keep in my desk in my active files. The letter has all the information I need—name, dates, address and phone number—for a quick review or call or any other follow-up I may need to do.

A lot of my correspondence, especially with people I know, I handwrite. I make a copy of their letter, handwrite my answer right in the margins and then send it back. People love this, and it saves lots of time and typing.

I can do these myself faster than going through the whole computer routine of typing and printing, or even e-mail. I can jot a note in a book, slip it into a manila envelope and mail it in a minute.

#### *Incoming*

I receive a great deal of correspondence, and I have a system for it. If you stop to respond to each letter you get the minute you get it, you'll be forever processing mail.

1. Don't attend to correspondence instantly, but don't let it build up. Not only is a pile of aged mail discouraging to process, but as time passes and the pile grows, we may get careless and bypass something important. The longer correspondence sits, the longer it takes to answer (we have to

add apologies and explanations and refresh our memories on the subject). So set a goal of processing correspondence regularly to keep the backlog to a minimum.

2. Go through each day's mail quickly and reduce the bulk—remove envelopes and other packaging (tape the address to the letter itself if you need to); toss the obvious junk, like extra flyers, enclosures and ads; and pitch items you don't need, like invitations you're not interested in that don't require a reply. Take that foot-high pile and reduce it to a 3" one.

If necessary (when you're away or deep in an urgent project), have someone else screen your mail and give you the condensed version—only the truly important stuff.

You can also reduce the items with scissors and tape to fewer pages yet to answer, respond or react to when it is convenient.

3. That 3" or smaller pile is now all you have to read, answer or otherwise act upon. I often answer mail on the road; you might want to put it in a folder and work on it whenever you get a chance.

4. File copies of letters you receive under the subject they pertain to, never in any kind of general correspondence file.

5. Your correspondence may include fan mail. I copy all fan mail and send copies to all concerned parties—such as editors, media people and managers of different departments of my publishing and mail-order company. I write "FYI" on the copies and file the original letter under the subject of the book it refers to. One of my top books, *Clutter Free! Finally & Forever*, is composed almost entirely of such correspondence that I faithfully kept and organized.

### A few more pointers on correspondence
- A prompt, brief letter is better than a long delay until "you have time to do it right."
- Short memos and letters (with the exception of love letters) are more likely to be read!
- Warmth and humor can remove the sting from a short response.
- Notes to someone you know well, or for the file, don't have to be letter perfect—a typo or hand correction or two adds a personal touch (and saves time that might better be used elsewhere).
- Don't assume that everyone has your phone number, fax number and address. Make sure these are in plain sight on everything you send out.

### For efficient and foul-proof mailing

Most mail-sorting and handling today is done by machine, and to those machines, *how* you do things makes a big difference.

• Since postal machines read top to bottom, never write anything below the zip code, or it may cause your letter or package to end up in the wrong place.

• Use abbreviations for states and things like street and avenue. Always use zip codes, and the add-on digits, too, when available.

• Don't put scotch tape over stamps, or they can't be canceled (and Uncle Sam will not like that).

• Address large envelopes sideways, not using the 9" side as the top. Don't include bulky metal things like paper clamps in envelopes, or your manuscript may be accidentally torn open in Tucson.

• When mailing photos, illustrations, tapes or disks, don't just slip them into an envelope—*protect* them. Add stiff cardboard, use a Jiffy bag or put them in a box with padding.

• Only address a package on one side—the obvious "top." And be sure the return address is *above* the mailing address. (If it's in the wrong place, adding "to" and "from" won't help!)

• Priority mail is often a good choice—you can send up to two pounds anywhere in the country quickly and inexpensively, and the packaging is free! (A priority-mailed manuscript stands out in an editor's pile, too.)

• For bulky things where speed is not an issue, don't forget the inexpensive fourth-class rate for manuscripts and other printed matter (which includes proofs, books and tapes).

• Before you send something by overnight mail or courier, bear in mind that in many cases the same thing done a day or two earlier costs much less in dollars and stress.

• Remember that it's not enough to package something up—you have to actually *mail* it to get results.

## WRITER'S STATIONERY AND BUSINESS CARDS

These days, stationery of any kind is inexpensive and easy to get or make yourself. For stationery and business cards you want something that is simple, attractive and professional looking.

• Don't use odd colors or textures here. Stick to light, neutral colors like white, off-white, light gray and tan.

• Have a graphic designer or local printer help you choose a font and design if you feel the need for help.

• On business cards and stationery, make sure you provide all the information people need to find or reply to you—complete name, address, e-mail, fax number, cell phone number, whatever.

• Don't print up ten thousand copies until you are sure your area code is not changing again soon. In fact, unless you have a large mailing or trade show in mind, a couple of thousand should be enough; or a hundred at a time off your computer.

• Displaying your name with a big "author" label will only make you look unprofessional or encourage others to engage you in conversation about writing (theirs!).

• Leave some room on your business card for people to write a short note. It's good to have some white space anyway.

• Choose good card stock for business cards if you can. No one likes a limp business card.

• Color can add to the expense of printing. A letterhead you can print out of your printer is very economical.

## E-MAIL

E-mail has revolutionized correspondence: It is much quicker and easier, more informal and a bit more ephemeral than traditional methods. There may not be many published collections of great classic e-mails in the future, but most of us appreciate getting our messages to and from people quickly! And many e-mail carriers allow features like return receipt requested, use of multiple font colors in an e-mail, attaching or embedding photos and copying an e-mail to multiple people at once. Some programs will even sort your e-mail for you and transfer it to your computer.

• E-mail can be saved to your computer so that you can retrieve entire hunks of text and never have to retype them. This makes it perfect for communication between authors and editors.

• One thing that makes e-mail so efficient is that if you instantly hit the reply key, you don't have to look up or type in an address of any kind; just type your response in the body of the letter and send.

• An e-mail program such Microsoft Outlook has a built-in reply form, so that when you get a letter, start reading it and have a thought, you can just hit "enter" and enter that thought in the proper place (it will appear in boldface, in brackets.) When you've made all the remarks you want to, you just hit "reply" and it goes back to the sender with all the answers right in place, and the person can even send it back again for another round, with answers to your answers.

• E-mail keeps a record of what date you receive and send things, but be sure to save or print e-mail that you may need to refer to because browsers may delete opened e-mails after a relatively short time.

• Don't assume that everyone has e-mail and that those who have it check it hourly.

• Check your e-mail regularly, and delete any junk mail immediately!

**Virus protection for e-mail:**
*Sometimes there are e-mails that put a virus in your system, when you open them. There are programs that check e-mail for viruses. Next time you're on the Internet, go to McAfee, to find out what they have available. That's the best anti-virus protection. Sometimes you may be notified about a virus by your server.*
*—Carl Mills*

**When fax is better:**
*Many of the "authorities" I deal with list their e-mail address and I write them by e-mail and ask them when it is convenient for me to call them for an interview. If there is no response, I use the fax. The truth is that many "experts" often forget to read their e-mail but their executive assistants put faxes on the experts' desks.*
*—Ruth Winter*

## LOVE THOSE LISTS!

Most of us would be lost without our lists. In every area of our lives, lists help keep us on target and producing. Without our lists, we would forget half of what we need to remember. In our writing, we can use them to keep things moving and in order.

Lists are a very individual thing—for writers or anyone else—and I doubt that any of us do our lists exactly the same. Some of us use lists as an organization map and schedule; others, just as a catchall so we don't forget anything.

### My listing system

I keep just three lists myself. Since I believe in writing all the time, I mix my writing items right in with everything else that's going on in my life. You might prefer to keep a separate list for writing objectives alone.

**Long-range list:** I keep this at home on my desk or in a file. It's list of long-range things to do, like building a barn, moving the power line, planning a trip to Spain, making a larger warehouse for my publishing company and holding my own writers seminars across the country.

**Current or carry-around list:** This is usually on a legal pad, and I list forty or fifty current goings-on here. I add about four things a day to it and delete about four. When it gets crowded, messy and beat up (usually in about a week or so), I recopy the remaining to dos onto a new list, date the old one and put a big X through it and put the old list in my autobiography file—what a perfect calendar and record to have for writing or legacy.

**Daily list:** My third list is where I jot down the things I plan to do and must not forget today, keeping them off both of my other lists. Such as:

> Pick up file this morning.
> Talk to Keep America Beautiful about my antilittering book.
> Overnight the new clutter manuscript to Carol.
> Write thank-you letter for the new cleaning antique.

I pitch this handwritten list at the end of the day and make a new one the next morning. Anything on this list that doesn't get done I transfer to my current list.

### A word on order

There are time management experts who say you should make a list of things to do, prioritize them and then discipline yourself relentlessly to that priority. That sounds logical, but priorities can change in minutes as calls and letters come in and events happen during the day. You can mark things 1, 2, 3, 4 or A, B, C, D on your list and try to follow that religiously, but when an express mail package arrives, *USA Today* calls for an article on a breaking subject or your interview subject finally calls back, you may not want to stick to your original priorities— maybe the new task should be done right away. There is a difference between efficiency and effectiveness.

Spending a lot of time trying to organize your lists into the perfect predetermined sequence isn't necessarily the way to go. Sometimes it's better to just list everything to be done and then tackle things by demand, spirit, mood or convenience and cross them off. Sometimes you just aren't in a position to do something that's a priority and will do it badly if you force it. Priorities change with the moment. Keep things on a list so you won't forget them, but don't let a list run you. It is just a mental assistant, a place to write your to dos down so you can glance at them and go for whatever.

**The battle of the backlog**

We've all noticed in our listing endeavors that the backlog of things we haven't done but are going to do someday when we get time (or money or someone to help) never seems to get any smaller. In fact, as time passes we only find more and more to do, and we want to do more, so we add all this to our list of "gotta get to soon things."

We almost always have too much to do, and lists can help us choose and execute the 20 percent we are going to do now, out of all we might or should do.

• When looking at all our lists like this, we usually pick by time and blowup factor. What about importance—long-range importance?

• Bottom of the list stuff will often age out—let it.

• Taking a few minutes at the end of the day to make a brief preliminary version of tomorrow's to do list will help keep you focused and on track, especially when timing is tight.

• Two lists that will help organize your writing endeavors: a list of all the projects and assignments you have in the works right now, that have been offered to you or that are imminent, by due date and urgency. And a list of all the stages and details of your current project, by when they have to be done.

• Very complete, lengthy lists, necessary as they may be at times, can actually obscure the big picture of what you're trying to accomplish in a given day or week. If this happens, after you write the whole list, put a note on stating your overall aim in a few words or couple of sentences on top of it. This will help keep you targeted, from losing the forest in the trees.

*List tip number one: When you make a list of things to do, put the things you want least to do at the top and, as time permits, do them first. For the things you really want to do, you don't*

*need a list. For instance, I don't need a reminder that says,*
*"Have wine." I never forget to do watercolors in the park,*
*because I love doing them.*

*Tip number two: Keep the list visible. Force yourself to look at*
*it. Let it obstruct your view. Have it pop up when you start your*
*computer (my calendar greets me every morning, so I can't for-*
*get a thing, unless I'm dumb enough not to read it).*

*I have a fluorescent lamp that hangs over my desk. On it I*
*hang lists of job details by category. But I still need reminders to*
*read those lists. So I put yellow stickies on my monitor. I can't*
*see anything—not even my calendar—until I do something*
*with them.*

*—Art Spikol*

### Getting and keeping a grip

How do you keep things from slipping through the cracks—messages not being relayed, calls not being returned, letters not being answered, things not being finished or followed through? This is an important part of office management, on a large or small scale. Anything undone is subconsciously undoing you.

I have an active pile next to the phone for things that need an action taken soon. I flip through the pile frequently to find the most timely, and when someone calls the active items are always right there so the caller doesn't have to wait while I go to the file.

When my office manager has papers that are waiting for something—such as an answer, approval, confirmation or signature—before they can be filed or processed, she puts them in a labeled file folder inside a special "holding pattern box" beside her desk. Each morning when the mail comes in, she checks the box for things whose missing piece has materialized so they can be on their way.

If you have a lot of things that need timely follow-up in your paperstream, you may want a "tickler" file to keep you from missing a beat. Such a file usually has files numbered 1 to 31, in which you slip things due for action on that date (key here is putting them in far enough ahead of the day they are actually due to give you time to do them, if needed). Behind folder 31 are folders holding things for all the rest of the months of the year, and when you reach the new month, you move them into their respective dates. In the long-range field of writing and publishing, you may want ticker files for farther ahead than just the end of the year—such as to remind you of copyright renewals, when book revisions will be due or the dynamite writing idea you came up with for your state's bicentennial.

There are also software packages (see page 242) that are designed to help you keep track of many of the operations and details of a writer's life.

## THE PHONE

We writers use the phone a lot, so take the time to check what rates you pay for long distance, what basic plan you have, what the rules are and whether you have the right plan. Read all the fine print in your phone bill (including all that mysterious stuff near the beginning), and talk to your phone company if you don't understand it. This will save you money and help you plan longer calls, such as interviews, for the best time.

### Be ready to record

Here's a principle that will multiply over a lifetime into the material for fifty books: simply have a pen and paper or other recording instrument on hand at the phone. Almost every call has something that needs to be recorded in some way.

The first information you get on something is often the most and the best. If you try to just remember it, you'll end up with unanswered questions or a phone number and address that are wrong. Multiply this process by many phone calls and you have a real problem. Don't wait till later to get it down or get it straight.

### Get it all the first time!

When you can pick up a name, number, address or further information right at the moment of initial contact, do it! Doing things later always takes longer, and too often they never get done. It took me years to learn this. When someone called or came by, I would grab just enough information to identify the issue or project, when in a couple minutes more I could have gotten it all. The need to look something up later will always come at a bad time. It will take an average of three calls, and now you have several sets of notes all on the same thing.

In the beginning, when someone called for me to speak or write an article for them, I always made this first call into a friendly visit about the weather or whatever, and told them I would think it over and get back with them. This was dumb. On the first call, when you and your caller are fresh, you'll get more information (and creativity, too) than on any second contact. At the end I always ask the person to mail further information, like brochures. Then it is all done, finished in one call, organized. Now I have all I need to know—such as how many people will be there and the potential for book sales, further contacts and spin-offs—so I can make an intelligent decision.

### A few more pointers on phones

• When calling, respect other people's time zones (we have a tendency, especially when eager to move on something, to forget them, or think that only ours really counts). But calling someone at what for them is 6:30 A.M. or 11:30 P.M. is not the way to win friends and get good interviews.

• For important calls, jot down a little outline of what you want to be sure to cover before you call.

• Record what was said in contract negotiations and other key conversations with editors and others the minute you put down the phone.

• To minimize phone tag, leave a complete enough message that the person does not need to call you back. Use e-mail. Or **answer the phone** when you know that important personage is likely to call back.

*I batch things rather than scattering them throughout the day. I try to make all my phone calls at once, for example. Since we live in Colorado, I sort them by East Coast, same time zone, then West Coast. I do my calling first thing in the morning when I'm the most "up" and I try for Tuesday, Wednesday or Thursday, as these are the best days to reach people.*

*Because I do an enormous amount of phone work—and more often than not get voice mail or an answering machine—I file the people I contacted by name in an accordion A–Z folder. Then when they call back I can quickly and painlessly find their paperwork. Note the date you called before filing it and audit your accordion file weekly so you can re-call those who haven't responded.*

—*Marilyn Ross*

*I keep a running record of every call in a loose-leaf phone log. The pages in it are forms I made up showing who I called, number of minutes I talked, rate per minute and cumulative phone costs for the month. When I've spent too much so far this month I stop calling!*

   *I do the same with faxes.*

*—Jim Joseph*

*We use e-mail and seldom leave call-back phone messages. (It is easier to re-place a call during our breaks than to have someone break in on our thoughts while we are writing. We keep separate lines for fax/Internet and voice communications. Toll-free 800 numbers for fax and voice also keep things simple."*

*—Clyde and Suzy Burleson*

## ORGANIZING THE THINGS WE OFTEN FORGET OR WOULD LIKE TO FORGET

• Set a time each day or week to do important but boring things that must be done, such as pay bills, fill out forms, make key phone calls and write for permissions or releases. It's usually best to do things like this while you're fresh—so you don't let them slide and you do them quickly and accurately—and get them over with. Then you can reward yourself by going back to writing.

• A safety measure for the absentminded or anyone: Keep all bills in one place. (Carol uses a red plastic envelope.) Put them there the minute they come in, review this frequently and keep everything current. This will keep your credit report in good standing and safely track the aftermath of even your most spendthrift month.

## TRACKING THOSE TAXES

Writers have to pay tax like everyone else—not quite as much, however, if we take the time to take advantage of the tax laws.

Writing is a business, as are self-employed people, and businesses are allowed to deduct the expenses of doing business from their gross income. For example, paying a 30 percent tax on the ten thousand-dollar advance you receive for a book will cost you three thousand dollars. If, however, in the process of writing the book you had to travel to

Pendleton, Oregon, to tour the Pendleton mills and study the making of wool shirts, buy lunch for three researchers, buy a certain software program to produce your manuscript, pay a pile of phone bills and motel bills from calling and traveling to collect information and pay an artist to produce visuals for the book, you have expenses to deduct. If all of this came to six thousand dollars, you have a net income of four thousand dollars to pay taxes on. Those taxes will now be only $1,200— a nice savings of $1,800.

Many people think it is too much trouble to document expenses, but in this day and age it is so simple it is almost done for you. All you have to do is note on the credit card receipt or other receipt the what, where, who and why. Keeping receipts in a box, file or drawer and entering income and expenditures in a notebook or computer is simple, fourth-grade arithmetic. There are other ways of keeping track as well, including special computer programs.

Since I am writing and speaking all the time, I expense almost everything—just about every trip anywhere—because I can produce undisputable proof that I was doing things related to my writing. I deduct a portion of both of my homes and their utility bills because I have a large writing office and a business phone line in both.

Start doing this if you aren't already. Track and take your deductions now, while you have a small-time operation, because as your writing gets more ambitious and your royalties and other writing income increase, so will your expenses. All this requires is learning and following the IRS regulations about home offices and how to allocate space and calculate deductions. With a little more effort, you can learn the rules and guidelines for keeping inventory and depreciating your business equipment and furnishings.

Keeping track is worth the hassle. Keeping track—other words: documentation, documentation, documentation—is the key to getting the tax benefits that are available. There are some tax caveats that limit deductions here and there, but in the main, if you keep track of expenses and can prove that they relate to the generation of writing income, you can deduct them. Every dollar of deduction saves about forty-five cents for you as a taxpayer, and why not take advantage of every deduction available.

### Common deductions for a writer

the part of your home exclusively devoted to your writing activities
office equipment and furnishings
office supplies
postage
research expenses
help hired to do office work or assist with editing or research
reference books
software
magazines or newsletters related to your work
dues or memberships in writers organizations
seminars or training sessions to help you learn something related to
    your craft
travel expenses (including food, lodging, mileage and parking)
photography and photo processing
artwork and design
entertainment related to your work (everything from taking an editor
    to lunch to throwing a party to celebrate your book's completion)

In writing, if your intent is to make a profit, you don't have to actually make one in order to deduct related expenses. Section 183 (the "hobby law") of the tax code suggests that you should make a profit three out of five years to be a legitimate business, but this is only a guideline. You can write and lose money for years and still deduct your expenses as long as you are really working at it.

If taxes worry you, just keep good records and evidence of all expenditures, and your accountant will know what to do. There is a high audit rate on home office tax returns, so do it right and be honest. Be aggressive where justified, too!

### Keeping records for your income tax

1. Have a clearly established (and secure) place to put all tax-related information during the year. When tax time comes around, the information will be at hand and make the job easier.

2. Keep track of all writing-related expenses—credit card charges and out-of-pocket items. Get receipts for everything, and note on them who you were with, the nature of the meeting, what assignment you bought film for, etc. Record all expenses in a running ledger—it will help you remember who and what you paid and when.

You don't need a special computer program to keep track of taxes on the computer. Just set up a file called something like Taxes 2002 and have in it a document for every deductible category of expense. Then when you get back from a trip to the local library to give them a copy of your latest book, you can quickly enter the cost of trip and the book before you forget!

3. Keep track of all article and book sales, royalties and advances, and the related receivables, agreement terms, payment due dates and when you actually received them. Don't forget any books you sell yourself, on the road or from home. All book sales, even of a single copy, should be reported as income. If you forget to charge sales tax (or don't want to bother), you will end up paying it out of your own pocket to be legal.

4. Keep track of your manuscripts and who you sent them to. Do this manually on a notepad, on a computer spreadsheet, or on one of the software packages available—like Lotus Organizer or The Writer's Software Companion (Novation Learning Systems, 190 Mt. Vernon Ave., Rochester, NY 14620) or The Working Writer (Dolphin Software Solutions, Suite 256, 1917 W. Fourth Ave., Vancouver, British Columbia, Canada V6J 1M7).

5. Two excellent software packages for keeping records for writing checks, invoices and statements are Quicken or QuickBooks. They are easy to use and will produce a variety of useful reports.

*I have a spreadsheet to help me keep track of my fees and expenses, that goes something like this:*

| Story | Publication | Editor | Fee |
|---|---|---|---|
| *Spring makeover* | Glamour | *Doe* | *$2,500* |

| Date put through | Rec'd payment | Expenses | Sent | Rec'd |
|---|---|---|---|---|
| *5/7* | *7/7* | *$32.58* | *7/1* | *7/7* |

*—Laurie Tarkan*

## OTHER THINGS TO RECORD AND KEEP AS YOU WRITE

There are other support things you need to preserve; some for your own P & L overview of your writing and some to get marketing ideas.

1. Keep all financial data together and do a summary at the end of a writing project. Be honest with yourself. You ought to know where you are at all times. Often we think we only spent a few bucks on some pursuit, and when we add it all up it turns out to be hundreds or even thousands of dol-

lars. Some books cost me five thousand dollars to get out and others cost fifty thousand dollars. Know where you are! It will help you make future decisions intelligently.

2. Any media representatives or businesspeople who have asked about your book or article before, during or after the writing process are valuable contacts, pure gold. Be sure to contact them when the right time comes. Many writers intend to do this, and then forget or can't find the names and addresses (or they are buried in with something else).

## STORING YOUR OFFICE SUPPLIES

The best place to store your pens and paper if you really want to be a writer is in your hand!

Seriously though, as for the rest of your tools and materials there is only one place for them: within reach. If at all possible, arrange supplies so that you can reach them without leaving your chair. A couple of drawers can hold enough writing materials to supply a five-year prison term. I'm talking about things like pens, paper, file folders, rulers, tape, glue, etc. Make sure you always have extras or a couple extra of all the things you use often, such as scissors (they walk), notepaper and copy paper, toner and ink cartridges. Remember, you want things reachable from the chair, bench, bed or wherever you do most of your writing.

## OFFICE OVERFLOW

What should we do with office overflow, such as drafts or earlier versions of things we can't pitch yet or mounds of material on books and articles we're finished with for now? Keeping the "slag piles" from big things like book projects slimmed down and cleared out is a constant battle because we have only so much space in the office for project piles and the like. (Carol had three ten-foot shelves filled with stuff—references, research material, memos, artwork roughs, cover roughs, earlier drafts of the manuscript, reader's reports, proofs—plus six computer file folders on one cleaning book we did.)

And how do we decide what is worth keeping? One of my readers provided an excellent answer:

> *When I finish a book or manual, I give the project a couple of weeks for the dust to settle, then I clean out the shelves, the file cabinets and computer of everything related to that project. I sort the notes (trashing everything that was incorporated into*

*the book or otherwise dealt with) and dump the remainder into a box with the page proofs, correspondence files, artwork and a complete disk backup of the word processing files. The box is then labeled with the name of the book or manual and moved to storage, where it stays until I do a revision or it looks like a good time to throw the whole thing out.*

If there are parts of a past project you might want to revise and perhaps market a different way (such as book material that might lend itself to articles), you can of course keep that on your computer, but everything truly inactive should move to storage.

## SAFEGUARDING YOUR BRAINCHILDREN

As deeply committed to our writing projects as we are, it's amazing how many of us fail to save and back up our computer files. Just exactly how much time and inspiration are you willing to lose at once? I wouldn't even give up fifteen minutes! If you keep a current backup and move it somewhere else every night, then you're fail-safe. If you let other people use your equipment at all, you're taking a risk. Many programs have a function that automatically saves the document every fifteen minutes or whatever interval you specify. Make it your habit to save at least once a page, if not paragraph.

You can use Zip disks to archive your books, one book per disk. This is a bit of an investment, but it's worth it. Copy all of the files for that book on that disk. If you have produced your own book, it's better to use the final layout version for the final manuscript (it is possible to extract the text from this back into your word processing program, if necessary), because so many small changes and corrections are made at the final layout stage that otherwise the "final manuscript" will be outdated. Even better is to have your printer burn a CD with your final layout, scans, fonts—everything you used to create your book.

*I don't quite trust computers, so I print out each chapter as I produce it and put it in a loose-leaf binder. When there's a new draft or version, I throw out the old and put in the new one. I do use a lot of paper!*

*—Elaine Schimberg*

It may seem that writing is a matter of working quietly and looking and waiting for words, information and inspiration. But there will come a day when things start flowing to you from every direction. Every investment of your time and energy and research will suddenly begin to give to you in abundance. A glorious day to look forward to, but it will mean a greater need for organization.

## CHAPTER 16

# *Organizing Your Work With Others*

Even though writing is an individual process, it is a social job in the sense that you extend yourself into the lives of those you are writing about, writing for and writing with. On the scene will come editors, artists, photographers, collaborators, contributors, researchers, limb chippers and critics—a whole platoon of other people who will be involved along the way to the final product. They are friends who may at times feel like foes and appear to treat you that way. Here is the way to save face and avoid foul-ups, to make the process of dealing with others as smooth and efficient as possible and get what you want with the fewest problems.

## GETTING OUTSIDE HELP ON YOUR WRITING

Is everyone (even those who claim to be) as enthusiastic about your writing as you are? Forget it! You'll find that support and help on a writing project is parallel to a political venture—everyone is generous with hoorahs and praise at your announcement, but cash and votes can be scarce as hens' teeth.

When you tap human resources, the response may be less than spectacular—even from spouses, relatives, people you employ and maybe even pay big bucks to and friends who claim they love you. Few people, for example, are likely to take the time to read and give opinions on your work, and complaining about this is pointless. People talk and promise big when it comes to helping you with your books and manuscripts, but in reality you are more likely to get a helpful response from about one in twenty.

The good news here is that the minority who do respond will often come up with pure gold. Much prime help can come from these people, and some of them do a lot. Appreciate those and make good use of them, and don't hate or divorce the ones who never come through.

## HOW TO GET THE MOST FROM OUTSIDE CONTRIBUTORS

So that you won't be disappointed or distraught by those two-legged resources you were counting on for some juicy stuff for your book, here are some things to bear in mind when soliciting outside assistance:

• Most people already feel stressed and put upon by the "too much" of modern life. So if they can't seem to find the time to respond to your solicitation or help you with your research problem, don't take it personally.

• Those you know (and have been helpful to in the past) will, of course, be a better bet than strangers you have to approach cold, unless you are a real charmer or your subject is so sensational it would turn any head.

• If you tap even the most productive sources too often, they may become assistance resistant. Don't wear out your welcome.

• People will usually be more willing to read a short manuscript or fill out a brief form than work on something long. In the case of a book, narrow your request to a section or a chapter or two that would most benefit from their attention.

• People you don't know well or at all are not likely to get around to sending you something later, so try to get what you need the moment you ask for it. I get much of my information from others—wonderful, brilliant and spontaneous stuff—right on the spot. Corner someone or call them, bring up what you are looking for and then start making notes like crazy. You'll get lots of good feedback, fast and free. And then you're finished (no need to write a letter and wait and hope for a response). See chapter seven for more on gathering in person.

• From your more reliable sources, asking for a written page or two will often beat interviews in time spent and the quality of what you get. Send a letter outlining what you want or need, and be very specific about it and what it will be used for. This avoids the need for long appointments and interviews. And their reply will be better composed, because it was written rather than just said. Even if you do end up interviewing them, it will go better and you will get more if they have in advance an outline of what you're after.

• When you put together a questionnaire or request letter, design it very carefully to elicit exactly the information you have in mind. Vagueness and generalities will give you off-target responses—a waste of the contributor's time and yours. Don't write questions that can be answered simply yes or no (unless you want a simple poll rather than details or in-depth information).

• Though people may not always respond well to written or interview requests, they may give you unsolicited assistance if you let them know what you are doing. Make your friends, family, co-workers and associates aware of the book or article you are writing, and often they will come to you with opinions and stories. Soon they may feel like they are writing it with you. People always like to be part of important goings-on.

• Offering a free book in exchange for contributions often helps to jog ambition. This doesn't cost much with the author's discount, it's tax deductible and it helps get your message out to the world. We often receive in accord with what we give!

• Offering contributors an acknowledgment in your book or article, a good word with your publisher, help with a project they may be working on or the like may encourage their assistance.

• When you need some serious help for your manuscript, pay for it; especially if it is something that might help your book or article sell and the person is credible and busy. They will respond and often give you twice as much as you asked for. And they may feed you information on the subject for years afterward. Those troublesome topics that would take you days to do and leave you on thin ice, just hire someone else to handle them. Money lends seriousness to the undertaking.

### Give credit where credit is due
Any help we get from fellow humans is a precious resource because it involves other people's lives and time. So don't hog all the fun and glory—give credit where credit is due.

Just be careful about promises you make to people for their help— mentions in the book or article, money, free books or photographs, etc. People remember every promise an author makes; and once the book is published and you are busy with tours, interviews and hard work on your next book, you may have trouble remembering all of those well-intentioned but optimistic promises you made to resource people. Or the budget may not allow everything you promised to do.

So think through ahead of time what you can offer and be realistic about it. Keep a clearly marked file of your promises, and honor them; in the writing business there is always a tomorrow.

### Helpers

Even in the largely solo business of writing, there are times when we may want to hire on a helper or two. Here are some ways to improve the results when you do:

1. Are you sure you really need a helper (have you been reading too many exhortations to delegate), or would it be simpler and quicker to just do the task in question yourself? Having too many helpers will slow you down because it is hard to get much done when you have to organize and direct others and retool them to fit your format. Keeping yourself efficiently channeled is tough enough.

2. On the other hand, if you really need helpers don't fail to use them because what they do may not be perfect. If they manage to do most of what you want and you only have to correct or add to what they've done, say 10 or 20 percent, you are still ahead.

3. Keep lists on your computer of things you want to discuss with helpers or assign to them. It will be easy to add to, delete from and update these lists.

4. Incomplete or inadequate instructions have wasted an incalculable amount of time, money and tooth enamel (as we grind our teeth over the results). Make sure your instructions are clear, complete and specific. Tell people exactly what you want, confirm it in writing, and if you still have any doubt, have them restate in their own words what you've asked them to do.

Make sure both you and your helpers understand the task at hand and how it will be accomplished. Try to answer all questions and eliminate any confusion. If there's a question in your mind, it will leave a question in theirs.

5. Note on your flowchart everything you delegate or assign to others, and put a name by each item.

6. At the very beginning, or early on, set the time or day when the response is due.

7. When working with researchers, don't just tell them what topics or

areas you need to have researched. Tell them exactly where you would like them to find the information—go on the Internet using certain search engines—what type of books or other references you want them to consult, the kinds of companies or organizations to contact and what general methodology you would like them to use. Since research is a potentially endless process, find out what their rate is and set at least a ballpark budget for the job, for example, $400 worth of information about sleep disorders.

8. To overcome the potential frustration and wasted time of trying to exchange copy by modem with helpers whose computer systems or programs are not compatible with yours, forget attachments to e-mails. Have everyone paste the copy they are sending right into the body of the e-mail.

---

**Casual asking, strong hints and sloppy requests to my helpers never worked for my first ten years of writing, and I figured they caused this. In the last ten years, since I realized it was me, I've had no problems.**

**My rules now for requests and communications with others:**

**1. They should always be written, never oral. Document everything and give a copy to everyone. Oral orders actually take longer, and they work about half as well as written ones.**

**2. Always make a copy of what you have asked someone to do, so there is no doubt.**

---

## THE ART OF FOLLOW-UP

*I shot an arrow into the air*
*It fell to earth . . . I know not where*

This is a verse with a message for writers. Those who assign and then assume are often disappointed. Giving orders and assignments and making requests is simple; getting the results you expected isn't. No matter what we ask for, it isn't always provided when, how and where we thought it would be. The key to success in business of any kind is accountability.

In writing, nothing is finished until the glue is on the covers in the printshop. Before that, most of our interactions, expectations and ventures require constant rechecking and evaluation. Forgetting a project once you've launched it is like throwing the warranty or receipt away after buying something. You have to stay connected to all that is going on and all that is supposed to be going on.

Here are some ways to do just that:

• I find that the best way to do follow-up is to scratch something off my lists or file it only after the assignment is finished. As long as it is active and in process, I keep it on my active lists. This means it still has my attention, and if it stops or slows down, I can make the contact and wake the situation up or deal with it again. If I toss the note when I make the assignment or place the order, I'm disconnected from it and no longer at the helm.

• E-mail is a quick, inexpensive way to follow up. Some people (not just your dentist) have good luck with postcards, too.

• Calling is a traditional follow-up method. The secret is not to call so soon that you annoy the person or so late that the schedule damage is already done.

• Put the ultimate deadlines on your calendar, day planner or computer tracking system, but make follow-ups well before those dates, to check progress. If you keep helpers aware of your own schedule and progress, it helps them coordinate their schedules and completion dates with yours. (When you make your project schedules, don't forget to allow some time for delays and screwups by others, not just yourself!)

• Friendly persistence is the ultimate answer. If what you need from someone is important enough to your manuscript, keep after them in a good-natured way (a little heartfelt flattery doesn't hurt, either). Carol didn't get a good answer to the question "How do I clean aluminum?" for one of my most popular books on cleaning until about the fourteenth time she asked me.

## NO WRITER IS ALONE

"They" don't disappear when you decide to write. Keeping the home fires burning and keeping your spouse, kids, boss and friends feeling as good about your new career as you do can be a challenge, especially once you get enthused by some successes or rewards—praise is pure gold to us and thin soup for others. The old adage that we cannot serve two masters really comes to life when you get serious about writing. As fun and ultimately rewarding as writing is, it can take a part of you away from others. Often in our excitement we don't see this, but others do. This is irritating to spouses or others who now see you diverting some of your energy, attention and ambition to "it" rather than them. People can be jealous of "it." (Trust me, it happens.)

When others are unhappy with you, they complain and may work against your or undermine you, silently at first and openly later. People become jealous, bored and irritated playing second fiddle to a few pieces of paper.

What can you do to minimize this occupation envy?

• Good communication is the best option you have here—sharing the whole process openly and involving them wherever you can. Offer to let them help with your writing activities if they want to. The more you assign to them, ask them to do or ask their advice on, the more they are likely to help and understand or at least retreat into being quietly thankful you are writing a book and will leave them alone.

When people know what's coming, they aren't as uptight about it and accept your "absence" better. A flowchart of what you've done and will be doing is a nice summary to share with those close to you. Secrecy tends to sire suspicion.

• Hide out from the hangers-on and give more of whatever "free" time you do have to your family.

• Hug your family more.

• Get up earlier. Few people resent your absence in the wee hours.

• Take full advantage of their schedules: Do your thing when hobbies, jobs, entertainments or school will have them well occupied.

• When separation anxiety is peaking, switch to something you can do sitting near them, like reading. This way you can at least be with them, rather than away at your keyboard.

• Watch out for the danger of letting your responsibilities (home and job) slide too far while you are riding the tide of some hot project or starting to use their time (when you were supposed go camping or to Disneyland) to write. At least be sure to pay the utility bills and do the key chores! And if you can't go camping in August, be sure to go in September, as you promised, after the manuscript is done!

*When I was working on my book I set deadlines and milestone dates for weeks ahead and I asked my family for support in helping me achieve them. This cleared the way for success and avoided conflicts. For instance, I provided my wife and children*

*with a list of weekend days I had scheduled for writing to verify*
*that they were fine with them before I committed to the schedule.*
                                        —Joseph Janiczek

## RE: READERS, EXPERT AND OTHERWISE

Since the ultimate purpose of writing is to have it read, it's not surprising that we hardly have something drafted when we have the urge to get someone's opinion of it. (Praise is what we're really after, of course.) And there are times when it makes sense to have outsiders read all or part of a project, especially in a specialized subject where we don't want to overlook anything or make a mistake. Here are some general rules for readers.

• Try hard to resist showing unfinished material to anyone. They will not automatically fill in the gaps and forgive the errors and ineptitudes of what they see. You will put people off, give a bad impression and maybe end up undoing your chance at something that matters to you, like publication.

• If you do have expert readers read something, you don't have to take every thing they say seriously or make every change they suggest. Use your own judgment.

• If you have more than one person read the same thing, take all readers' remarks into account at the same time, page by page, to avoid wasting time and backtracking (you might discover something different or better in the next reader's remarks).

• Remember that all opinions on written material are just that: opinions. If sixteen people read your story and say the same thing about it, what they say is probably worth listening to. But all opinions are not equal. The opinion of a professional editor in the field you are writing for is usually worth more than your best friend's opinion of the same manuscript (though even editors and agents are not infallible and can have differing opinions). Above all, do not take the praise of mothers and sweethearts too seriously or take the complaints of rivals to heart.

*One of the reasons my book turned out so well is that I sought*
*help from others and was open to constructive criticism.*
*Whether you are a fiction or nonfiction writer, you need to*
*decide whether you are open to such criticism. If so, get as much*

*help as you can from intelligent people eager to help.*

*If you aren't open to same, ask no one, because if they do read it and comment you will argue, disagree and make enemies (or lose friends). Be willing to take advice if you ask for it, or don't ask.*

—Jean Loftus

## One last word about others' opinions of your words

One of our biggest fears, and surely the main reason many of us never get our writing out into the light of day, is fear of what others will say or think about it. Writing is pretty personal when you get down to it. People can criticize our car, dog, yard, state or dress code, and most of us can live with that. But our writing is close to our inner being, and comments can really get to us. That goes both ways, of course—whether others praise our writing or pooh-pooh it.

You write something really good about an event at your company meeting, for example, and one of the supervisors who happens to like it tells you, "Hey, Morgan, that was pretty good. You ought to make up a bunch of copies and hand them out at the closing event of the conference." You are absolutely elated; this is almost like being published! So you polish up that article, run off a hundred copies on some nice beige paper and pass them out to all of your employees and their families at the meeting.

After the closing ceremonies everyone is gone, but your article isn't. They took the menus, the notepads, the matches and the awful hotel mints, but there right out in front of most places on the tables lie your wonderful words. Some copies have been used as napkins or coasters; others are doodled on or made into airplanes; even your spouse left hers sitting there. Talk about rejection in print!

What do you do about this? Give the perceptive supervisor who recognized your genius a promotion to CEO, fire the rest? That might be the emotion that floods over you, but remember, even the all-time masters have had their stuff tread on by the unappreciative public. Let it go and keep writing. Several people did read your piece and took it home to share with their families. And of course you inspired the other young or timid would-be writers and showed them what to do and how. And your words may have touched the minds and affected the lives of many. Even if the majority of those copies were left on the table . . . you did right!

## CLIENTS

In an ideal world, we would all see eye to eye and have no arguments or misunderstandings. But in the real world, we disagree and miscommunicate with our writing clients. Here are some ways to minimize conflict and maximize understanding.

• You may not want to work with every client that comes along. Most of us have encountered over time some personalities that mean problems—people who nitpick and complain constantly, fail to come through with things, stir up trouble or try to cheat us. In the end this means a lot of handling is involved, and it's not fun, either. When you're talking to a prospective client and those little red flags go up, don't ignore them. When someone is a pain or a drag in the early stages of something, don't expect them to get better as the project advances and pressures mount. People will be as much trouble, if not more, at every stage as they were at the beginning.

• When we end up in an adversarial role with someone, it is often because of gray areas in agreements we had with them. This can result in anything from bad feelings to lawsuits. Don't let this happen. Before you start a project or sign a contract with a client, spell out who does what and what each job includes. When in doubt, overexplain rather than underexplain.

• Learn from what went wrong last time. Experience, though it may be expensive, is one of our greatest sources of improvement. When something goes wrong in a relationship, understanding or contract agreement, don't just file it away in your mind. Change the attitude, the communication, the wording—whatever caused the problem. Make sure you gain something from the experience.

## COLLABORATORS

*Undertaken wisely, and with luck, collaboration has advantages. You produce a book that, probably, you would never have written alone. With a good collaborator you find that two heads are indeed better than one. The work becomes exciting and highly productive, the two minds striking ideas off each other like flint and steel.*

*—Raymond Hull*

Some key points on organizing your relationship with a collaborator:

• Bear in mind that while working with a collaborator is less lonely and sometimes more fun, in general you are multiplying the work, not dividing it!

• As with choosing clients, watch for "red flags" when choosing a writing partner. If someone is always late or never returns your calls now, don't expect that to change when you are in harness together.

• Do a small project, or several small projects, with someone before signing on for a long haul such as a book. Find out whether or not you work well together, whether you have similar—or at least meshing—values and goals.

• You may both think you know what your understanding is, but not until you see a draft of it on paper, will those questions and doubts surface, so they can be addressed and dealt with. Make a detailed and well-thought-out agreement before you start.

• Have regular meetings.

• The more organized a form you can get your collaborator to put his or her raw material in, the more merciful the whole process will be, and the less time you will have to spend on noncreative "drudge" work.

*When working with my collaborators on my book, we scheduled "team meetings" (with deadlines) every few weeks to bring everyone together for a synergistic day. The communication that occurred helped advance the project light years each time.*

*At all times we followed the philosophy of using talent where and when it was needed. We tried to avoid people taking on tasks they were not passionately talented to complete.*

*—Joseph Janiczek*

*I write direct and to the point with few words. I like to write the foundation, the outline, the first draft. My collaborators both love to add details and description, and edit. I don't. When you write with someone else you need to know your strengths and weaknesses and hopefully find a collaborator who complements you.*

*—Mary Jo Rulnick*

*Be sure you put on paper who is responsible for what, the division of labor. Make sure one person only is responsible for the writing, has the final say on it. I am always in charge of the writing and want no one besides my agent or editor telling me what do here.*

*Keep your appointments with your collaborator promptly and don't waste time when you're with him or her. Don't try to make a friend of them—be very professional and work, work, work!*
—Frances Spatz Leighton

## WORKING WITH EDITORS

Editors are the others we most want to be dealing with. Once we get in that enviable position, organization can help us to open doors and get green lights.

• Do market research to organize your marketing efforts. Sending editors or publishing houses things they would not possibly use or consider is a waste of everyone's time, but it is done every day. Don't send *The Complete Book of Atheism* to Word Publishing, or *How to Catch and Cook a Snail Darter* to the Sierra Club.

• If you make multiple submissions by mail, take the time to make sure the right letter gets into the right envelope. When your letter addressed to the editor in chief of *The Writer* reaches the *Writer's Digest* editor, it will not improve your submission's chances with her.

• Make sure that you make submissions in a form the publisher wants to see, whether that be a proposal, query or finished manuscript. For the proper format for any type of submission, see references like *Writer's Market* and *The Writer's Digest Guide to Manuscript Formats* and *Formatting & Submitting Your Manuscript*. And don't even think of sending anything handwritten, single-spaced or without page numbers (all common mistakes of beginners)!

• Prepare the table of contents in your book query or proposal carefully. If the order of the topics is logical and well thought out, it will give the editor confidence that you can produce a well-organized and satisfying final product.

• Good organization—a sound structure—in your article or book itself (see chapter nine) will make the editor's job much easier and repeat assignments more likely.

• No editor wants to receive a jumbled mass of photographs or illustrations. Make sure any illustrations that accompany your words are well organized (see chapter ten).

## More pointers from the pros on editors

> *Networking is probably the thing that has helped my writing career the most. A good relationship with one editor yielded me over thirty stories this year.*
> *—Kyle Minor*

> *I market my writing in a variety of ways, the most useful of which is trips to New York to meet the editors in person.*
> *—Maxine Rock*

> *What has helped my writing career the most? I'm businesslike, punctual, dependable. Editors can rely on me.*
> *—Maxine Rock*

> *You build a trust with an editor or agent. You give your word, then you stick by it. If you go the extra mile, people remember you.*
> *—Mary Jo Rulnick*

> *E-mail is the best way to correspond with editors and keep a record of your transactions with your them. I save all e-mails I think I might need (especially those in which there is a mis-meeting of the minds between an editor and myself). It's important to have a record like this. I do eventually delete them, usually about six months after the copy they refer to has been published.*
> *—Seli Groves*

> *Your position with editors should be this: You need to realize that you are an expert in your topic, not in book or magazine publishing. Editors know how to publish a book or magazine and what sells it best. You must separate your emotions from this, and be excited to have their help, not defensive. This may have been easier for me because I am a surgeon, and when you*

*are a resident you are criticized constantly. You finally realize
they are doing all this because they want to help you be and do
better.*

*It helped me immensely through the whole process of writing
a book to read things written from an editor's or agent's perspective. It helped me understand, to see where they come from, and
made communicating with them easier. You want to foster these
relationships if you intend to keep on writing.*

—*Jean Loftus*

*I never let editors see my manuscripts until they're in fairly pol-
ished form. I'd rather be late and clean than on time and a
mess. I've found that it's best not to assume that somehow they
will perceive the lovely statue in the grubby hunk of marble
you're sending. Give them the statue.*

—*Charles Mann*

*When dealing with editors, don't be a pain—this is a collabora-
tive relationship. As much as possible, keep your personal problems to yourself, don't share them with your editor. Try to keep
the moaning and groaning to yourself. You're a professional—
concentrate on doing your job, and delivering.*

*I always picture how many other authors and nonauthors are
making demands on an editor, so I try to bother them as little as
possible. If I'm feeling insecure, I remind myself that he or she is
my editor, not my mother. Editors are not baby-sitters.*

—*Janice Papolos*

## WORKING WITH ARTISTS AND ILLUSTRATORS

Artists, illustrators and designers are important partners in the job of
getting our message across with maximum impact. For smoother, more
efficient working relationships with them, and better results:

• Start thinking early on about what in your manuscript cries out
to be illustrated, and look for someone to do it.

• Make sure that person can produce professional-quality illustrations, or let your sister-in-law get her start somewhere else.

• Working with someone nearby will make meetings more convenient, and make it easier to establish rapport. But many top-notch illus-

trators have never met the clients they work for. You *can* communicate ideas and feedback on sketches and concepts across distance; it just takes a lot of clear words on paper to do it well.

• If you have an idea of what you want, in style or subject, show the artist a sample of it—such as a book with illustrations that creates the effect you have in mind.

• Before work starts, make a written agreement that establishes how many illustrations will be done for what price and who will have what rights to them.

• Catch any problems or oversights in the rough—always review roughs before the artist does a final. (If your illustrations have labels or dialogue in them, remember that many artists did not get an "A" in spelling.)

• Bear in mind that artists and designers are always mainly concentrating on graphic effect—you have to guard the meaning, check for accuracy and make sure the emphasis is where it should be.

• Whenever possible, let the art do things the words can't.

*I have a very close, personal relationship with my photographer; we've been a team for twenty years. Smithsonian Magazine introduced us, and we hit it off. He lives in NYC. I find that you have to have good chemistry between the participants for good collaboration.*

*—Maxine Rock*

*Get a local artist; it's not hard. Here's how I did it. First I sat down and determined that I needed 138 sketches for my book. Then I looked through published books for art of the type and style I had in mind and photocopied samples. I made up a packet that described the whole job I needed done, showed examples of the style I wanted and listed a few specific illustrations my book would need.*

*Then I called a local art school and got the names of three prospective artists and sent the packet to them. I asked them to do a sample illustration of the first item on my list and to give me a price quote to do the whole job. The quotes ranged from two thousand dollars to fifteen thousand dollars, and the two thousand-dollar person was actually the best.*

*After I decided which artist I wanted and she did her initial sketches, I sat down with her and the pile of roughs and explained that this was wrong, and this was how I wanted that, and why, etc. This worked very well, and you can't do it when the person is across the country.*

*When you send in photos, make sure you send them with a recommendation to the designer as to placement, and identify them on the back with the heading in the book, and the manuscript page, where they belong. This will help assure that all photos end up in the right place.*

*—Jean Loftus*

*This is what I provided for the illustrator of my book, and it worked wonderfully: I made a list of all of the illustrations needed, described each one and provided a photo of the item to be illustrated if possible. If the illustration was to show a hanging shoe file, I didn't just provide a photo of it but explained exactly what I wanted it to be holding. Then I put all of the descriptions and photos in a report cover and handed it to him.*

*—Pauline Hatch*

---

**Writing may be a solitary pursuit, but solitude must be set aside for the good of the project—and your collaborator's sanity!**

**CHAPTER 17**

# *Organizing Your Growing Career*

When we first start writing, most of us don't have a clue how much fun and good is going to come from it. Writing makes you a whole new person if you take it seriously. The rewards of writing are never ending, whether your writing changes one life (even your own!) or the lives of millions.

Like you, I've had a pretty exciting life—I've met people, gone places, raised a family and built businesses. I almost didn't think there could be more out there. But just start writing, and another brand-new world will open up. You'll discover parts you didn't even know you had, awaken drive and emotions that had long gone dormant, and maybe even earn some money to save or to spend on something you've always wanted. Where will it end up? It won't! One book or article leads to two or three more, and then to five or six. Speaking assignments and classes and seminars may follow.

Writing is a golden shovel waiting to be picked up and used well, and the earth you will move here is your readers' minds and hearts and everything they do afterward. Writing can even become addictive because we all like to be loved, needed and busy.

Before long you will have a career; you start out with one good book or article idea, and that singular soon becomes a plural and a multitude. Ideas and energy will pour into pages and more pages, maybe even to the point that you end up hiring others to help you and even building a writing or publishing business of your own. Writing is a career that will give a lot to you even as you give to it. You'll be as content to stay home or in your office as to tour the world; you'll be happy to write while others shop and run all over.

## BE READY TO MAKE THE MOST OF THE MEDIA

In this book of advice for writers, preparing for the media is one of the areas I feel most qualified to write about. This brag can be backed up by the more than five thousand media appearances I've made and the eight thousand speeches, classes and workshops I've done in my life—usually with excellent ratings. Because my system seems to work and many others have copied it, I will be a little opinionated here. But it will help you enormously when your turn comes to face a TV or radio interviewer, or a live audience.

The bottom line here is that media exposure sells books. It sells you so that you can sell books. The better you do with the media, the more attention you will get and the more books you will sell.

The media can and will make a big contribution to the success of your writing if you let them. But you need to take some initiative here. Just about anything you can write about has some media appeal—you need to find it and feed it to them. I've sold TV producers more than five thousand segments and interviews on the dull subject of cleaning!

There are no set rules here, so relax and when you get a chance to do media, grab it. Is it scary? Not a bit, even the first time, **if you know your subject and are prepared**. For my first book, a media tour was set up immediately, starting out big in San Francisco. I had a little radio experience, but none with TV or print media, yet still I did well. You will do well, too, if you remember the following. (If your book is being published by a publisher, they may do some of these steps; but since a publisher's media staff is always stretched thin, it pays to enhance their efforts in any way you can.)

**1. Compile your own list of media**. Start by contacting the local media and work your way up the list to the size of show and audience you want to reach, and distance you want to travel. You might not get *Oprah*, CNN or *Larry King Live* on your first shot, but maybe you will eventually if your work is really good and you hang in there (or you are Merv Griffin's niece).

**2. Make a media kit.** I've done all of mine with a simple pocket folder. A media kit has something (gimmick, slogan or promise) on the cover to get people to open it. Remember, the media need news!

Include a sample list of questions or facts that they can use to stir interest in your subject or book, a published article or two on you, if available, a picture of yourself, a brief resume of your credentials as they relate to this book and a copy or two of the book.

Having your press kit on a Web site makes it easy for the media to download photos and get your bio, stories and all the information on you and your book at any hour of the day or night at their convenience.

**3. Send information ahead.** Before an appearance or interview, send some information and extra copies of your book to the show or studio or whatever, with sample questions about the subject and often a full media kit. Once the media have this, they do all the rest.

**4. Be ready.** Have your material for your appearance—ideas, stories, instructions, questions and answers, whatever—written out ahead of time. Put your ideas in concise, outline form, using as few words as possible to describe things, so you will remember all you need to about them. That way you'll be able to just glance at the page to get your "script" and bearings, rather than having to read your responses.

Concentrate on the most obvious areas of interest and the things the hosts or interviewers are most likely to ask about, and generally they will follow your lead. Have some extra ready, too, in case things go quickly or the interview runs long.

The amount of time you will have to get your message across may not be long in any media appearance, particularly on TV, so be prepared to make the most of these few minutes by having your best material condensed down into short, punchy "bites."

**5. The more time the better.** The more time you get when you appear, of course, the better. TV generally offers two kinds of slots for author appearances: a six-minute segment, which may be run at any time, and an appearance on the morning or noon news, usually two and a half to three minutes.

Two segments are better than one, and a whole hour or half a show, is great. The TV people may even come to your "book site" (home office) if you have something interesting to show.

**6. Rely on the hosts.** They are real pros and will usually manage to make you look good even if you are shy or scared or get in over your head.

Let the host take charge of the interview. Most of them are really good and know how to get the best out of you, and they will. Let them do your book pushing for you—don't keep saying "in my book." Trainers may tell you to do that, but the media pros hate it.

**7. Go for phone interviews, too**, and don't make light of them. People tend to think author appearances are only in TV studios or at the newspaper office. Not so; most of mine now, and many of the best, are done by phone.

Most radio stations like little token free gifts, like one or two copies of your book to the fifth caller or to the caller who can correctly answer some question. This gives the book more exposure and pleases both listeners and the host.

**8. Help make sure your book is available.** When possible, call the local bookstores where your interview is being held and make sure they have some of your books on hand. Offer to provide them with copies if you have extras or get some from your publisher.

**9. Dress for success.** I'm not sure that you can overdress for a TV appearance, but you can dress too casually. I always wear a suit and tie, no sport clothes. Wear conservative Sunday-go-to-meeting clothes so that you don't stand out—keep the focus on your book and its message, not you.

**10. Stay ready.** Remember that media attention is not necessarily a onetime thing. After an initial big bang of publicity engineered by your publisher when your book comes out, there may be later follow-up interest as long as your book is still selling and the topic is still hot. I still do plenty of interviews for my book *Clutter's Last Stand,* which was published in 1984.

## MAKING POINTS WITH THE MEDIA

Remember, too, that the media are the lords of their domain. They know what they want, when and how. Don't try to persuade them otherwise once they give you the word, or you won't be asked back. On one *LIVE! With Regis & Kathie Lee* show in New York, I was showing how a garbage disposal worked and had a wonderful visual for it, a little model of a disposal. Nope, they wanted the whole kitchen cabinet and sink with disposal on the set (five hundred pounds total!) and for me to bring it there. It was silly, but I did as they asked. Things like this have happened to me many times; I just salute and do what they ask, and they like me for it. Authors who argue and insist on getting their way are rarely repeat guests.

The only real chance of getting your way is to carefully outline in detail the segment you wish to do, explaining how and why it will work, and send this to them weeks or months ahead. If you do a good job of selling they may buy into it and do it your way, if it appears professional enough. For example, when the Discovery Channel asked for a couple of segments I knew wouldn't have enough meat to satisfy the audience,

I sent them some different ones. They took some of my suggestions, and all went well.

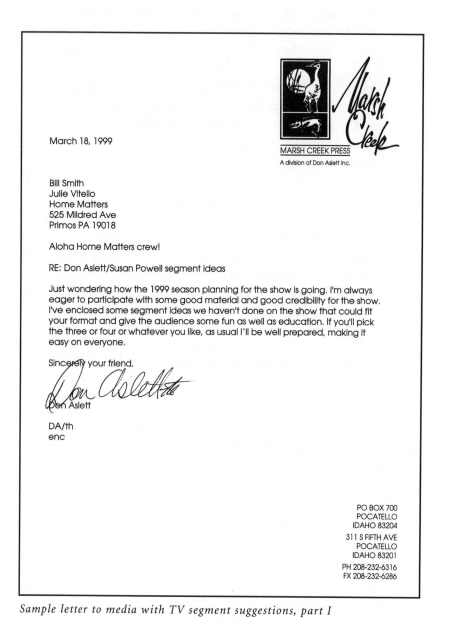

March 18, 1999

**MARSH CREEK PRESS**
A division of Don Aslett Inc.

Bill Smith
Julie Vitello
Home Matters
525 Mildred Ave
Primos PA 19018

Aloha Home Matters crew!

RE: Don Aslett/Susan Powell segment ideas

Just wondering how the 1999 season planning for the show is going. I'm always eager to participate with some good material and good credibility for the show. I've enclosed some segment ideas we haven't done on the show that could fit your format and give the audience some fun as well as education. If you'll pick the three or four or whatever you like, as usual I'll be well prepared, making it easy on everyone.

Sincerely your friend,

Don Aslett

DA/th
enc

PO BOX 700
POCATELLO
IDAHO 83204

311 S FIFTH AVE
POCATELLO
IDAHO 83201

PH 208-232-6316
FX 208-232-6286

*Sample letter to media with TV segment suggestions, part I*

**Some good segment ideas I can give you a detailed outline of, if they strike a note of interest:**

**1. Success in high places:**
Reaching high places—inside and outside a home—to clean or repair one of the toughest challenges for homeowners. The number one home accident is falling. We could do a great segment on all of the dos and don'ts here, and the right and wrong things to use for climbing and reaching, from ladders, to extension handles, to home scaffolding, and stools and chairs. This would be extremely visual and a good chance for Susan to participate and super helpful for viewers, most of whom haven't considered the risks of reaching high places.

**2. Office clutter:**
I have a good new segment (seminar presentation) on dealing with Office Clutter, the accent being on paper. The majority of homes now have an "office" or even a home business that is run out of them and homeowners are fighting the machines, files, materials, and furnishings necessary to run things here. This would be a fun how-to, hands-on session of why and what and where and how to keep things neat and in good working order. Lots of visuals across a big table or desk.

**3. Junk and clutter:**
It's strange, but we've never done a clutter segment on Home Matters, yet this is my best subject and the country's most needed one! Susan and I could do a quick dejunking of the "drawers" at home, showing people how to cope with and get rid of clutter, to live better and find more room.

**4. Environment-minded cleaning:**
This is a hot topic and a big worry in the country right now. And it lends itself to some good visuals and great demos of what we can use and how to use it, some techniques and rules we can use to help preserve the environment in our cleaning and home care overall. Again this could be a big table spread with lots of good surprises and participation with Susan.

**5. Cutting things around the house:**
Here is a super segment concerning all the cutting we do at home (mostly doing it dangerously and wrong!). We could show quick and safe ways to cut the 10 or 12 things we most often need to cut, and what tools to use, etc. We could lay out some items that are often cut, lay the tool needed for each beside it, and with my instructions have Susan go down the line and cut each of them perfectly and easily (this should get some ooohs and aaaahs out of even the camera crews!). We could stick to hand tools or touch on electric cutters. This is a great safety segment, also.

*Sample letter to media with TV segment suggestions, part II*

## WORKING WITH PRINT MEDIA

Interviews for the print media have less pressure, because the interview doesn't go out live, immediately. Anything you say that needs to be confirmed or double-checked can be. I find print media the easiest to deal with and the most willing to provide copies or transcripts of what you said. One thing you can count on with print media is that no matter how much you send them (how many books or whatever), they will always want to talk to you to get quotes. The newspapers and magazines I've appeared in a dozen times still interview me, though mostly by phone now.

They are often interested in being able to run some of the copy or artwork from your book, so be generous; check with your publisher first, if your book is not self-published, to learn the policy on this. The easier your material is to understand and use, the more coverage you will get.

Print media often want photographs, too, and large papers usually take their own. They own the photographs if they take them, so don't wear yourself out trying to get a copy—sometimes (about one time in fifty) they will yield and provide one.

---

**Never tell print media "this is off the record"; if a comment isn't going to put you in a favorable light, don't make it!**

---

## SECRETS OF SUCCESS WITH THE MEDIA

When people ask me for the secret of my success with the media, I make it clear that having good material and being well prepared come first.

The one thing beyond this, however, that has generated the best relations with and most confidence from hosts is the fact that we do everything early, way ahead. I don't tailgate deadlines. When I'm told to be there by eight o'clock, I'm there by seven o'clock—always early! That relaxes them, can result in more interview time, and they will be remembered. Being dependable is the flag I carry, and you can, too.

*Your job is not done when your book is delivered to the publisher. You have years of publicity ahead of you.*

*When dealing with a publisher's publicist, don't be difficult, a prima donna. If you had a choice of who to work with, whose book to spend your time on, would you choose someone you love or someone you can hardly tolerate?*

*When my publisher's publicist left just as my book was coming out, I had a decision to make. I was afraid of TV, but more*

*afraid of a failed book. If you find yourself in a similar situa-*
*tion, you will need to step in yourself, or forget the book party*
*and hire a publicist.*

*When doing publicity, no radio station or cable show is too*
*small to be worth doing. Don't neglect local and regional*
*shows—it doesn't have to be a major market to count. When*
*doing publicity on your own, be gracious and don't step on the*
*publisher's publicist's toes.*

*—Janice Papolos*

## THE MEDIA CAN HELP YOU WITH YOUR WRITING, TOO

Media interest can do more for you than just sell books. As you appear
and discuss your subject, both hosts and audiences will come up with
plenty of fresh ideas and angles on it. They are good, and they will surprise and delight you. Don't lose any of this; these often spontaneous
additions to your writing bank are worth their weight in gold, so be
sure to capture them. I've gained at least two whole books' worth of
material from my twenty years of media tours. Just when I think there
is nothing new about clutter or cleaning, I learn something more this
way, much of it stimulated by good jobs done by newspaper writers and
radio and TV hosts.

## KEEP THE MEDIA IN MIND WHEN WRITING

You can wait until a book is finished to go back and think through the
possibilities, but better yet is doing it as you go along, tossing ideas into
a file marked "media" with your files on that book. I often model my
media ideas on audience participation ideas and routines that I've
found get roars of laughter or approval in my cleaning and dejunking
seminars.

Except for language differences, media in the other countries I've
been in so far seem to be about the same as in the U.S. I've done a great
many appearances in Great Britain and in Canada and Australia as well,
and they have much the same formats, audiences and ideas as their U.S.
counterparts.

## WHAT WORKS ON THE PAGE AND ON THE STAGE!

One big advantage of giving speeches and other live presentations on what you're writing about is that you get an immediate reaction ("votes") from your audiences as to what they like, what really turns them on. Once you have this, you can use it in other appearances and in developing your repertoire, and take it into account in your writing, too. If they like it on stage, they'll usually like it on the page! Here are some things whose audience appeal has been proven over and over in my public appearances:

1. **Humor, humor, humor!** It never fails to please the audience, even at funerals. People have a chance to participate physically when they laugh, and humor will help almost any subject go over.

2. **Give them two stories (anecdotes) for every fact, principle or instruction** you give them.

3. **People like visuals**—art and illustration—on the stage and on the page.

4. **They like to participate, even a little.** If you ask them to help out, they will and love it. On the stage, you can ask them to answer questions, come up with ideas, help with props or compete with each other. On the page, you can challenge and question your readers or give them quizzes and self-tests to take. People really like tests and contests, especially quick, simple ones.

5. **Give them a source.** People always want to know where they can get what you are talking about or recommending. So whenever you can, give them a source: store or company name, product name or whatever. They want specifics, not generics.

6. **Let them know where they can contact you.** Good writers don't have to be mystery writers. If your audiences or readers can find you, they will bless you with material, opinions and questions that generally result in a better (or another!) book.

7. **Keep to the time limit.** Even if you are the best in the world, if you go to overtime you will turn them off. Too many extra words or too long a chapter will do the same thing.

## MAKE A RECORD OF EVERY CONTACT AND APPEARANCE

Remember that with the media, there is always a tomorrow. If you are good, they will use you aggressively forever. The first thing I noticed when I started doing interviews was that many authors, and publishers, kept little or no records of appearances (except maybe the date and program involved). But if you get a follow-up call from a program or station for another interview when you happen to be in that city again, you may have a hard time remembering what the last show was like, what you said or did. And repeating yourself (doing an accidental rerun) in a situation like this is not the way to win friends and please audiences.

So I came up with a sheet like the following and use it to record every interview, appearance and speech I do. It is filled out and then filed. I have thousands of these on file now, and when a show calls for an interview I have an instant history of what topics I covered before and when. Plus we have everything we need for future contacts, sales and thank-yous.

A form like this can also help with tracking book sales. If you or your publisher happen to see an area where sales and orders come in more heavily than elsewhere, you can look back and see what show you did there and what you did on that show—what worked.

*Just before and during publication, I start a binder called "Publicity." I note every transaction on the book here under the headings: Date, Contact, Phone Number, E-mail, Address and Notes; and write in every radio, TV, newspaper or magazine article, interview or mention of it. I write everything down so I have a list for the next book. I pass these sheets on to fellow authors, who then share their media lists with me, and thus, we exponentially increase our contact lists. Also, anytime I think something would be a good lead, I enter it here and write down the results of the phone call.*

*—Janice Papolos*

*I set up a separate group of marketing folders as soon as I think of a new book idea: reviews, PR, catalogs, premium possibilities, Internet, bookstores, possible endorsers, etc. When it's time to think about launching the new book, I have a ready-made marketing plan.*

*—Marilyn Ross*

Sample interview record

## OTHER KINDS OF RECORDS

In the print media, newspapers or magazines, it is customary to ask for a tearsheet of the article by or about you, and the publication will usually send you one for your records in case you miss the issue. However on radio or TV it is a bit pushy to hit them up for a copy of the show. If they don't volunteer to provide one, the best thing is to have a friend or acquaintance in the area record it for you. I often make good use of the material from my print appearances, but of the many TV and radio tapes I have collected, I use only a few.

## FILE YOUR FEEDBACK

All of your fan mail and the feedback on your media and personal appearances are well worth preserving. Hopefully you can call this file "love letters." It will serve you well if you need to produce testimonials or evidence for any reason. It can help your writing, too—I've done entire books composed largely of reader's comments and questions. And even negative feedback or criticism can help you get more on track in any areas you might need to improve.

1. Keep any reviews or articles about a book or about you as a writer carefully filed under whatever heading fits your filing system best. Be sure to note the names of the publications they appeared in and the dates they appeared. Get several copies of the publication in question if possible, so that you still have two clean, crisp copies for the record after giving one to your mother and sticking one in your "press kit original" file.

2. Read letters with a highlighter in hand and mark anything profound, worthwhile or funny. This way, after you've filed or saved them for something, you can quickly spot the lines that ring your bell. If the letter applies to two or three published books or subjects in general, copy the letter, highlight as needed and put a copy in each of those files.

3. I always answer letters from my readers. Anyone with enough spunk to write you will be a forever fan and sell forty books to friends. One real admirer out there is worth two bookstores any day. I often send a copy of their letter back to them with a short note or thank-you handwritten on it, and I often include a free autographed book for those who have contributed valuable information or truly touched my heart. This only takes a few minutes and a couple of dollars and builds a great reservoir of help and friendship.

## TWO LAST NOTES

Being asked to do something by the media is a heady experience, no doubt about it. But bear in mind that you don't have to take all media offers. Sometimes spending two days to fly somewhere, do a three-minute appearance and then fly home is just not worth it. So use your own judgment.

Lastly, don't be overawed by all the celebrity authors you may meet in your media adventures. Don't think you're a failure when you hear their big stories. (You could try some of your fantasies on them in return!)

## CHRONICLING, AND ADVANCING, YOUR GROWING CAREER

As your experience grows, be sure to keep a clear record of it. Keep clean copies of all your published articles and books. Make yourself a writer's resume and perhaps a brochure on your skills and services. List yourself in any directories, print or online, that may lead to new assignments. Make a mailing list of your most reliable and likely clients and keep them aware of your latest accomplishments. Write a short and long version of your "writer's bio" and keep them updated and handy. Take yourself seriously, and the world will, too.

## HOW YOUR FIRST BOOK CAN HELP THOSE THAT FOLLOW

Using your first book to lead the way for others is smart, and using your first book to market itself and others is also good book sense. So use your existing books for

1. **Gathering:** I add a solicitation page to the back of all my books now, welcoming, encouraging and outright asking readers to contribute anything they might have to say about the subject at hand. Make this as clear and simple as possible, and make it easy for readers to respond.

2. **Selling:** I always include a little catalog or order blank in a couple of pages at the back of the book telling readers how they can get additional copies of this book or any of my others by mail from me.

These things do work, but don't expect to be deluged with responses, either correspondence or cash. But the responses you do get will be good ones, and they add up over time.

When it comes to selling from the back of books, two things have proven more effective than just an order blank:

1. **Show the cover** of any book you are offering, if you can, and tell something about it; include a little description, or at least a blurb or brief salesy summary of the book, not the title alone. A paragraph is better than one line. Make this as provocative and compelling as possible so the reader *must* have this book.

**2. Offer a deal.** People love deals, such as two $12.99 books (worth $25.98) for just $20. With no middleman, you can make good money this way with little effort. It might even be worth offering free postage.

## ORGANIZING FOR REVISIONS OF YOUR BOOKS

No book is ever done—any and all "adds" or improvements to it are well worth having. Organize now for revisions and updates. Every book of mine has a revision file. Whenever you think of, hear or see something that should be taken into account in the next edition, write it up or copy it, and drop it in the file. When you're reading over your choice chapters some evening and find a few typos or some other mistake or an oversight, note them, too, and put them in the file. Don't assume that someone else will surely see and fix them. Almost all nonfiction books will need updating sooner or later, and if you keep saving things, you'll be half ready when the publisher asks you to do a revision.

The best time to start a revision file is right when you are finishing up a book in the first place. The things you meant to do in this first edition are 110 percent clear to you then, but you don't have the time, space or maybe even the knowledge to do them right now. Very fresh in your mind, now, too, is anything you didn't like about the physical book itself when you got that first copy from the publisher. Something here might possibly be fixable in a new edition, so write it down, make a record of it before your mind moves on to other things.

You can also keep a master copy of your book to note corrections and make edits, changes and revisions in it as you go along.

## TUNING IN TO THE BIG PICTURE

After you get a few things published, think about the big picture, if you haven't done it before now. Planning your career is organizing, too. You don't want to drift into things; ideally you should choose the direction of your writing and make sure that where you are headed with your writing career is where you want to be headed.

Be careful not to get typecast in one subject (unless that's what you want), because publishers will definitely typecast you. This can be an advantage and lead to repeat assignments; it can also be a drawback or an obstacle.

Also remember that it's not just how much money you make or fame you achieve that counts, but how you will feel in the final chapter of your life or up on cloud nine when you read the little entry on you and your works in *Contemporary Authors.* If you want to change anything in that entry, start changing it now!

## THE WIN-WIN OF BEING A WRITER

This is what makes the whole writing business worthwhile: You start out sending your writing places, and it ends up taking you places, as you write about what you live and end up living what you write.

Writing has a guaranteed return as your readers enter your life and share their thoughts and times and places with you. Once the public knows you and your feelings and your talents, they will contribute by calls, letters, conversations and even criticisms, and all of this makes your life pretty darn exciting. Plenty of professional output is talent tossed to the wind—a few people catch it or benefit from it, and it is gone. But a writer leaves hard evidence on a page somewhere that others clip and keep, and ten years later they may call or write you with heartfelt thanks or send you something or jump on your bandwagon.

When we write we do something that matters, and knowing that you matter is the best reward imaginable.

---

**Writing won't just become a big and important part of your life; it will enrich it, as well as the lives of others. There is no stopping place for good writers. They never retire; they just number their pages more creatively. You won't have to take your writing career anywhere; it will take you, if you write for the right reasons and at the right time— which is now!**

## RECOMMENDED BOOKS

### Marketing guides/overviews

*Writer's Market* (Writer's Digest Books), edited by Kirsten Holm

*Literary Marketplace* (R.R. Bowker)

*The Writer's Handbook* (Writer, Incorporated), edited by Sylvia Burack

*The Writer's Market Companion* (Writer's Digest Books), by Joe Feiertag and Mary Cupito

*Poet's Market* (Writer's Digest Books), edited by Chantelle Bentley

*Writer's Guide to Book Editors, Publishers, and Literary Agents* (Prima Press), by Jeff Herman

*International Directory of Little Magazines and Small Presses,* (Dustbooks), edited by Len Fulton

*Novel & Short Story Writer's Market* (Writer's Digest Books), edited by Barbara Kuroff

*Children Writer's & Illustrator's Market* (Writer's Digest Books), edited by Alice Pope

*The Market Guide for Young Writers,* 5th ed. (Writer's Digest Books), by Kathy Henderson

*Guide to Literary Agents* (Writer's Digest Books), edited by Donya Dickerson

*A Writer's Guide to Book Publishing* (Plume), by Richard Balkin

*Writer's Digest Handbook of Making Money Freelance Writing* (Writer's Digest Books), by the editors of *Writer's Digest*

*Make Your Knowledge Sell: A Complete Guide to Selling Nonfiction on the Web,* by Ken Evoy and Monique Harris, http://myks .sitesell.com.

### Guides to professional presentations

*How to Write a Book Proposal,* rev. ed. (Writer's Digest Books), by Michael Larsen

*How to Write Irresistible Query Letters* (Writer's Digest Books), by Lisa Collier Cool

*Your Novel Proposal: From Creation to Contract* (Writer's Digest Books), by Blythe Camenson and Marshall Cook

*Kirsch's Guide to the Book Contract* (Acrobat Books), by Jonathan Kirsch

*The Writer's Digest Guide to Manuscript Formats* (Writer's Digest Books), by Dian Dincin Buchman and Seli Groves

*Formatting and Submitting Your Manuscript* (Writer's Digest Books), by Jack and Glenda Neff, Don Prues and the editors of *Writer's Market*

### Writing fiction/scripts

*How to Write & Sell Your First Novel*, rev. ed. (Writer's Digest Books), by Oscar Collier with Frances Spatz Leighton

*How to Write Best-Selling Fiction* (Writer's Digest Books), by Dean Koontz (out of print)

*Fiction Writer's Workshop* (Story Press), by Josip Novakovich

*Building Better Plots* (Writer's Digest Books), by Robert Kernen

*Creating Short Fiction* (St. Martin's Press), by Damon Knight

*Story* (HarperTrade), by Robert McKee

*Story Sparkers: A Creativity Guide for Children's Writers* (Writer's Digest Books), by Debbie Dadey and Marcia Thornton Jones

*The Complete Book of Scriptwriting*, rev. ed. (Writer's Digest Books), by J. Michael Straczynski

*Screenplay* (Dell), by Syd Field

### Writing nonfiction

*How to Write the Story of Your Life* (Writer's Digest Books), by Frank P. Thomas

*Writing Articles From the Heart* (Writer's Digest Books), by Marjorie Holmes

*Writing From Personal Experience* (Writer's Digest Books) by Nancy Kelton

*How to Write and Sell Your Personal Experiences* (Writer's Digest Books), by Lois Duncan

*You Can Write a Cookbook* (Writer's Digest Books), by J. Kevin Wolfe

*You Can Write a Column* (Writer's Digest Books), by Monica Cardoza

*Writing Creative Nonfiction* (Ten Speed Press), by Theodore A. Rees Cheney

*Writing Articles About the World Around You* (Writer's Digest

Books), by Marcia Yudkin

*How to Write & Sell Your First Nonfiction Book* (St. Martin's Press), by Oscar Collier and Frances Spatz Leighton

*Getting the Words Right: How to Rewrite, Edit, & Revise* (Writer's Digest Books), by Theodore A. Rees Cheney

### Self-Publishing

*The Complete Guide to Self-Publishing* (Writer's Digest Books), 3d ed., by Marilyn and Tom Ross

*Jump Start Your Book Sales* (Writer's Digest Books), by Tom and Marilyn Ross

*The Self-Publishing Manual: How to Write, Print, and Sell Your Own Book* (Para Publishing), by Dan Poynter

*U-Publish.com: How Individual Writers Can Now Effectively Compete With the Giants of Publishing*, 2d ed., by Dan Poynter and Danny O. Snow

### For a more productive writing life

*Write Where You Live: Successful Freelancing at Home* (Writer's Digest Books), by Elaine Schimberg

*Secrets of Self-Employment*, (G.P. Putnam's Sons), by Sarah and Paul Edwards

*Teaming Up: The Small Business Guide to Collaborating With Others to Boost Your Earnings and Expand Your Horizons* (Tarcher/Putnam), by Paul and Sarah Edwards and Rick Benzel

*Working From Home*, 5th ed. (Tarcher/Putnam), by Paul and Sarah Edwards

*Keeping Work Simple* (Storey Communications), by Don Aslett and Carol Cartaino

### Guides to making more time for writing (by Don Aslett)

*How to Have a 48-Hour Day*

*How to Handle 1,000 Things at Once*

*No Time to Clean!*

*Is There Life After Housework?*

*Clutter's Last Stand*

*Not for Packrats Only*

*Lose 200 Lbs. This Weekend*

*The Office Clutter Cure*

## CONTRIBUTOR BIOGRAPHIES

**Lynne Alpern** is the author of *Oh, Lord, I Sound Like Mama,* from Peachtree Press.

**Isaac Asimov** is the author of more than three hundred books in fields such as physics, astronomy, chemistry, biology, history, biography, humor and fiction.

**Nicholas Bakalar** is a New York-based freelance writer and book editor who has worked as an acquiring editor for Doubleday, HarperCollins and other houses. He has authored or coauthored ten books, including *A Writer's Guide to Book Publishing, The Baseball Fan's Companion* and *The Wisdom of John Paul II.*

**Samm Sinclair Baker,** called "America's Leading Self-Help Author" by *The New York Times,* wrote hundreds of articles and authored or coauthored more than thirty books, including some of the best-selling diet books of all time.

**Jenny Behymer** is a freelance writer, researcher and essayist from Hillsboro, Ohio.

**John Brady** has written and published four books, including *The Craft of Interviewing.* He is a veteran magazine editor and publishing consultant in the Boston area.

**Dian Dincin Buchman, Ph.D.**, wrote more than sixty books, including *The Writer's Digest Book of Manuscript Formats* (coauthored with Seli Groves). Dian was also the founder of the Council of Writer's Organizations and a past president of the American Society of Journalists and Authors.

**Clyde and Suzy Burleson** are the authors of the best-seller *The Jennifer Project, The Day the Bomb Fell on America, Flight from Dhahran, Effective Meetings: The Complete Guide* and many other nonfiction books, as well as screen treatments and novels.

**Sheila Davis** is a lyricist and composer. She is the author of *The Craft of Lyric Writing* and a contributor to the *Encyclopedia of Rhetoric and Composition.*

**Don Donaldson** is the author of six forensic mysteries in the Andy Broussard/Kit Franklyn series, and medical thrillers for Berkeley including *Do No Harm* and *In the Blood*.

**Paul and Sarah Edwards**, who contributed some thoughts to the discussion of collaborators, are columnists, and the coauthors of thirteen books, including *Working from Home* and *The Practical Dreamer's Handbook*. Their Web site is http://workingfromhome.com.

**Rohn Engh** is the director of Photosource International (http://www .photosource.com), publisher of *PhotoSourceBook*, a directory for stock photographers, and author of *Sellphotos.com* and *Sell and Re-Sell Your Photos*.

**Ken Evoy** is the coauthor of *Make Your Knowledge Sell*, a complete guide to selling nonfiction on the Web.

**Kenneth Green** is the director of the environmental program at Reason Public Policy Institute. He has a doctorate in environmental science and engineering from UCLA.

**Seli Groves** is the author of six books, including the *Writer's Digest Guide to Manuscript Formats* (coauthored with Dian Buchman), and a syndicated columnist for King Features and North American Syndicate.

**Pauline Hatch** is a professional organizer and coauthor of *It's Here . . . Somewhere*, a room-by-room guide to decluttering.

**Dave Hermansen** is the chief financial officer of Varsity Contractors, Inc., and an organizing wizard.

**Michael Patton Hoover** is a retired publishing executive who spent more than twenty-five years developing and implementing cost-saving methods for publishers.

**Lois Horowitz** is a retired research librarian who was formerly head of acquisitions at the San Diego Public Library. She is the author of *Knowing Where to Look: The Ultimate Guide to Research*.

**Raymond Hull** was the coauthor of *The Peter Principle* and many other nonfiction books and articles, and plays.

**Martha Jacob** is a freelance writer and researcher in Hillsboro, Ohio.

**Joseph Janiczek** is a highly successful financial analyst and the author of *How to Achieve Absolute Financial Freedom.*

**Jim Joseph** is an investigative journalist, syndicated columnist and author of twenty-four books. His fellow writers in the American Society of Journalists and Authors have called him "an organizing genius."

**Terra Koerpel** is a scriptwriter and producer.

**Jean Lawrence**, who lives outside Phoenix in Chandler, Arizona, is a full-time health and technology freelancer, newsletter publisher and screenwriter.

**George Laycock**, freelance author and journalist, has written more than fifty books, including *The Mountain Men, Autumn of the Eagle* and *Grizzly: Wilderness Legend.*

**Frances Spatz Leighton** is the coauthor (with Oscar Collier) of *How to Write and Sell Your First Novel* and *How to Write and Sell a Nonfiction Book,* as well as many best-selling celebrity biographies and "as told tos."

**Jean Loftus** is a plastic surgeon in the Cincinnati area and author of *The Smart Woman's Guide to Plastic Surgery.* ("When people ask me what I do, I tell them I like to say I'm an author, but I'm really just a plastic surgeon.")

**Charles Mann** is the author of a number of books on science and technology and contributing editor to *Atlantic Monthly* and *Inside.com.*

**James A. Michener** was the Pulitzer Prize-winning author of more than forty books, many of them best-sellers. He was a tireless researcher, and many of his books, such as *Hawaii, Centennial, The Source, Poland* and *Covenant,* were more than one thousand pages long. The quotes in this book are from his autobiography, *The World Is My Home.*

**Carl Mills** is a linguist who does quantitative research on human language and then writes papers about it. He writes up to 100,000 words a year, plus committee reports. (And he's a good man to have at hand when your computer acts up!)

**Kyle Minor** is a freelance writer and film producer based in Palm Beach.

**Keith Monroe** has sold articles to *Reader's Digest, The New Yorker, Fortune, Sports Illustrated* and *New York Times Magazine,* among others. He is the author or ghostwriter of eight published books.

**Ernest Newman** was an English music critic, biographer and translator whose real name was William Roberts.

**Beverly Nye** is a media personality and the author of the best-selling books *A Family Raised on Sunshine, A Family Raised on Rainbows* and *Everyone's a Homemaker,* among others.

**Janice Papolos** is the author of four books, all considered definitive in their field, including *Overcoming Depression, The Bipolar Child* and *The Performing Artist's Handbook.*

**Sandra Phillips** is a freelance writer and editor from Whittier, California.

**Kirk Polking** is a former editor of *Writer's Digest* and director of the Writer's Digest School, as well as an author of nonfiction books for children and adults, including *Oceanographers and Explorers of the Sea* and *Writing Family Histories and Memoirs.*

**Elizabeth Pomada** is a literary agent and author of the *Painted Lady* series, about San Francisco landmarks.

**Ed Rach** is a retired architect who designed several million square feet of office space in his career and did computer design installation for many businesses on Wall Street.

**Maxine Rock,** journalist and author, is the winner of eighteen writing awards for work published in magazines and books worldwide. She lives in Atlanta, Georgia.

**Marilyn Ross** is the coauthor of *The Complete Guide to Self-Publishing* and *Jump Start Your Book Sales.* Her Web site is http://www .about-books.com.

**Mary Jo Rulnick** is the author of *Write Well & Sell: Easy Writing, Easy Money* and *Write Well & Sell: Self-Publishing Made Simple.*

**Kelly Boyer Sagert** is the managing editor of the northern edition of *Over the Back Fence* magazine.

**Elaine Schimberg** has written for numerous magazines including

*Reader's Digest, Woman's Day* and *Glamour,* and written or coauthored more than a dozen books of instruction and self-help, including *Coping with Blended Families* and *How to Get Out of the Hospital Alive.*

**Deniece Schofield** is the author of *Confessions of an Organized Homemaker* and *Confessions of a Happily Organized Family.*

**Peter Seidel** is an architect, and the author of *Invisible Walls: Why We Ignore the Damage We Inflict on the Planet... and Ourselves.*

**Robert Sloan**, who has published many short stories and poems in literary quarterlies and journals, does a regular "audio column" on Kentucky Public Radio and teaches creative writing at Morehead State University. He lives and writes on an Appalachian farm.

**Art Spikol**, a former columnist for *Writer's Digest* and former editor of *Philadelphia* magazine, can write anything. He is also one of the fastest watercolorists in the world and would probably be famous if he would just take his time.

**Hollis Stevenson** is a writer, designer and educator.

**George Sullivan** is the author of a good-sized shelf of books for children and young adults (well over one hundred books!).

**Laurie Tarkan** is a journalist and author of *My Mother's Breast: Daughters Face Their Mother's Breast Cancer.*

**Frank Thomas** is a teacher of writing and the author of *How to Write the Story of Your Life,* the most heartfelt, best-written and psychically sound book on the subject.

**Anna Lee Waldo** is a writer of historical fiction who grew up among Blackfoot and Crow Indians in Montana. Her novels include the bestsellers *Sacajawea, Prairie* and *Circle of Stones.*

**Carol and Mike Werner** are writers, commercial stock photographers and graphic illustrators.

**Ruth Winter** is the author of thirty-four books and hundreds of print and Web articles. Her Web site is http://www.brainbody.com.

## ANSWER KEY FOR "THE MANX CAT" OUTLINE

From page 148 in text:
What a Manx is (1 page)
Where breed originated (1 paragraph)
Other popular breeds of cat (1½ pages)/getting off the subject
Why many cats have stripes (⅔ page)/definitely off the subject
Manx Appreciation Society of America (1 paragraph)/should
    probably be last topic in the article
Genetic problems of Manxes (¾ page)/should go with
    breeding Manxes
The Manx personality (½ page)/put with or after what
    makes Manx different
The appeal of Manxes/should be second or third topic in the article
The shame of abandoning cats (2 pages)/off the subject again!
Breeding Manxes successfully (1 page)/put after the appeal of Manxes
What makes Manxes different: they have no tail, and move differently
    (2 paragraphs)/put right after the lead

## ORGANIZING IDEAS WANTED!

*If you have a better way, please let us know what it is!*

Do you have an idea for organizing the writing life (maybe one better than anything here!) that you'd like to share with readers in future editions of this book? Please send it to

*Get Organized Ideas*
*PO Box 700*
*Pocatello, ID 83204*

or e-mail it to aslettdon@aol.com or cartaino@aol.com

If we find your thoughts especially helpful, we'll be pleased to send you a free copy of "Writer on the Road," a helpful booklet on organizing your professional travels, in return.